British Economic and Social History since 1700

THE AGE OF INDUSTRIAL EXPANSION

British Economic and
Social History since 1700

THE AGE
OF INDUSTRIAL
EXPANSION

A. J. HOLLAND MA

Second Edition

NELSON

THOMAS NELSON AND SONS LTD
Nelson House   Mayfield Road
Walton-on-Thames   Surrey KT12 5PL

P.O. Box 18123   Nairobi   Kenya

116-D JTC Factory Building
Lorong 3   Geylang Square   Singapore 1438

THOMAS NELSON AUSTRALIA PTY LTD
480 La Trobe Street Melbourne Victoria 3000

NELSON CANADA LTD
1120 Birchmount Road   Scarborough
Ontario M1K 5G4

THOMAS NELSON (HONG KONG) LTD
Watson Estate   Block A   13 Floor
Watson Road   Causeway Bay   Hong Kong

THOMAS NELSON (NIGERIA) LTD
8 Ilupeju Bypass   PMB 21303   Ikeja   Lagos

ISBN 0-17-445138-5
NCN 240-2825-7

Printed in Hong Kong

Contents

PART THREE *The Twentieth Century*

Preface

This book is intended mainly for students preparing for Ordinary level of the G.C.E. or for the C.S.E. It is hoped that it will also prove useful to students who begin this subject in the sixth form, and for those who need a simple introduction to the main trends of the economic development of England since 1700. The divisions between 'history', 'economic history', and 'social history' are artificial ones, but I have tried to emphasise the development of this country into an industrial state, rather than the actions of politicians. The book is divided into three parts so that the reader can use it for both topics and periods.

Many of the great problems of economic history are still a cause of dispute among those engaged in research, but in a textbook an author must attempt to arrive at some definite conclusion. Changes in the size of the population before 1801, the birth-rate in the eighteenth century, living standards during the first or classical industrial revolution, or even the whole concept of an industrial revolution, are all subjects which can be interpreted in different ways; in the present century, state control and private enterprise can be viewed in different lights by any two economists. I have tried to keep a steady course, despite the navigational hazards.

I am most grateful to Thomas Nelson and Sons for their encouragement, faith and patience, and especially to W. T. Cunningham and J. V. Steele for their very practical help. I owe a very real debt to the general editor, T. J. P. York, for his courteous, scholarly and helpful guidance throughout. Finally, I am most grateful to my wife who has given me considerable help throughout.

King Edward VI School,   A.J.H.
Southampton.
October 1967

Preface to the Second Edition

Apart from a few minor corrections, this second edition differs from the first only in parts of the last three chapters. Events come quickly, so that recent history needs constant revision. The intervening years have seen a weakening in the optimism of the 1960s, though the age of greater expectancy has not yet died. This book now ends on a rather less optimistic note, which is but a reflection of the mood of the times.

No changes have been made to take account of decimalisation or metrication, as readers will still be familiar with the terms actually used in the past.

A.J.H.

December 1974

Acknowledgements

Our thanks are extended to the bodies and individuals listed below for their help in providing illustrations and for permission to reproduce them. The sources of the plates and of the pictures in the text are as follows:
Alma Components Ltd: plate 47.
American Iron and Steel Institute: plate 12.
M. Brassington: plate 51.
British Museum: page 60.
British Rail: plate 44.
English Electric Co. Ltd: plate 61.
Esso Petroleum Co. Ltd: plate 58.
Giles and the Daily Express: page 264.
Gourock Ropework Co. Ltd: plate 39.
Imperial War Museum: plate 46.
Mansell Collection: plate 43.
John Miller Ltd: plate 60.
The Directors of the Goodwood Estate Company Ltd: plate 2 (original, Goodwood MS.E31, in the West Sussex Record Office).
National Maritime Museum: plates 23–7.
Newport Museum and Art Gallery: page 174.
Newton, Chambers and Co. Ltd: plate 35.
Nuffield Organisation: plate 50.
Punch: page 227.
Radio Times Hulton Picture Library: plates 1, 52–4.
Rochdale Art Gallery: plate 41.
Frank Rodgers: plates 6–8, 37.
Royal Agricultural Society of England: plates 3, 4, 13; pages 21–2.
Science Museum: plates 15–17, 29, 33–4, 55; page 71.
Seaspeed Ltd: plate 30.
Shaw Savill and Albion Co. Ltd: plate 28.
Southern Newspapers Ltd: plate 56.
S.P.C.K.: pages 42, 54.
Steel Company of Wales: plate 59.
Headmaster, Taunton's School, Southampton: plate 57.
University of London Library: plates 5, 31–2, 36, 38, 40, 42; pages 30–1, 33, 36–7, 46–7, 72, 94, 98, 111, 127, 141, 144–7, 150–3, 158, 164, 199.
Wedgwood and Sons Ltd: plates 9, 10.
Reece Winstone: plates 11, 18–22, 48–9.
G. Bernard Wood: plates 14, 45.

Plates

Figures and Diagrams

Maps

PART ONE

The Eighteenth Century

CHAPTER 1

The People of England, 1700–1815

THE SIZE OF THE POPULATION

Today we are very aware of the fact that the population of England, and indeed of the whole world, is rising. Government departments make plans on the assumption that our population will continue to rise, and that we will need more houses, more schools, and more food. In the United Kingdom an official count, or census, of people is made every ten years, so that we now have accurate statistics to show the growth of population. But the first British census did not take place until 1801; any figures for population before that date are the result of guesswork. During the eighteenth century some people were trying to calculate the size of the population (it has been called an age of 'political arithmetic'), and scholars since then have devoted much time to the problem. But even now we are not absolutely certain of the size of England's population during the eighteenth century, and the further we go back in time the more hazardous the guesswork. However, it is reasonable to suppose that the population of England and Wales grew relatively slowly during the centuries before 1700: from 1·8 million in 1086 (the year of the Domesday Book), to 2·2 million in 1377, and 4·1 million in 1600.

In 1696 Gregory King, a map-maker and surveyor, estimated the population of England and Wales as 5·5 million. He used the Hearth Tax returns in making his calculations, and it is probable that he underestimated. As far as we know, there was no significant change in this slow upward trend during the first half of the eighteenth century. Between 1700 and 1720 the total may have fallen slightly, but by about 1750 it was 6·4 million. Assuming that these estimates are correct, a graph will show that the rate of growth was much as

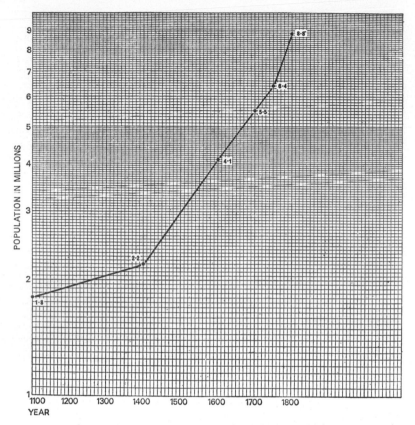

The probable growth of the population of England and Wales, 1100–1800. This graph is logarithmic on the vertical axis and has a natural scale on the horizontal axis. The student should draw a graph using the natural scale on both axes.

before. During the second half of the century the population probably grew as follows:

	millions
1760	6·7
1770	7·4
1780	7·9
1790	8·6
1801	8·8

This rate of growth was greater than that of any previous period. It is true that it was slight compared with that of the nineteenth cen-

1 Hogarth's Gin Lane, *a horrific representation of the evils of cheap spirits. The arch,
bottom left, bears the legend 'Drunk for a penny, Dead drunk for twopence, Clean straw
for nothing'. There was a companion print which showed that beer-drinking had healthier
results.* (p. 6)

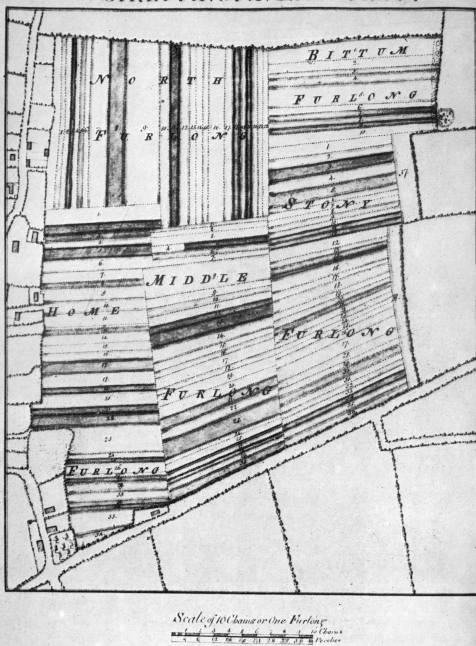

2 *A page from the survey of open fields in a Sussex village, made by the Enclosure Commissioners in 1781. The numbers on the furlong strips denote ownership before consolidation.* (p. 17)

tury.[1] (From 8·8 million in 1801 the population of England and Wales grew to 17·9 million in 1851, and to 32·5 million in 1901.) But to people in 1800 it appeared that the population was growing spectacularly and rapidly.

Malthus' Warning

It had been customary to regard the growth of a country's population as a sign of growing strength. 'People is riches' was the succinct if ungrammatical phrase. More people meant more workers, more customers, more soldiers. A bigger population meant that a country could embark upon more ambitious enterprises because its labour force could become more specialised. However, in 1798 the Reverend Thomas Robert Malthus (1766–1834) published a book entitled *An Essay on the Principles of Population*.[2] This book had a great influence on the people of the time, as the author looked at the problem from an original standpoint. Malthus argued that a thriving people tended to multiply more rapidly than its means of subsistence. He foresaw a shortage of agricultural land, and considered that disease and famine would follow if nothing was done to check the growth of population. Among other things, he suggested that people should not marry at an early age, and that they should be aware of the dangers of too large a family. (He did *not* advocate birth control, as did Francis Place thirty years later.) Malthus' book was published three years before the first census, which appeared to give further point to his argument. Fortunately, although the population grew far more rapidly than Malthus had predicted, his gloomy forecast did not come true. The nineteenth century saw improvements in farming and in transport which enabled England to feed its population better than before, though this meant that the country had to rely more upon imported food. But his warning was a salutary one. The old adage 'with every mouth God sends a pair of hands' has a corollary— with every pair of hands a mouth to feed. The problem which Malthus saw may have been postponed rather than obviated.

The Reasons for Growth

What were the causes of the increase in the population of England and Wales during the last decades of the eighteenth century? To

[1] See p. 85.   [2] See p. 297.

answer this question it is necessary to begin with general principles. A country's population increases or decreases according to the balance between births and deaths (*natural increase*) and the balance between immigration and emigration. There is no evidence to suggest that the rise was caused by an influx of people into England. Jews and Protestants came to England from central Europe to escape persecution. A more numerous group of immigrants came from Scotland after the Act of Union in 1707, and from Ireland. But these were at least balanced by Englishmen who went overseas to the West Indies, India and America. The answer must, therefore, be found in the natural increase.

During the first half of the eighteenth century the death rate showed little significant change. Each age finds its own killer (in our day, for example, the cigarette and the motor car). The bubonic plague, which had decimated the population in the Middle Ages, disappeared from England after the Fire of London in 1666. But disease and epidemics still swept through the country. The number of deaths from smallpox declined very slowly after 1721 as inoculation and later vaccination became more common among the wealthy; but the effect of this in the eighteenth century was very slight as the poor could not afford vaccination. Other diseases caused by unhygienic conditions were widespread: malaria and dysentery thrived in an age which lacked a sewage system, in which refuse choked the ditches, and in which paupers' communal graves remained open until they were full. The temporary arresting of the growth of population during the first three decades was probably due to deaths from influenza and smallpox.

Excessive consumption of alcohol may have shortened the lives of some of the poor in the first half of the century. The wars against France in the reigns of William III and Anne made the importation of French brandy difficult, and this resulted in an increase in British-distilled gin and whisky. As the production of these spirits entailed the use of wheat and barley, and aided the British farmer, only a low duty was imposed, and the price was well within the range of all. Gin drinking became a scourge, particularly in London. William Hogarth (1697–1764) satirised the scandal in his famous caricature *Gin Lane*. In 1742–43 the output of British spirits was 8 million gallons (including 7 million gallons of gin). In 1751 the government

placed a high duty on spirits, and thereafter the consumption of gin
fell rapidly (in 1780 it was 1 million gallons).

Another reason for the high death rate was the lack of medical care
given to women in child-birth, and to very young children. In 1739
half of all those who died in London were children under eleven
years old, whilst 38 per cent were aged three or under. At the British
Lying-in Hospital in London, between 1749 and 1759, the mortality
rate was 1 in 42 for mothers, and 1 in 15 for their babies. By the end
of the century the rate was 1 in 938 for mothers, and 1 in 118 for
children.

However, the good done by the Lying-in (or maternity) Hospital
in London was not paralleled in the achievements of other hospitals,
despite their growing number. Nine new hospitals, including Guys',
were founded in London in the period 1720 to 1760. Outside London,
in 1720, the only hospitals were in Rochester and in Bath. By 1760
there were sixteen provincial hospitals, and by 1800 the number had
grown to thirty-eight. Dispensaries for the poor were also established
at this time. The first was founded by Dr Armstrong in 1769 in
London, and in the next twenty years a further twelve were established in the capital. But these foundations did little to prevent
deaths. The methods of the medical profession were still primitive.
A lack of knowledge of hygiene and the causes of infection led to
epidemics and deaths. Surgical methods, until the discovery of anti-
septics and anaesthetics in the nineteenth century, were such that one
out of every two amputations led to the death of the patient. Indeed,
entry into a hospital during the eighteenth century probably decreased rather than increased a sick person's chances of survival.

The reason for the decline in the death-rate in the second half of
the eighteenth century was a rising standard of living. There was
more fresh meat and vegetables, and an improvement in the food
supply, so that not so many people died of starvation or diseases
caused by malnutrition; transport improved, so that food shortages
in a particular area could be remedied. The development of overseas
trade led to a more balanced diet. New houses, though poor by our
standards, were built of bricks and mortar, instead of timber and
mud; they had slate roofs instead of thatch, and the effect of these
changes was to reduce disease-carrying pests. More coal was hewn,
and it could more easily be transported; coal fires and drier houses

led to a decline in deaths from rheumatoid complaints. Personal cleanliness was improved by an increase in the production of soap and of cotton clothing (the latter could be washed more easily and more frequently than woollen garments).

It is probable that the birth-rate rose between about 1740 and 1790. Various reasons for this have been suggested. The decline of the apprenticeship system may have led to earlier marriages. A young man serving his seven years usually had to sign an agreement that he would not marry until his time was up, and he would then need to work for a few years before he could support a wife. The poem *Sally in our Alley*, written by Henry Carey, has these lines:

> But when my seven long years are out
> O then I'll marry Sally.

Many domestic servants had to remain single or lose their employment and their 'homes'. As the eighteenth century progressed, married quarters for domestic servants became more common. As transport improved, young men and women, who would in former times have remained unmarried because of a lack of marriage partners in their own class and locality, were able to find a spouse. Also, the decline of landholding meant that parents did not need to discourage early marriages, which formerly would have led to further division of the property. Whatever the reasons, a great increase in the birth rate, coupled with a much smaller decline in the death rate, was causing the population to grow at an unprecedented rate by the end of the eighteenth century.

Geographical Distribution

In 1700 the most densely populated, or rather the least sparsely populated area of England and Wales was the south, roughly comprising those counties which fall within lines drawn from Worcestershire and Norfolk to Somerset and Kent. One-tenth of the total population lived in London, Westminster and Middlesex. This London area, with over half a million inhabitants in 1700, continued to grow in the eighteenth century. Outside London, the biggest town in England in 1700 was Bristol, with 40,000 people. Norwich had 28,000, York and Exeter about 12,000, Worcester and Nottingham 10,000, Shrewsbury 7,000, Southampton about 5,000, and Birmingham,

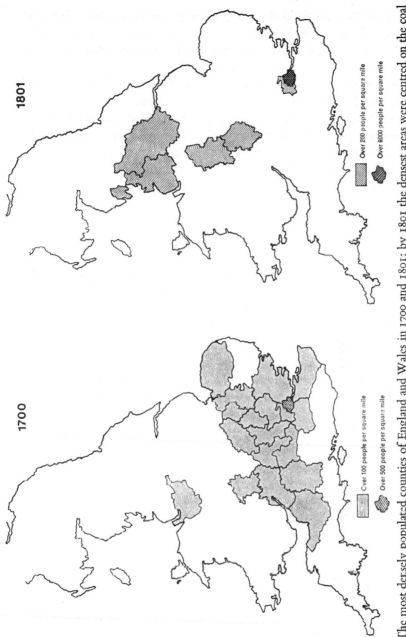

1700

Over 100 people per square mile

Over 500 people per square mile

1801

Over 200 people per square mile

Over 9000 people per square mile

The most densely populated counties of England and Wales in 1700 and 1801: by 1801 the densest areas were centred on the coal and iron fields. These maps are based on average density. In fact some parts of each county were much more thickly populated than others; north Lancashire, for example, had very few people.

Liverpool and Sheffield about 4,000. In the course of the century the centre of population began to shift from the south to the midlands and the north, as industry developed. The iron industry, once important in Sussex and Gloucestershire, moved to Shropshire, Worcestershire, Staffordshire and south Yorkshire. The cotton industry grew in Lancashire, silk weaving in Cheshire and Coventry. By 1800, London had nearly one million inhabitants, and was still by far the biggest town in England. But Manchester, Birmingham and Liverpool had grown to about 90,000, small when compared with the capital, but large by the standards of the day. Bath and Norwich, for example, had about 40,000 people. In 1800, as in 1700, the majority of the people lived and worked in rural surroundings.

CLASSES OF PEOPLE

Although there were no rigid barriers between the classes in England during the eighteenth century—there were no feudal duties, no serfs, no villeins—and although it was possible for the clever and the lucky young man to better himself, it cannot be denied that there was little equality of opportunity. There was a vast difference between rich and poor. On the one hand were the great landowners with an income of as much as £20,000 a year (about £200,000 in our money), on the other there were poor labourers earning about £20 a year. There were, indeed, two nations—the rich and the poor.

The Aristocracy

The peers and their relatives were able to hold many of the highest offices in the government and in the Church. Some of these posts were very highly paid. The famous Duke of Marlborough, for example, received £6,000 a year as Captain-General and Master of the Ordnance. The aristocracy, as well as owning vast areas of land, were very active in business enterprises, unlike most of their European counterparts. As they had vast incomes, they were able to provide the capital necessary for new concerns. The Dukes of Devonshire put much money into coalmining; the Dukes of Bedford engaged in speculative building in London; the Duke of Bridgewater built the first important English canal; Viscount Townshend took an active interest in farming. They were not 'idle rich', but leaders of Church and state, and pioneers in industry and commerce. They also led comfortable lives. They spent some of their time in their country houses. During the eighteenth century many of the 'historic homes' of today were built or improved. Blenheim Palace was built; Woburn Abbey, Welbeck Abbey, and Palace House, Beaulieu, were enlarged. The aristocracy spent some of the year in London, and the eighteenth century saw the development of fashionable areas in the capital. In 1700 Soho and Bloomsbury were fashionable; by 1800 Mayfair was the most sought-after district. Within this time Berkeley Square, Devonshire House, Harley Street, the original Regent Street and Regent's Park were built. In London the rich could work and play. They could visit the coffee houses, such as White's, Boodle's, the Cocoa Tree, or Almack's. They gambled and they drank. (The expression 'drunk as a lord' was an apt one.) Their wives and daughters engaged in many pursuits which in the nineteenth century were regarded as 'unlady-like'. They went hunting, took part in electioneering, drank and gambled. Cricket was a popular pastime among ladies; when they played they wore white dresses, and coloured hair ribbons distinguished the two sides.

The Middle Classes

Next to the aristocracy were the middle classes, engaged in the professions and in farming. Gregory King tells us that there were 23,000 families in 1696 with an income of between £70 and £200 a year. Many of the inventors and the founders of manufacturing businesses belonged to this class. Jethro Tull, who patented a seed-drill, was a lawyer; Samuel Whitbread, the brewer, was the son of a landowner; Jedediah Strutt, the hosiery manufacturer, was the son of a farmer; John Wilkinson, the iron master, was the son of a hardware retailer. Businesses and trades were mostly family concerns. An ironmaster's sons became ironmasters, and married daughters of ironmasters, and so on. One remarkable feature of 'captains of industry' in the eighteenth century was the large number who were Nonconformists (i.e. Protestants who were not members of the Church of England). Among these were Abraham Darby, Benjamin Huntsman, Jedediah Strutt, Aaron Walker, and Josiah Wedgwood. The success of the Nonconformists in business was due to the excellent technical education they received in their schools, the 'dissenting academies', their strict upbringing, and their exclusion from public office because of their religion.

The Lower Classes

The lower classes can be divided into three main groups. First there were the skilled craftsmen, such as the shipwright, the blacksmith, or the wheelwright. These could make a reasonable living, for there was work for the skilled man, and they could play some part in local affairs. Secondly there were the unskilled or semi-skilled, such as porters and labourers, who lived at little more than subsistence level. Their work was often seasonal, and bad weather could cause them prolonged unemployment. They lived in poor houses of wattle and daub, with clay floors and low roofs. The poor countryman could gather wood for a fire, but the poor townsman often had a hot meal only on Sundays, cooked in the nearest bake-house. Such unskilled men earned from £14 to £20 a year at a time when rent of a hovel cost about 6d. a week, beer ½d. a quart, and wheat bread 1d. per lb. A third group were those who were unable to earn even a bare living. Gregory King calculated that in 1696 there were 400,000 such families in England and Wales. It is no wonder that there were so many thieves and beggars among 'the rabble'.

Even those poor who were in regular employment found it difficult to keep out of the hands of the moneylenders. Farm servants were usually paid annually, shipwrights were paid half-yearly (one quarter in arrears), and casual labour was usually paid at the end of the job. The worker needed to borrow at a high rate of interest until such time as he was paid, and he needed to plan his expenditure with some care. In one way the development of the factory, where the men were usually paid weekly, was the salvation of the poor.

Because there were so many people who were very poor, and some people who were very rich, domestic servants—both men and women—formed a very large occupational group. The very wealthy employed a variety of servants: cooks, butlers, footmen, grooms, chambermaids, housemaids, laundry maids, and scullery maids. Their hours were long, and their wages low, but they were no worse off than the countryman working in his cottage or the factory-worker in the town. The domestic servant had some chance of promotion. The young girl, starting in the lowest rank, as a scullery maid, could become a housekeeper or a lady's maid. The boy, starting as a page or postillion, could become a butler or even a bailiff. Moreover, the domestic servant had two great advantages over other workers. He (or she) often had better living conditions, and in time of trouble would be looked after by the master. The aristocracy usually did for their servants what the welfare state does today. The great disadvantage of domestic service was the lack of freedom. Marriage might cause dismissal, for example.

The amusements of the poor can be termed escapist. Drink was the means whereby they sought to forget their miseries. Cock-fighting and bull-baiting were popular pastimes—more typical of eighteenth-century England than country dancing. Brutality and hedonism were the keynotes of the age. Towards the end of the century there were signs of improvement. The Society for Promoting Christian Knowledge, founded in 1698, through its Charity Schools was teaching some of the poor to read and write. The London Society for the Reformation of Manners and the Sunday Observance Society were attacking the loose morality of all classes. The rumbustious England of *Tom Jones* was to give way, in the nineteenth century, to a more disciplined and ordered society.

CHAPTER 2

The Land, 1700-1815

THE PRODUCE OF THE LAND

In 1700 the majority of the English people lived in rural surroundings; today the majority live in towns. Whereas we are, generally speaking, unlikely to spend much of our working life in the production of food, people in the eighteenth century (and indeed the nineteenth century) had to devote much of their energy to it. Apart from those who lived in London, all the inhabitants needed to know something about how to grow food. Farm-workers were by far the largest occupational group in England. In addition, craftsmen, such as blacksmiths, wheelwrights and wainwrights, were engaged indirectly in agriculture. Work on the land was done by the whole family—by the man, his wife and children. Children had to dig, use a sickle, spread manure, feed and look after pigs and poultry. Cottager's wives did much of the manual work in the garden, milked the cows, collected manure and helped with the sowing and the harvest. Women worked as farm labourers; farmers' wives looked after the dairy and the accounts, as well as doing manual labour in the busy times. Women did this work in addition to the brewing, the baking, the sewing, the spinning, the cooking, and looking after their children.

The people had to produce their own food. It is obvious that before the invention of refrigeration, before the development of quick transport, and before the invention of air-tight tins, most perishable foodstuffs could not be preserved. Ice-pits and salt-bins were used to preserve meat, but it was not possible for a Londoner to have milk from a cow in Wales, or for a Bristol family to be supplied with eggs from Northumberland. The produce of the land was mostly consumed by people living locally. And in order to eat, the people had to produce meat and grain. They could not specialise, as we do today, and so most farms were what are called 'mixed' farms, i.e. both pastoral and arable.

However, agricultural produce did not merely consist of meat and grain. The land, and its products, played an even more important role. Wheat, used in the south of England for making bread, was more than food. Some wheat was needed by the distillers for making spirits. Wheaten flour was used by stationers, bookbinders, and paper-hangers as paste; it was also the chief ingredient in the making of starch, which was used by housewives, hairdressers, paper-makers and washer-women. Barley was grown chiefly to produce drink, namely beer and ale. Rye was used for cheap bread and as meal for animals and poultry; it was also used by the tanners in the processing of leather. Animals were more than a source of meat. Sheep provided wool as well as mutton, and cattle provided leather as well as beef. At the beginning of the eighteenth century wool was the chief raw material used in the textile industry, whilst leather was needed for shoes, breeches, gloves and harness. The horns of sheep and cattle were used for making cutlery handles, and the bones for glue-making. The fat was needed by the soap-boilers and was used as grease for lubricating cogs and wheels. Sheep fat was used also by the tallow-makers, who made candles for the poor—the rich used wax and whale-oil.

THE AGRARIAN REVOLUTION

During the eighteenth century, especially in the second half, there was a need to increase agricultural production, owing to the rise of population, and to a greater number of people being needed as full-time industrial workers. Because 'necessity is the mother of invention', changes took place in agriculture which are sometimes called 'the agrarian revolution'. This is a term which we use with reservations, as the changes took place very gradually, over a long period of time. The changes were as follows: the use of more land for farming, higher productivity, an increase in the size of farms, the investment of capital in farming, new techniques of farming, and the invention of new tools.

Enclosures

One of the means whereby more land was brought into better use was that of enclosure. This process meant one of three things. First, it was used to denote the redistribution of landholding so that each farmer's land was consolidated, instead of consisting of scattered strips. Secondly, the term was used when land, already consolidated, was enclosed by hedge, fence, or wall. Thirdly, it meant that land which had been used only for grazing by all the villagers, i.e. common land, was enclosed for arable purposes. Enclosure was not an 'invention' of the eighteenth century. It was a process which had been going on for several centuries, but one which was accelerated after about 1750.

The old *open field* method of farming, with its scattered strips of arable land and communal pastures, had disadvantages. Minor defects were the time lost in walking from a strip in one open field to another, and the difficulty of introducing new methods of cultivation. But, more important, land was wasted as each year one-third of the open fields were left fallow, and scientific breeding of cattle, by selective mating, was almost impossible.

During the sixteenth century there was an 'enclosure movement', in spite of opposition from the government, aimed at the improvement of sheep-farming. The enclosure movement in the eighteenth century was encouraged by the government, and attempted to improve arable farming. If the scattered strips were replaced by a system whereby each man held his land in one parcel, then each man's land could be surrounded by a hedge or fence, and he could drain it, rotate the crops, and carry out selective breeding.

The parts of England most affected by the enclosures of the eighteenth century were those where the land was used in the main for arable purposes, or where land which had hitherto been waste-land could profitably be put under the plough. In general, this comprised a region from the coasts of Dorset and Hampshire northwards to the south of Yorkshire. About half the arable land in this central wedge was enclosed before 1700. The number of Acts of Parliament passed authorising enclosures gives some indication of the impetus of the movement after 1760. However, the number of Acts does not tell the whole story of the extent of enclosures, for enclosures were carried out by two other methods besides: (1) by consent, where all the landowners agreed; (2) by the purchase by one man of all the land in the open fields.

	COMMON FIELDS		WASTE	
	no. of Acts	acreage	no. of Acts	acreage
1700–1760	152	237,845	56	74,518
1760–1801	1,479	2,428,721	521	752,150
1802–1844	1,075	1,110,302	808	939,043

When enclosure was effected by an Act of Parliament, the method was as follows. A public meeting, usually called by the biggest land-owner, and attended by all the landholders, was held in the village. If the owners of three-quarters of the land agreed, a petition was nailed to the door of the parish church. Landholders signed this petition, for and against. If the same majority of the landowners (which could be one or two very rich men) favoured enclosure, a Bill was prepared by lawyers and sent to Westminster. The Bill was debated in the House of Commons and the Lords, signed by the King, and became an Act. The Act appointed three, five or seven commissioners to carry out the enclosure; these commissioners were usually gentry, who acted as 'umpires', and they in turn appointed paid surveyors and valuers. In due course, the land was reallocated among the landholders, roads and drains were made, and hedges planted or fences erected. When the task was completed, the cost was divided among the landholders, in proportion to the value of their land. The costs were often large, and many of the small landowners had difficulty in finding their share of the expenses. In 1801, the General Enclosure Act was passed; this laid down model clauses for enclosure acts, simplified the legal procedure, and considerably lessened the costs.

What were the effects of enclosures? On farming as a science, they were entirely beneficial. By the rotation of crops, land yielded more grain an acre. As land which had hitherto been waste or common land was ploughed up, the total area of arable land grew. Hedges helped to protect the crops from high winds, and from damage done by stray animals. A greater variety of food could be produced, including more vegetables. Also, more animal fodder could be grown, so that it was no longer necessary to slaughter so many beasts each Michaelmas. This meant that there was more fresh meat to be had in the winter, and that the breeds of cattle and sheep could be improved. More animals meant more manure, more manure meant more fodder, more fodder more animals. . . . It was far better to have a flock of sheep folded on a field which would in turn be used for arable purposes, than to have them roaming on waste or common land. As the productivity of farm-land grew, the possibility of profit grew, so that rich men were willing to invest capital. These rich farmers were the pioneers of new methods, and without their investment English farming would have developed more slowly than it did. Enclosures were certainly a factor in enabling England to feed her growing population.

The Results of Enclosures

How did enclosures affect people? In the long run, everyone gained, as greater productivity per acre meant more food. But at the time some people suffered. The rich landowner was certainly able to make farming more profitable. The small landowner, or 'yeoman', was not adversely affected by enclosures. The number of smallholders, farming a few acres, and employing one or two men did not decline in the eighteenth century; it is possible that the number rose. The smallholder was, however, hard hit by the conditions which prevailed at the end of the Napoleonic Wars (1815), and he tended to disappear. But to blame enclosures for the disappearance of the yeoman farmer is unjustified. Those who suffered were the squatters, who kept animals on land to which they had no legal right, and those cottagers who kept a pig or some poultry on the common land. As they had no documentary proof of ownership (indeed it is most likely that their family had never possessed any), they found themselves, after enclosure, without any land. Another group who suffered were the casual labourers, who found that the new farmers wanted full-time workers. But there is no evidence that the number employed in farming fell, and it is highly probable that more farm-workers were needed with the introduction of new methods. There is no evidence either that villages became smaller because of enclosures; it was simply that the towns grew much more rapidly. And, as industry developed, the sons of farm-workers could seek employment in the nearest town, where they might enjoy a higher standard of living. People are usually disturbed by change, even if the changes are beneficial. Some eighteenth-century writers give the impression that enclosures brought untold misery to the villagers. Oliver Goldsmith wrote a poem in 1770 called *The Deserted Village*, which contains these lines:

> Ill fares the land, to hastening ills a prey,
> Where wealth accumulates, and men decay . . .
> But a bold peasantry, their country's pride,
> When once destroyed, can never be supplied.

Arthur Young, a champion of enclosures, wrote in 1801 that:

by nineteen enclosure acts out of twenty the poor are injured, in some grossly injured. . . . Go to an alehouse of an old enclosed country, and there you will see the origin of poverty and the poor rates.

It seems likely that hardship was caused to some as enclosures co-incided with the rise of population, but that unemployment and poverty would have existed even if enclosures had not been carried out.

Techniques of Farming

The advances in farming techniques in England in the eighteenth century were important ones. Whereas in 1700 Englishmen went to Europe to study new methods, by the end of the century England had become the model for the rest of the Continent. The changes came about slowly, and were largely the result of systematic and scientific experiment by noblemen or rich gentry with large estates, and capital to invest.

One problem was making light sandy soil suitable for growing crops. A traditional method was to plant shrubs, usually broom, and after about two years to cut them and dig in the branches. This was, however, an expensive method, as it involved the employment of much labour and the land could not be put under cultivation for several years. Early in the eighteenth century the use of marl as a fertiliser was revived in Norfolk. Marl is a mixture of clay and carbonate of lime, and was found in quantity in the fenland districts of East Anglia. But although some progress was made in recovering poor sandy soil in the eighteenth century, it was not until the nine-teenth that a great advance was made.

There was a gradual improvement in the scientific rotation of crops. If the same crop is grown on the same piece of land year after year, the soil will become poorer and poorer. In the open field system, the usual practice was to leave one field fallow every third year. This rested the soil, but was obviously wasteful. During the seventeenth century Sir Richard Weston (1591–1652) had noticed that Dutch farmers used a system of crop rotation whereby some crop was grown every year, and he experimented on his own estates. During the eighteenth century the idea gradually spread. Richard Bradley, Professor of Botany in the University of Cambridge, carried out further experiments, and his ideas were later put into practice by Viscount Townshend (1674–1738). Townshend was a Whig, brother-in-law of Robert Walpole, and he held several high government offices until 1730, when he resigned after a quarrel with Walpole. He retired to his estates at Rainham, near King's Lynn in Norfolk, and spent the remainder of his life improving them. The land was sandy, with some coarse grass which afforded poor pasture for sheep. By the time of Townshend's death, Rainham was producing grain, and had rich sheep pastures. The land was marled and manured. A four-course rotation of crops was used, which came to be called the 'Norfolk System'. In a four-year cycle, wheat, turnips, barley and clover were grown. Turnips helped to clean the ground of weeds, and sheep could be folded on them as they grew in the field, so that whilst the sheep were provided with fodder, they in turn manured the field. Clover, as well as being animal fodder, fed the soil with nitrogen and made it richer for growing corn. This rotation gradually spread through Norfolk, for it was particularly suited to sandy soil, and then, with variations, to other parts of the country. In lieu of clover, other grasses, such as sanfoin and lucerne, were grown; towards the end of the eighteenth century the Swedish turnip (or 'swede') was introduced.

An increase in animal fodder meant that improvements could be made in livestock. By selective breeding, farmers were able to produce sheep and cattle with shorter legs and necks and smaller bones, so that more meat was obtained from each animal. One pioneer in stock-breeding was Robert Bakewell (1725–95) of Dishley, Leicestershire. He improved Longhorn cattle, and bred fine horses, but he is most famous for a breed of sheep, the New Leicestershire. His methods were used by other breeders, including Charles and Robert Colling, of Darlington, who developed Shorthorn cattle; John

3   *Robert Bakewell, the stock-breeder.* (p. 20)

4   *Thomas Coke (on the left), inspecting some of his South Down sheep on his estate at Holkham, Norfolk.* (p. 23)

5 *Thorncliffe Ironworks,*
1810. They were established
in this pleasant valley some
eight miles north of Sheffield
in 1793. Today the valley is
covered by industrial
buildings. (p. 32)

6 *England's first cotton*
mill, established by Ark-
wright in 1771 on the river
Derwent at Cromford,
Derbyshire. (p. 40)

Ellman of Glynde, who improved Southern sheep; and the Quartleys who improved Devon cattle. Other breeders imported Chinese pigs in order to improve the English stock.

Farming Tools

Coincidental with these improvements in arable and pastoral farming were experiments with new farming implements. Jethro Tull (1674–1741) of Berkshire published a book called *Horse Hoeing*

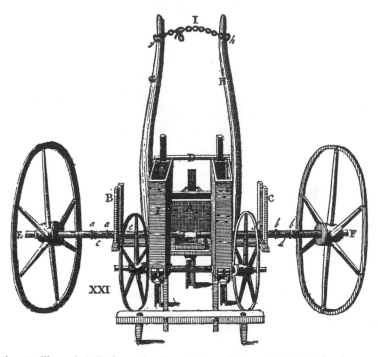

Jethro Tull's seed-drill, from the first edition of *Horse Hoeing Husbandry*, 1731. This drill sowed at a controlled depth, and the spacing was determined by the seeds being dropped from a ratchet-wheel on the axle.

Husbandry in 1731, in which he described two tools which he was using. The first was a seed-drill, which planted at a uniform depth and distance apart. (He had conducted many careful experiments with various crops to find the best depth and width.)[1] The second

[1] James Cooke improved the seed-drill in 1782.

of Tull's inventions was a horse-drawn hoe, which removed weeds and broke up the soil near growing crops, thus allowing oxygen to reach the roots. Another important development was the introduction of a new plough in about 1720, copied from the Dutch, and usually known as the Rotherham (Rotterdam?) plough. This plough was smaller and lighter than those used hitherto, with an iron coulter and share, so that it needed fewer horses or oxen to draw it. It was a swing plough, i.e. the coulter could be set at a different angle after each furrow. The Rotherham plough was widely used in the north

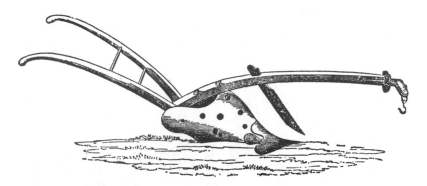

The Rotherham plough, developed after 1720, was later improved by Robert Ransome of Ipswich in 1785, when he patented a cast-iron share—immeasurably better than the traditional wrought-iron ones.

and the east. Towards the end of the eighteenth century other farm implements, such as clod-crushers and harrows, were made of iron. As some of these were too big to be made by the local craftsmen, specialist firms developed. One of the earliest was that of Robert Ransome, who established a factory at Ipswich in 1789.

Propagandists

The new techniques, and the new tools, spread only slowly throughout the country, despite the activities of the propagandists. One of the most important of them was Arthur Young (1741–1820), who was born in London, and educated in Suffolk. After failing to make a success of running a small farm, he became an agricultural journalist, and between 1767 and 1815 published over thirty books.

In these he advocated large farms, enclosures, and the new methods. He toured various parts of England, as well as Ireland, France and Italy, amassing material for his books. From 1784 to 1809 he edited *Annals of Agriculture*, to which George III contributed. In 1793, at the outbreak of the war with France, a Board of Agriculture, which lasted until 1821, was established as a private venture with some help from the Government, in order to increase the food supply. Arthur Young was appointed as Secretary to the Board, with Sir John Sinclair, a Scottish landowner, as President. William Marshall (1745–1818), a Yorkshireman, published *A Survey of Rural Economy* in 1787 —an important analysis of the state of English farming. The first issue of *The Farmer's Magazine* had appeared in 1776. Another important propagandist was Thomas Coke (1752–1842), a practical farmer who was very wealthy. He inherited his estates at Holkham in Norfolk in 1776. When he began, the annual rents of his property were worth £12,300 a year; in 1816 they had risen to £25,700. He used the new methods himself, and encouraged his tenants to do likewise. To stimulate investment in the land and in equipment, he gave his tenants long leases. From 1778 he held an annual sheep-shearing meeting, known colloquially as 'Coke's Clippings'. At first these gatherings were intended only for Coke's tenants, but they became so famous that visitors came from all over England and from some parts of Europe. At the last meeting in 1821, 7,000 people were present. At these meetings, farm implements, improved breeds of animals and varieties of crops were to be seen. The Holkham sheep-shearings were, in effect, the forerunner of the agricultural show.

Farming became a fashionable enterprise. King George III, whose example was followed by many others, farmed part of Windsor Park, and deserves his title of 'Farmer George'. The increased interest in farming is shown by the establishment of a Chair in Agriculture in the University of Edinburgh in 1790, and a Chair of Rural Economy at Oxford in 1796. And the increased production of food helped England to feed her growing population, to fight the long wars against France, and to develop industries.

CHAPTER 3

Industrial Growth, 1700-1815

During the eighteenth century, especially in the latter half, a series of improvements were made in some branches of industry which resulted in Britain becoming during the nineteenth century a predominantly industrial nation. In 1881, Arnold Toynbee gave a series of lectures entitled 'The Industrial Revolution of the Eighteenth Century in England' to a group of working men. The phrase 'Industrial Revolution' became popular, and in various books the term is still used to denote the changes which took place during the period from about 1760 to about 1830. The term, convenient enough when first used, is today open to several objections. The course of industrial change has speeded up in the twentieth century, so that we are very conscious that we live ourselves in an age of 'industrial revolution'; to us the changes which took place in the eighteenth century appear to have evolved relatively slowly. Further, whilst some industries saw radical change, e.g. cotton, others such as shipbuilding remained relatively static. A more convenient term for us to apply to the eighteenth century and the early nineteenth century is a phrase using imagery of our own era—the 'take-off into an industrial society'.

The improvements which took place led to the application of science to industry, to the growth of factories and works in large towns, to the beginnings of mechanisation, to an increase in industrial production, and to a rapid growth in overseas trade.

The Impetus for Change

Why did these improvements take place when they did? 'Necessity is the mother of invention.' Because the demand for manufactured goods increased, means had to be found for greater production, and innovation bred innovation. The demand was stimulated by several factors. The people of England needed more goods, because the size of the population rose simultaneously with a rise in living standards. During the period from 1700 to 1815, England spent many years at war with France. Whilst these wars retarded the steady growth of industry in general, certain industries and some regions were stimulated. As an example, whilst the tin-mining industry in Cornwall declined, iron production in the midlands grew. In both cases, the wars made quite a difference to their fortunes. But the wars against France also added to Britain's overseas empire; you will have read of Wolfe and Quebec, and of Clive in India. The British Empire had become, by 1815, a world-wide one, and was important to Britain's economy as a source of raw material, and as a market for manufactured goods. Also, as Britain began to industrialise before the rest of Europe, she had in addition a large number of customers on the Continent.

Britain began to industrialise before other European countries because she had many advantages. As the wars were fought on foreign soil, or on the seas, the country was not ravaged. England had comparative political stability, and some semblance of internal order. Further, the country possessed rich men who were willing to invest capital in new enterprises. Capital is essential to industrial expansion: inventors, founders of factories, builders of expensive machinery, all needed ready capital. These 'captains of industry', versatile hard working men, often risked their entire fortunes, and lived frugally, so that succeeding generations reaped the full benefit of their labours. The country banks, which had developed at the end of the seventeenth century, also played an important part as suppliers of capital.

England had the labour force necessary for industrial expansion because of the rise of population. Further, as serfdom had virtually disappeared (it still existed in several European countries), the people were relatively mobile, and were able to seek employment in new or expanding industries in regions other than that of their birth. The decay of guild restrictions, and the comparative absence of government regulation, also contributed to the conditions essential to change.

The improvements in transport, especially the building of canals

NEWCASTLE
Coal

KENDAL
Woollens

Woollens   LEEDS
                    Woollens   HULL

MANCHESTER
Cotton   SHEFFIELD
                  Cutlery

Lead

CHESTER   *Lace*
Woollens   NOTTINGHAM   *Woollens
Salt*   *Hosiery*   *(declining)*
Pottery   LEICESTER   NORWICH

Hardware   BIRMINGHAM

Iron

LONDON
BRISTOL

*Lead Woollens
(declining)*   *Iron*

Tin

The location of industry, *c.* 1750. England was still a mainly agricultural country
and her industry was scattered. Compare this with the map on p. 139.

and better roads, made industrial expansion easier. Invention and
technical improvements were stimulated by the growth of scientific
knowledge in the preceding century, which had seen the foundation
of the Royal Society. Also, as steam power became an essential of
increased production, England was fortunate in having coal and iron
in abundance.

IRON

There were no great problems in mining the iron ore. As the mines were usually shallow, the miners were not troubled by flooding or by poisonous or inflammable gases. Miners were able to split the rocks by heating them and then cooling them rapidly with water, or by using gun-powder. The men used cast-iron tools such as picks, wedges and crowbars. Many of the old workings, usually rectangular shafts, can still be seen in the Mendips, or in the Peak District of Derbyshire.

It is true that England's iron ore contains much waste, sometimes as much as 50 per cent. But despite this, the country had in the eighteenth century plenty of natural mineral for its purposes. The expansion of the iron industry was impeded by three problems. First, iron ore is a bulky commodity, and until canals were built and roads improved after 1760, transport was difficult. Until then, local iron-stone had to be used, or mineral which could be brought by water. Secondly, power was needed in some stages of iron manufacturing, e.g. for working the bellows in order to increase the heat of the furnaces, and for lifting the great hammer in the forges. Until the development of the steam engine in the second half of the eighteenth century, ironworks were sometimes sited at 'hammer-ponds', so that hydraulic hammers could be used, but water was not always available at certain times of the year. Thirdly, and most important, there was a shortage of fuel.

The manufacture of iron required intense heat at each stage. First, the iron ore had to be smelted in furnaces; the molten iron was then run into rectangular troughs or 'pigs'. Pig iron contained impurities and was brittle. It was either taken to a forge where it was reheated and hammered whilst red-hot into bar iron, or it was heated again in a furnace and poured into loam or clay moulds to make cast iron. Bar iron was malleable, and could be used for making nails which were used in great quantities by shipbuilders. The bars were cut into plates and the plates into thin strips at a slitting-mill. Cast iron was harder but more brittle, and was used for making items such as pots and pans, or pipes.

The fuel used in the various stages of iron manufacture was charcoal. This was expensive and scarce because timber was used for so many other purposes. Wood was the staple fuel for private houses, and for industries such as glass-making and brewing. Wood was the main constructional material for houses, bridges, docks, furniture, military fortifications, farming equipment, gates and fences, and shipbuilding. In 1700 English ironmasters were unable to supply more than half the iron needed because of lack of fuel. Bar iron was imported from the Baltic, especially from Sweden, as a partial solution to the problem.

The fuel problem was the more frustrating as England had a wealth of coal. Various experiments were made in the seventeenth century to use coal in the iron industry, without success. It was found that the sulphur content of coal made the pig iron brittle and, therefore, virtually useless. A solution was found in the eighteenth century by a Quaker family named Darby.

The Darbys of Coalbrookdale

Abraham Darby I (he must be called thus, as his son and grandson bore the same name) was born in 1678, the son of a Worcestershire nailer. After serving his apprenticeship he worked in iron foundries in Bristol and in the United Provinces. In 1709 he bought an ironworks at Coalbrookdale, Shropshire. Coalbrookdale had natural advantages: there was coal, iron and timber close at hand; the river Coalbrook, a tributary of the Severn, afforded both a means of transport and a source of power. There, in his short lifetime (he died in 1717 aged 39), Abraham Darby I founded the fortunes of a firm which is still in existence (as part of Allied Ironfounders Limited), and began experiments which his son continued. At some time after 1709 Abraham Darby I found that the local 'clod' coal had a small sulphur content, and that if this coal was subjected to a controlled burning, the 'coke' could be used in the furnace for smelting iron ore. This coke had several advantages over charcoal. It was cheaper and more plentiful; it could be used in a bigger furnace without choking, so that a higher temperature could be attained. The smelted iron was more liquid, and could be run into smaller pigs. Coke had, however, one great disadvantage—its phosphoric content. Phosphorus makes iron brittle, and most English iron ore has phosphorus in its natural state. Abraham Darby, by using coke for smelting, increased the phosphorus in the pig iron, which was suitable only for casting.

Because of this serious limitation, and perhaps because Darby kept his process a secret, the use of coke in smelting did not spread rapidly throughout the iron industry.

Abraham Darby II (1711–63) became manager of the Coalbrookdale ironworks in 1738, and took over sole control in 1745. In 1749 he improved upon his father's method and used coke to produce pig iron suitable for the forges (i.e. bar iron). Nothing is known of the actual techniques he used, but he could only make small quantities. Coalbrookdale was also the scene of other improvements and new methods. The firm made atmospheric engines, and later cast components for Watt's steam engines. Thomas and George Cranage, works foremen, invented the reverberatory furnace, later developed by Cort, in 1766. Abraham Darby III is famous for making cast iron rails, and for building (in collaboration with John Wilkinson) the first iron bridge in the world in 1779. The bridge spanned the Severn, and the small town which grew up near Coalbrookdale has been known as Ironbridge ever since. By 1800 the Coalbrookdale ironworks had over one thousand employees.

The Darbys of Coalbrookdale had pioneered the use of coal furnaces for pig and cast iron. But in the forges charcoal was still used for reheating the pig iron to make bar iron. The more the iron was reheated and hammered, the better the quality of wrought iron obtained. It was a slow and laborious process, and the enforced use of charcoal added to the expense. The bottleneck was the more irritating as pig iron could now be produced in great quantity. During the Seven Years' War (1756–63) attempts were made to use coal in the production of bar iron by Dr Roebuck of the Carron ironworks, but he was no more successful than Abraham Darby II had been. Bar iron remained scarce and expensive at a time when demand was increasing. England became more than ever dependent upon importation from Sweden and Russia—a dependence which had dangers in time of war.

Henry Cort

The problem was at last solved by Henry Cort (1740–1800), who patented the 'puddling' process in 1783 and 'rolling' in 1784. Henry Cort was born in Lancaster, and spent much of his life as an agent and contractor for the Navy in London. As he had difficulty in obtaining enough bar iron, he decided to experiment in its production himself. He moved to Fontley, near Fareham, Hants, and established an iron mill there. Fontley had certain natural advantages. There was a stream to turn the water wheels, timber was close at hand, and materials could be taken by sea from and to Fareham creek. In addition, a considerable amount of naval shipbuilding was taking place in Hampshire, particularly at Portsmouth, Bursledon and Buckler's Hard. The Navy needed iron in great quantity, for anchors, nails, knees and guns. Cort's inventions made it possible for iron to be produced in sufficient quantity to meet the demand. An iron mill could now produce fifteen tons in twelve hours where formerly a forge hammer could produce but one ton in that time.

In the puddling process the pig iron was heated in a coke-burning reverberatory furnace, so that the fuel and the iron did not come into contact with each other. When the iron was molten, it was stirred

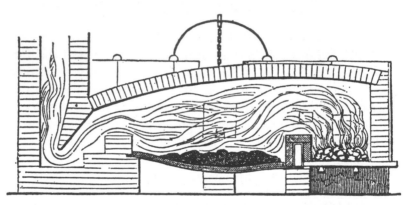

Diagram of a reverberatory furnace. A bridge separated the furnace on the right from the iron on the left. The puddlers stirred the molten iron through a door in front.

by a puddler through an opening in the front of the furnace, and the air which came into contact with the iron removed the carbon and other impurities. Puddling was a skilled trade, for the workman had to stir thoroughly as the iron began to cool. When it was partially cooled, and therefore neither liquid nor solid, the puddler formed it into lumps called 'blooms'. These were taken from the furnace, hammered to remove the dross, and then passed through grooved

Puddlers at work. The man on the left is stirring; the man right-centre is removing red-hot iron. As the tools became almost red-hot, they were thrown into a trough of water, and exchanged for cold ones.

rollers which shaped the metal into thin bars or plates. It should be stressed that the two inventions were complementary: both were essential in the production of cheap iron.

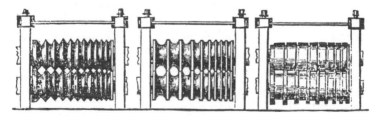

Grooved rollers, through which the red-hot 'puddled' iron was passed several times and made into rough bars.

Cort's inventions were important to others besides the Navy. Iron could now be used for rails, machines, ships, pipes, bridges, and innumerable objects for which wood had been used hitherto because of the shortage of iron. Cort himself gained little material benefit from his inventions. His partner, Samuel Jellicoe, had obtained money to finance the firm by dishonest means, and the patent was terminated by the Navy. Cort became a bankrupt, and spent many years in penury until he was eventually granted a government pension of £200 per annum.

As a result of Cort's inventions the iron industry became concentrated near the coal fields, especially in South Wales, Shropshire, the Black Country, south Yorkshire, and the lowlands of Scotland. Also, ironworks tended to become larger units.

One ironmaster who benefited directly from the puddling process was Richard Crawshay of Merthyr Tydfil. When Cort's patent lapsed, he used the new methods in the Cyfartha ironworks with such effect that the production of bar iron there rose from a mere 500 tons in 1784 to 10,000 tons in 1809. The annual output of pig iron for the whole of England rose as follows:

	tons
1720	25,000
1788	61,000
1796	109,000
1806	227,000

John Wilkinson

It was, indeed, an exciting age in which to be an ironmaster. The career of John Wilkinson, the most famous and the most colourful eighteenth-century ironmaster, may be used as an illustration. John's father, Isaac Wilkinson (1704–84), worked in an iron foundry in Cumberland. He then decided to set up his own business—according to him because his masters raised his wages!

My masters gave me 12s. a week; I was content. They raised me to 14s.—I did not ask them for it. They went on to 16s.—18s. I never asked them for the advances. They gave me a guinea a week. I said to myself, if I am worth a guinea a week to you, I am worth more to myself. I left them.

John Wilkinson (1728–1808) expanded the small business which his father had founded. He married a wealthy woman, and became a 'captain of industry'. His many iron mills, mainly in Shropshire, made components for Boulton and Watt's steam engines: he collaborated with Abraham Darby III in the building of the first iron bridge;

in 1787 he built an iron canal barge; in 1788 he constructed iron pipes for the Paris water supply. In order to run his business more effectively, he acquired ships, farms, ale-houses (these gave him a supply of coin at a time when hard currency was short), and brickworks. He invented a new method of boring cannon—and whilst he was making guns for Britain, his brother was in France arming his country's enemies! John Wilkinson, 'Iron Mad' as he was called, saw clearly

The Coalbrookdale Company's forge at Horsehay, Shropshire. On the right, a 'bloom' of red-hot iron is being dragged with tongs. On the left, several bars have been beaten together at the forge-hammer to form a sheet. Finishing rollers are at work in the centre. Behind the forge-hammer on the right a puddler can just be seen working at the furnace door.

the potentialities of iron. He forecast that buildings and roads would be made of iron. When he died, he was buried in accordance with the directions of his will, in an iron coffin.

Wilkinson, Cort, Crawshay, Roebuck, the Darbys, and countless others, had made England the leaders in iron production. By 1800 the country was exporting iron to Europe, and iron was to be an important asset in the industrial age which was to come.

Steel

The production of cheap steel was not effected in the eighteenth century. The difference between iron and steel is the carbon content.

Cast iron contains carbon, and is hard but brittle: wrought iron contains no carbon, is malleable but soft. Obviously a product which is both hard and flexible has great advantages. To produce this superior iron ('steel') it was necessary first to extract all the carbon, and then to add about 1·5 per cent carbon. The only known methods of doing this were very expensive. Benjamin Hunstman (1704–76), a clockmaker in Doncaster, had difficulty in obtaining good quality steel for watch springs, and he began to experiment in steel production. He moved to Sheffield, and perfected the 'crucible' method in about 1750. Bar iron was heated slowly for several days in order to harden it: the resultant product was known as 'blister steel'. This blister steel was then smelted at a very high temperature in sealed clay crucibles lined with charcoal and ground glass. This produced crucible steel which was hard and flexible. Hunstman was unable to interest Sheffield cutlery manufacturers in his product at first, but when the French began to use crucible steel, the English cutlers were forced to use it in order to withstand foreign competition. Hunstman later established near Sheffield what was in effect the first English steelworks. He soon had rivals. Samuel Walker, who had established a small forge at Rotherham in 1741, discovered the secret of Hunstman's method of producing cast steel, and began making it. By the time he died in 1782, he owned many workshops in and around Rotherham, and a mansion at Masborough. But though Samuel Walker made a fortune from cast steel, and though it was used by cutlers, watchmakers, and the makers of cutting tools, it was not until the third quarter of the nineteenth century that steel was produced cheaply and in large quantities.

COAL

The demand for coal grew in the eighteenth century mainly as a result of the expansion of the iron industry, and the development of steam engines. It was also used in many other industries, such as brewing, soap-boiling, brick-making and glass-blowing. In addition, the growing number of people living in towns needed domestic fuel and were unable to get wood cheaply.

The most important coalmining area was centred on Newcastle; coal was also mined in Durham, south Yorkshire, Lancashire, Nottinghamshire, Derbyshire, the Midlands, the Forest of Dean, and

Somerset. As coal is heavy and bulky, it was best carried on water. So the hewn coal was taken in horse-drawn wagons either to the sea, if it was close enough, or else to the nearest river, where it was loaded into barges known as 'keels'. It was taken downriver in the keels to sturdy, shallow-draught sailing ships, called 'colliers'.

Dangers of Mining

Although the coal industry expanded its annual output from 2·25 million tons in 1660, to 6 million in 1770, and 10 million in 1800, there were few revolutionary changes in technique during the period. Pits remained small, for deep mining was prohibited by the twin dangers of flooding and explosion. Most English coal is found in narrow seams in hillsides. At first the surface crop was taken, and this presented few difficulties. Then, where it was possible, shafts sloping upwards ('adits') were dug from the hill-side, so that the water could drain away. But as the demand for coal increased, and the surface coal was taken, it was necessary to find a method of pumping water from vertical shafts. Man and bucket were replaced by horse gins, and then by steam pumps.[1] The problem of ventilation proved more difficult. In shallow mines choke-damp[2] was a danger. Choke-damp, air deficient in oxygen, caused miners to lapse into unconsciousness. Miners were able to detect its presence by using candles: since fire needs oxygen, the candle-flame grew dimmer as choke-damp increased. Thus the miners were warned and could leave the shaft. In deeper mines the danger was an inflammable gas comprising methane (CH_4) and air, known as 'fire-damp'. Many miners lost their lives in explosions caused by a naked flame igniting fire-damp. In an attempt to minimise the danger, 'firemen' were employed in small mines. Their task was to make a preliminary inspection of the coalface, and to ignite any fire-damp which might be present. They wrapped themselves in wet sacking, and used poles with lighted candles on the end. Attempts were also made to disperse the fire-damp by inducing an air-flow. To do this, a second shaft was dug, and either children were employed to operate trap-doors and produce a draught, or else a brazier was lit at the bottom of it so that the rising hot air should encourage circulation. In 1807 Buddle patented a suction air pump, which

[1] See p. 51.   [2] Compare German *dampf* meaning fog or vapour.

achieved better results. But as pits became deeper, the danger of explosion increased. In 1813 the Reverend John Hodgson, alarmed at
the accident rate in the north-east, formed the Sunderland Society
for the Prevention of Accidents in Mines. In 1815 the Society approached Sir Humphry Davy at Newcastle, whilst he was on his way
to a shooting holiday in Scotland, and within three months Davy
had invented a safety lamp, in which the flame was protected by

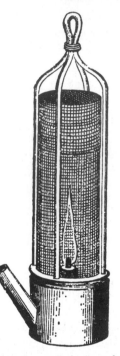

Davy's safety lamp. The wire gauze had 784 holes per square inch.

wire gauze. The secret of the lamp was that the heat from the flame
was reduced by the gauze, so that any fire-damp present was not
ignited. Davy's safety lamp, which was improved upon by George
Stephenson and others, made it possible for miners to go deeper—
obviously they needed light to do their work. If mining had remained at its former level, the safety lamp would have reduced
accidents. But as the lamp made deeper mining possible, mining
disasters continued as frequently as before.

7 The remains of a pair of tilt-hammers at Abbeydale Forge, Sheffield. (p. 27)

8 England's first iron bridge, built by Abraham Darby III in 1779. It is still in use for pedestrians to cross the Severn at Ironbridge, Shropshire. (p. 29)

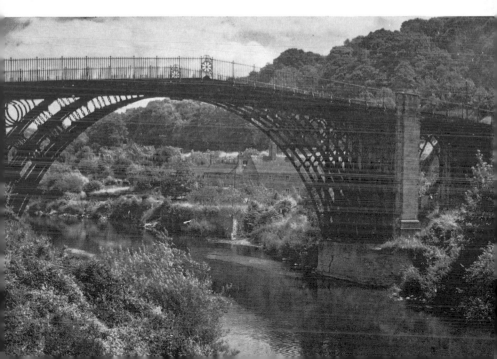

9 Wedgwood's Etruria works at Burslem, Staffordshire. Note the horse on the tow-path: Wedgwood was a pioneer in the use of canals. (pp. 44, 67)

10 Plates from the famous Queen's Ware service made by Wedgwood for Catherine II of Russia, 1773–74. Many pieces are now on show at the Winter Palace, Leningrad. (p. 45)

Mining Techniques

Methods of hewing and drawing the coal changed little during the eighteenth century. The men won the coal with picks, crowbars, and wedges; sometimes they split the seam with gun-powder. Coal pillars were left to support the roof, but as these hindered ventilation the use of wooden pit-props for shoring became more common. The hewn coal was placed in wicker baskets on wooden sleds and drawn by boys to the shaft. In the second half of the century wooden rails

From the Children's Employment Report, 1842 (see p. 163). The youth on the right is pushing a wagon load of coal. The child on the left is a trapper; he opened and shut the door—a monotonous task in damp and dark conditions.

were used, and after 1763 pit-ponies were used for hauling. The coal was brought to the surface either by using a horse or horse windlass which pulled up the baskets on a hempen rope, or by women who scaled ladders with wicker baskets on their backs. The women, regarded as a 'wild lot', began working in the mines at the age of six or seven, served first as 'trappers', then became haulers until they were about nine years old. Then and into adulthood, they were regarded as strong enough to climb up the ladders with the heavy baskets. As they dressed in trousers and coarse flannel shirts, they were barely distinguishable from the men except for some feminine adornment, such as beads or earrings.

Mining was a hard and dangerous life for men, women and children. But by their efforts the black diamond was won from the earth to become the source of power for the new machines.

TEXTILES

Wool

In 1700 the manufacture of woollen cloth was the most important branch of the textile industry. By 1815 cotton, which made rapid advances after 1780, was paramount. Wool had been the chief source of England's wealth during the Middle Ages; symbolically the Lord Chancellor still sits in the House of Lords on the Woolsack, as a token of the debt owed by the nation to wool. By 1700 the woollen industry had become largely concentrated in three main areas—the west of England from Gloucestershire to Devon, East Anglia, and the West Riding of Yorkshire. It was organised largely as a *domestic industry*, i.e. the work was done in the home and not in a factory, and the workers did not own the raw wool or the finished product. In the west of England and East Anglia, there were merchant clothiers who paid the woollen workers on a piece-rate basis; in Yorkshire, the unit of production was usually smaller, comprising one or two families, although even there the richer clothier was becoming increasingly common. The domestic system was particularly suited to rural areas, where the concentration of a large number of workers would have proved difficult. The system was one which usually entailed the whole family working together. Children were employed in carding or combing the wool, women did the spinning (hence the term 'spinster'), and men the weaving. The finishing, i.e. fulling, bleaching and dyeing, was usually done in small workshops under the direct supervision of the employer. Those processes performed in the home had, of course, to be done by hand, and by means of small tools. Wire carding brushes, distaffs and spinning wheels, and hand-looms could be accommodated in the small houses of the workers, whereas steam engines and rivers could not! One reason for fulling being done in a workshop was that water-power was often used, whilst large tenter-frames had to be erected on which to hang the finished cloth. Because the woollen industry was well-established along traditional lines, it changed very slowly during the eighteenth century. More use was made of water power, especially in Yorkshire, and carding was done mechanically after 1792, when Edmund Cartwright invented a combing machine. But spinning and weaving by machinery was not common practice in the woollen industry until after about 1820.

Linen and Silk

There was little significant change during the eighteenth century in the manufacture of linen and silk. Linen is made from flax, which was grown in various parts of the country. In Ireland, where labour was cheap, mechanisation did not offer great advantages. Some power-driven mills were in operation in Leeds by the 1780's, and in the next decade some successful flax-spinning machines were in use. But the weaving was still done by hand. The manufacture of silk had developed in England during the last years of the seventeenth century, but as all the raw material had to be imported—neither the mulberry nor the silk-worm take kindly to the English climate—this branch of the textile industry did not make rapid strides. John and Thomas Lombe established a factory on the River Derwent, near Derby, in 1717, and installed a silk-throwing machine copied from an Italian invention. This factory was 500 feet long and had 460 windows, and can be called the first 'modern' factory in England. Thomas Lombe, who outlived his brother, employed 1,500 workers, and made a fortune. Other silk factories were established in London, Stockport and Macclesfield.

Cotton—Problems of the Industry

The cotton industry, comparatively small in 1700, was concentrated largely in Lancashire and Cheshire. Most cotton materials—used by the upper classes for petticoats, curtains and cushion covers, because patterns could be printed on the cloth—were imported from India. The English cotton industry was given an unintentional boost when, in 1701 and in 1721, Acts of Parliament were passed prohibiting the wearing of Indian calicoes. The aim was to aid the woollen industry: the effect was to help the Lancashire cotton industry. But despite this help, the cotton industry advanced only slowly until about 1780 because of two limitations—the supply of raw cotton and the slowness of hand-spinning. During the course of the eighteenth century the supply of the raw material was improved (imports of raw cotton increased twenty-eight-fold) first from the Levant, then from the West Indies, and after 1783 from the U.S.A. The supply from America was aided by the invention of a cleaning machine, called a 'cotton gin', by Eli Whitney in 1793.

The problem of the supply of yarn—it took ten spinners to keep one weaver supplied—worsened when, in 1733, John Kay invented a device called the 'Flying Shuttle'. This weaving machine passed the shuttle across the warp automatically, enabling the weaver to make broader cloth without the aid of an assistant, and to double his output. The need for a spinning machine was therefore intensified. There was a demand for cotton cloth, there was sufficient raw cotton, there was a means of speeding up weaving. But the supply of yarn remained a bottleneck to increased production for over thirty years. In 1738 Lewis Paul and John Wyatt invented a method of roller spinning, but they failed commercially. Then, in 1764, James Hargreaves, a Lancashire carpenter, built the 'Spinning Jenny', whereby one man could work eight spindles. Later the Jenny was modified so that as many as eighty threads were spun simultaneously.

Richard Arkwright

Both the Flying Shuttle and the Jenny were small enough to be used in the homes of the workers, and they were operated by hand. But soon power was applied to cotton machines, and this led to the development of factories. In 1769 Richard Arkwright took out a patent for a water-driven spinning-machine, the 'Water Frame'. This machine was based on Paul and Wyatt's roller principle, the yarn passing through two pairs of rollers, the first turning more slowly than the second. The Water Frame had several advantages: it spun a strong thread so that cotton could be used for the warp (hitherto a woollen warp had been used); it spun quickly; and it could be handled by children. In 1771, in partnership with Jedediah Strutt, Arkwright established a factory at Cromford, near Derby, a few miles from Lombe's silk factory. At Cromford the river passes through a narrow gorge, and runs swiftly; in addition, the warm water from Matlock prevents it from freezing in the winter. As water power was used in the first factories, they were known as 'mills', a term still used today. By 1775 three hundred people were employed at Cromford Mill, England's first cotton factory.

With both spinning and weaving speeded up, there was urgent need of a mechanical means of carding. Arkwright took out a patent for a combing machine in 1775, which carded the cotton by means of three cylinders with bent metal teeth. (This machine, like the spinning and weaving machines, could not easily be used for wool, as different sheep do not produce a fibre of uniform size.)

Richard Arkwright became the first real cotton magnate. In 1773 he established weaving shops in Derby, and in 1776 set up a third mill at Belper, and a fourth in Manchester. In 1784, in partnership with David Dale, he started the New Lanark Mills on the banks of the Clyde. He died in 1792, leaving assets of £500,000. Considering his start in life, this was a remarkable achievement. He was born in 1732 in Preston, the youngest of a poor family. He was apprenticed to a barber and wig-maker, and at the age of eighteen he set up his own barber's shop in Bolton. He taught himself to read and write, but he had little technical knowledge. Because of this, he has always been suspected of 'pirating' the inventions of others. He was involved in a law-suit in 1785 concerning his patent rights for the Water Frame, and the jury gave a verdict that he had stolen ideas from other inventors. It is, however, to his credit that he withstood misfortune courageously. For example, in 1779 his mill at Chorley, Lancashire, was wrecked by spinners who feared for their livelihood. He was both too harshly condemned and over-praised by his contemporaries. When he was knighted in 1786, one wrote that 'a great mill-owner is newly *created* a knight, though he was not *born* a gentleman'. Sir Robert Peel, senior, wrote 'We all looked up at him'. If Arkwright was unscrupulous, he was a man who worked hard, who was a brilliant organiser and a far-sighted businessman, and one who can claim to be the 'father of the factory system'.

Further Inventions

The story of cotton inventions did not end with Arkwright. Samuel Crompton of Bolton patented the Spinning Mule in 1779. This machine combined the best features of the Jenny, which made thin thread, with those of the Water Frame, which made strong thread. By using the Mule, English spinners were able to make thin, strong thread, from which fine cotton goods (e.g. muslin) could be manufactured to compete with those made in India.

The inventions of Hargreaves, Arkwright and Crompton upset the balance between spinning and weaving, for Kay's Flying Shuttle was comparatively slow. In 1784 the Reverend Edmund Cartwright, a former lecturer in classical literature at Oxford, and then a country parson, invented the first power loom. It was a clumsy machine, but by 1787 he had improved on its design and set up a weaving shop in Doncaster, with twenty steam-powered looms. Cartwright's business failed in 1792. Although other attempts were made to perfect a power loom, success came slowly. Inventors met with considerable opposition from the handloom weavers, who in 1792 were earning 35s. a

Printing calico by hand, using engraved wooden blocks. Bell's printing machine greatly speeded up this process (see pp. 43, 141).

week. The weavers, as well as fearing a reduction in their high wages, were reluctant to work in factories rather than in their own homes. But the demand for cloth, stimulated by the wars with France, meant that mechanisation had to come. In 1803 William Horrocks of Stockport made a metal power loom, and the use of this machine, despite violent opposition and even machine wrecking as in the 'Luddite riots' (1812–13), gradually spread. In 1822 the firm of Roberts, Hill and Company was established for loom-making, to meet the growing demand for cotton machines.

Technical changes in finishing were simultaneous with those in carding, spinning and weaving. In 1784 Thomas Bell patented a machine by which cotton cloth, or calico, was printed by copper rollers. In 1785 James Watt, the famous steam engineer, introduced to England the French discovery of the use of chlorine as a bleaching agent. (Previously bleaching had been done by exposing the cloth to sunlight and by the application of sour milk—a long and laborious process.) In 1798 Charles Tennant produced chlorine as a dry, easily transportable powder.

Growth of the Cotton Industry

Cotton had become a most important industry by 1800: imports of raw cotton, which amounted to £2,000,000 in 1700, had risen to £56,000,000 in 1800. In the same period, cotton exports had grown from a mere £24,000 to £5,800,000. The cotton industry developed more quickly than wool because it was a comparatively new industry, unhampered by regulations and tradition. Also, cotton fibre was a standard size, whilst wool, which came from diverse English flocks, varied in texture, so that machinery for it needed to be more complex. Moreover, wool is elastic and needs uneven pressure. These technical difficulties, together with the dispersal of the woollen industry away from the coal fields, and the public demand for cotton, inevitably led to the emergence of cotton as the leading textile industry. By the time suitable machinery had been evolved, there was a temporary shortage of raw wool, and this lasted until after 1830 when the ranches of Australia and New Zealand became the suppliers. For people in England, cotton clothing was cheap and hygienic; for England's customers in Africa and India, cotton was more suitable than wool.

By 1815 ninety per cent of the cotton industry was located in Lancashire, with the remainder in the Paisley area. The reasons for the heavy concentration in Lancashire were many. Local workers were experienced in textile manufacture, and there were few restrictive guild regulations; the climate was favourable, being humid with a small range of temperature variation; pure water was available for bleaching and calico printing, and abundant coal for steam power; as in all mining areas, there was plenty of female and child labour to be had; trading links with the outside world already existed and in

Liverpool there was a good and easily accessible port. No doubt too the barrenness of the soil, which was unproductive for agriculture, had encouraged Lancashire folk to seek other ways of making their living.

OTHER INDUSTRIES

The emphasis on iron, coal and textiles must not lead us to imagine that these were the only industries in eighteenth-century England, though they were the major ones. Changes occurred in other industries also.

Wedgwood and Ceramics

The pottery industry saw changes in organisation rather than in technique, and these changes were due almost entirely to Josiah Wedgwood (1730–95). Wedgwood, born in north Staffordshire, was the thirteenth son of a mediocre master potter. Josiah started work in the family pottery business when he was nine years old. When he was twelve he contracted smallpox, as a result of which he later had to have a leg amputated. The pottery industry was already well-established in Staffordshire, where there was plenty of clay and coal. But the pottery made there was poor in texture and design, and rarely sold as far away as London. Josiah Wedgwood shrewdly saw the possibilities for expansion. Improvements in roads and canals allowed easier transport of heavy commodities such as coal and clay, and safer transit of fragile pottery. The eighteenth century saw a rise in the population, and an increase in the standard of living. Tea, coffee and chocolate drinking, already popular with the rich, was becoming increasingly the habit of the less well-to-do. There was a ready market for a man of enterprise. The rich wanted high-quality ware, whilst the rest of the population sought less expensive sets. Plate was expensive, pewter was scarce, porcelain too fragile. Wedgwood's pottery was to supply the needs of all tastes. His success was due to the quality of his produce, his original designs, the specialisation of labour, and his sales organisation.

Wedgwood established a new factory at Etruria, near Hanley, in 1769. There, using the new discoveries of green glaze, cream-ware and jasper-ware, he produced quality goods for the rich. The most famous were the elegant vases with a white decoration on 'wedgwood blue' backgrounds. As Italian or classical motifs were in vogue, he employed the great designer, Flaxman. Also, current events or famous contemporary personalities were depicted, such as Wesley preaching, Captain Cook and the signing of the Treaty of Paris. With an eye to the European market and beyond, Wedgwood used the heads of Popes for ware which sold in Spain, Italy and South America. He sought the patronage of royalty, and interested the nobility in his products. He had a display room at Etruria, and in 1765 opened a showroom in London. Four years later he was selling £100 worth of goods in London a week. He made a dinner service for Catherine the Great of Russia (the bulk of which still survives despite her habit of throwing pieces at servants); the one thousand pieces each had a different English scene. Wedgwood's vases were frequently used by the great artist Romney as background in his canvases.

Wedgwood was a perfectionist. He used to walk around the factory smashing with his stick any piece which was sub-standard, and chalked on the bench 'This won't do for Josiah Wedgwood'. His workmen, with good habits and pride instilled into them by the growth of Methodism in Staffordshire, responded well. He increased production by a division of labour. Instead of one man performing every process, Wedgwood employed specialists—some mixed the clay, others worked on the potters' wheels, some saw to the firing, some to the glazing.

Sales were increased by a variety of methods. In order to cater for the popular taste, the 'willow pattern' was produced. Advertisements were inserted in newspapers; special discounts were given; catalogues appeared in Europe in translation. His sales methods have a strikingly modern ring. Catherine's dinner service, for example, was displayed in the London showroom in 1774 before it was sent to Russia. Wedgwood was called in his own time 'Vase Maker General to the Universe.' He died in 1795 worth £500,000.

Other makers of pottery followed Wedgwood's example. The most notable was Josiah Spode (1754–1827) who became famous for jasper, cream, and black-ware.

Chemicals

The greatest advance in the chemical industry was in the production of sulphuric acid. J. R. Glauber (1603–70) had discovered that lead would resist sulphuric acid, and in the following century this discovery was put to use. John Roebuck (1718–94) with his partner Samuel Garbett (1717–1805) established the Birmingham Vitriol Manufactory in 1746 in order to supply the demand. Sulphuric acid was needed for making soda and alkalis for the textile industries. Also it was needed by candle-makers and match-makers. It was used for cleaning metals, or for stripping silver from copper; and it was an important component in the making of superphosphates for agricultural fertilisers. In 1790 a Frenchman, Nicholas Leblanc, produced sodium bicarbonate (soda) for soap-makers by treating salt with sulphuric acid, heated with coal and limestone. British manufacturers quickly adopted Leblanc's process.

A chamber for the manufacture of sulphuric acid. It was made of wood and lined with lead.

Whilst the production of sulphuric acid was the greatest advance made by chemists, the isolation of metals was important. Nickel was isolated in 1771, manganese in 1774, molybdenum in 1781, titanium in 1794, and chromium in 1797. Further advances in chemistry were stimulated by the French Wars (1793–1815). The shortage of tallow led to experiments in gas lighting, and Westminster was lit by that means in 1812. Methods of preserving food by sterilisation by heat, a French invention, were adapted by Bryan Donkyn (1768–1855). Whereas the French had used bottles, Donkyn used tins. In 1813 he presented the Prince Regent with samples of tinned food. An improved method of refining sugar, using steam-heated metal coils, was invented by E. C. Howard (1774–1816) during the wars.

Chemical engineering was to play a more important role in Britain during the nineteenth and twentieth centuries, but the birth of the industry during the eighteenth century led to the foundation of chemical factories in Lancashire and on Tyneside.

Soda crystallising works, Birmingham, c. 1840.

CHAPTER 4

Power, 1700-1800

Any machine, however simple, requires power. During the eighteenth century machines were worked by men, by horses or oxen, by wind and water, and finally by steam. Except for steam, the other means of power all had severe limitations, for there is a limit to the strength of man and animal, and wind and water are unreliable servants. The harnessing of steam was a prerequisite of an industrial society, but the successful development of the steam engine was delayed until materials, mechanical skill and some degree of precision engineering were all available. It was not until about 1780 that steam power could be seen clearly as the power source of the future. It is not surprising, therefore, that much time was spent in improving the more traditional means of power.

WATER AND WIND

Water power remained important during most of the century. The first textile and iron mills were established on the banks of rivers, as flour mills had been centuries earlier. Water was used to turn large wheels, usually made of wood and iron, and these wheels drove the machinery. Water power had several defects: in time of drought or ice the power was not available, and in time of flood the flow could prove too strong and the level too high. The location of the machine was limited also, with the result that too many water-wheels were built on the same stretch of river. But water had to be used until steam power was perfected. John Smeaton brought about an improvement in water-wheels by experimenting with models. In 1759 he demonstrated to the Royal Society in London that undershot wheels in which the water made contact at the bottom of the wheel were only 22 per cent efficient, whilst overshot wheels were over 60 per cent efficient. Later undershot wheels were improved to an effi-ciency of 65 per cent by erecting them so that the water entered the paddles just below the midway point between top and bottom. The importance of water power is shown by the fact that many of the first steam engines were used to pump water, with the water and not the steam engine providing the direct motive force to machines.

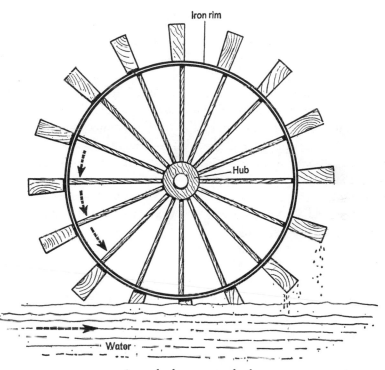

An undershot water-wheel.

Improvements were also made to windmills. Windmills were used for pumping water, milling flour and sawing wood. They were made almost entirely of wood until 1754, when Smeaton made one using cast iron parts. In wooden windmills the large worm wheels were cut with saws and finished with chisels; these wheels were lubricated with animal grease to prevent excessive wear and to remove some of the friction. The huge sails were usually about 40 feet long, and made a great noise as they turned. In 1745 Edmund Lee patented the fantail, which kept the sails pointed into the wind. In 1772 Andrew Meikle patented a more efficient sail with hinged shutters, which could be adjusted according to the wind strength. The invention of

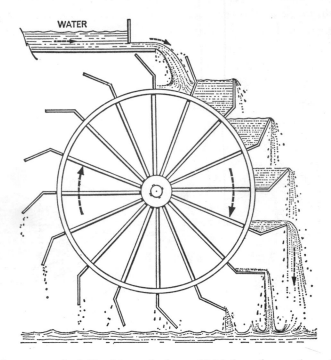

Overshot water-wheels like this required an artificial channel to produce a 'waterfall' (see Plate 12).

a centrifugal governor by Thomas Mead in 1787 made windmills virtually automatic, since the speed could be controlled without manual adjustment. Eighteenth-century windmills rarely developed more than 15 horse power; they were large and cumbersome, and often stopped working when the wind was light. They had two main advantages: millwrights knew how to build them, and they were cheap to run and maintain.

STEAM ENGINES

Savery and Newcomen

The first steam engines were invented because of the need for a means of pumping water out of mines. The first successful one was patented in 1698 by Captain Thomas Savery, a military engineer from Cornwall. In mechanical terms, one would call it a pulsometer pump, for it had no moving parts other than valves. It utilised two characteristics of steam: when steam condenses into water in a closed cylinder, a vacuum is produced; when steam expands, it will push away barriers in its path.

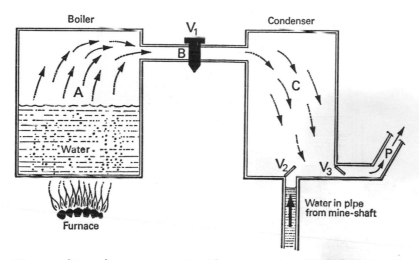

Diagram of Savery's steam pump, 1698. The water was heated in the boiler A with all the valves closed. When V1 was opened, steam travelled along pipe B into the condenser C. V1 was then closed, and cold water poured on the outside of C, so that a partial vacuum was created. V2 opened and water from the mine-shaft was drawn upward by atmospheric pressure. When C was nearly filled with water, valves V1 and V3 were opened, V2 closed and the steam pushed the water up pipe P. This simple description of Savery's engine demonstrates its main principles.

Savery's engines were used in copper mines in Cornwall and in Staffordshire collieries. One Savery engine, in Sion House, near London, pumped 52 gallons a minute to a height of 58 feet. But Savery's engine had two major defects: a low thermal efficiency (0·5 per cent), and a high risk of explosion. The danger was increased as the boiler had to be in the mine shaft, and a pressure of 150 lb. to the square inch was sometimes reached.

Savery's engine was soon superseded by an improved pump invented in 1711 by Thomas Newcomen, a Dartmouth blacksmith and locksmith. In one way Newcomen's engine took a backward step technologically, as it was an atmospheric engine only, i.e. the expansive power of steam was not used.

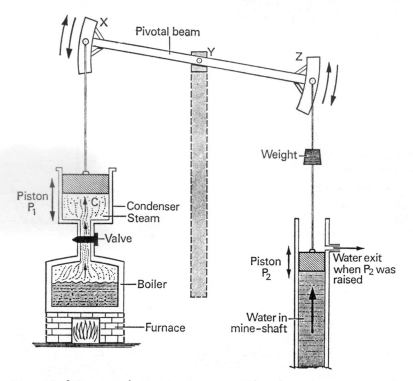

Diagram of Newcomen's steam engine, 1711. When the engine was at rest, P_2 descended since the arm of the pivotal beam YZ was heavier than XY. When a vacuum was created in C, P_1 came down and P_2 went up. Then the valve was opened, the condenser was filled with steam, and P_2 descended again.

As Savery still held the patent right for 'fire engines', Newcomen went into partnership with him in order to be able to manufacture and sell his pump. The first was erected at Dudley Castle, Stafford-

11 *An eight-sail windmill, built in 1830 for grinding corn, at Heckington, Lincolnshire. Note the mill stone on the left of the door. (p. 50)*

12 *The Saugus Ironworks, Massachusetts, U.S.A., now restored as a museum. A number of overshot water-wheels for powering the forge hammers are visible. (pp. 27, 48)*

13 *The Barton Aqueduct which carried the Bridgewater Canal over the river Irwell. This picture appeared in one of Arthur Young's many books*—Six Months' Tour Through the North of England (*1770*). (p. 66)

14 *A barge descending the famous Five-Rise locks on the Leeds–Liverpool canal at Bingley, Yorkshire.* (p. 67)

shire, in 1712. The engine made ten strokes, and raised 100 gallons of water over 153 feet each minute. Three men were required to work it: one man opened and shut the valves, another poured water outside the condenser, whilst a third stoked the furnace. Within a few years three important modifications were made. First, condensation was achieved by the injection of water inside the cylinder, thus increasing the stroke rate. Secondly, the valves were regulated automatically by a string attached to the main beam. (Legend has it that this was discovered by a lazy boy named Humphrey Potter, who tired of his boring duties.) Thirdly, in 1717 Henry Beighton of Newcastle added a safety valve. When Newcomen's patent expired in 1733, similar engines became widely used. One was used by the Thames Water Supply Company to feed a reservoir. Some were used to supply fountains for country mansions. But the main use of the steam pump was in coal and lead mines, for which John Smeaton built a considerable number, especially in Cornwall and in the north-east. Engines were exported to France, Prussia, Spain, Sweden and the Netherlands. The Newcomen engine, however, had two serious deficiencies: it was expensive to run (an average coal bill was about £1,000 per annum), and it could not be applied to rotary motion.

James Watt

The steam engine was further improved by James Watt (1736–1819). He was the son of a master carpenter and shipwright of Greenock, and served as an apprentice to an instrument maker in London. In 1757 he was appointed as 'Mathematical Instrument maker' to the University of Glasgow, and in 1763, as part of his duties, he was required to repair a Newcomen engine. He noticed that the engine could only perform a few strokes without stopping owing to the great loss of heat, and that the condensation of steam was far from perfect. He began to experiment with an engine in which the boiler and the condenser were separated, and in which steam could be used to work the piston. As he had to earn his living, and to experiment in his limited spare time, he was unable to make very rapid progress for a few years. He also lacked the capital to build an engine, and in making his first experiments he had run up debts of £1,000. Professor Black of Glasgow University gave Watt some small financial assistance, as well as much scientific help,

as he was an authority on latent heat. Dr Black did a further service
to the inventor when he introduced him to John Roebuck, the owner
of the Carron ironworks. Roebuck needed a pump for his coal mines
in Scotland; Watt needed time and money. They formed a partnership which resulted in the erection of Watt's first steam pump, the
'Beelzebub', near Edinburgh in 1768. Unfortunately it was not very
successful, and Watt's experiments were halted once more.

A Boulton and Watt steam engine, c. 1780.

In 1773 Roebuck went bankrupt, and his ill-fortune was to be a
blessing to James Watt. Matthew Boulton, who in 1765 had completed the building of a large hardware and toy factory at Soho,
Birmingham, wanted steam power for his machines. He bought
Roebuck's share in Watt's engine, had it removed from Scotland
and re-erected in Birmingham, and persuaded the inventor to supervise it. In 1774 the engine, after modification, was working satisfactorily. In the following year the two men, one the inventor, and
the other the supplier of capital and the organiser, entered into a
further partnership.

At first they made steam pumps, supplying them to collieries, tin mines and water-works. One was made for John Wilkinson's blast furnaces. But Matthew Boulton saw the use that could be made of the steam engine if it could be applied to rotary motion, and he inspired Watt, and the works foreman, William Murdock, to turn their minds to this problem. In 1781 Watt invented the sun-and-planets gear, by which a crankshaft attached to the piston turned a wheel. In the following year three further improvements were made. By means of a steam inlet valve at both ends of the cylinder, the piston was pushed by steam in both directions (i.e. it was made double-acting); a throttle was devised; and a centrifugal governor was added. Steam engines could now be used for purposes other than pumping.

The first Watt rotary steam engine was put to work at the Albion Flour Mills at Blackfriars in 1785. These mills were built by John Rennie, a pupil of Andrew Meikle. There Watt's engines were used for working hoists, for turning twenty pairs of millstones, and for driving fans. The age of steam had begun. Erasmus Darwin wrote:

> Soon shall thy arm, unconquer'd Steam! afar
> Drag the slow barge, or drive the rapid car;
> Or on wide-waving wings expanded bear
> The flying-chariot through the fields of air.

Soon Watt's engines were being used in a paper mill, a corn mill, a brewery, in Wilkinson's ironworks, and in a cotton mill. It must not, however, be thought that suddenly everyone was using steam. It was to take fifty years before steam power became the norm in factories. Also, the pressures in Watt's engines were comparatively low, and it was left to others, notably Richard Trevithick, to experiment with high pressures.

James Watt can be called with justification the 'father of the steam engine'. He was also the first to use the power unit of one horse power, equal to 33,000 foot pounds per minute.

THE BEGINNINGS OF ENGINEERING

The advent of the steam engine caused the development of a new profession—engineering. The first engines and machines were built by men drawn from a variety of skilled trades—such as carpenters, blacksmiths and clock-makers. But the civil engineer really developed from the ancient trade of the millwright, in which many of the inventors of the eighteenth century served an apprenticeship. This was a natural evolution, for millwrights built windmills, water-wheels and bridges. James Brindley, who became famous as a canal-builder, was a millwright. So was William Murdock, the foreman of Boulton and Watt's works at Soho. Murdock, as well as playing a major role in the development of the steam engine, built a model steam locomotive in 1784 which achieved a speed of 8 m.p.h. He experimented with the production of gas lighting from coal at a house in Redruth, Cornwall, and in 1798 installed some gas lighting in the Soho works. Other 'engineers' were equally versatile. Joseph Bramah made a water closet in 1778, a screw propeller in 1785, a hydraulic press in 1796, a rotary wood-planer in 1802, and also patented a burglar-proof door lock. Walter Taylor, of Southampton, who had a tiny workshop over the West Gate, where he made wooden blocks for the Navy, invented a circular saw in 1780.

The name 'engineer' did not become common outside the army until the eighteenth century was well advanced. John Smeaton (1742-1792) was the first to call himself a 'civil' (i.e. non-military) engineer, and was largely responsible for forming the Society of Engineers, which held its first meeting in Holborn in 1771. Smeaton is mostly remembered as the builder of the third Eddystone Lighthouse, con-structed between 1756 and 1759. This lighthouse was made of inter-locking stone, and lasted until 1877, when it was removed because the rock on which it was built was wearing away. Smeaton's light-house was re-erected on Plymouth Hoe, where it may be seen today. Smeaton also built several bridges in Scotland. John Rennie (1761-1821), the father of Sir John Rennie, was a student at Edinburgh University, and then a pupil of Andrew Meikle, the millwright. Rennie built the Albion Flour Mills, the Kennet and Avon Canal, the East and West India Docks in London, Holyhead Harbour, and extensions to the naval dockyards at Sheerness and Chatham. He was largely responsible for the revival of the Society of Engineers in 1793, after it had ceased its activities upon the death of Smeaton in 1792.

Although the skill and the achievements of these pioneers of engineering was much admired on the Continent, it was a long time before they found true recognition in British universities. The first

Chair of Engineering in Britain was established in Glasgow in 1840. University College and King's College, London, soon did likewise, but the University of Cambridge did not establish its Department of Engineering until 1875.

The engineering workmen, those who made components for engines or machines, were not members of the Society of Civil Engineers. Their association, the millwrights', did not survive the Combination Acts of 1799–1800.[1] When workmen's associations became legal again in 1824, the men of the engineering trades were dispersed among several different small societies. They came together in 1851, when the A.S.E. (the forerunner of the Amalgamated Engineering Union) was formed. The full title of the A.S.E. was 'The Amalgamated Society of Engineers, Machinists, Smiths, Millwrights and Pattern-makers'.

As early as 1828 the function of the civil engineer was described as 'the art of directing the great sources of power in Nature for the use and convenience of Man'. The engineers and the skilled mechanics were a priceless asset to England during the nineteenth century.

[1] See p. 168.

CHAPTER 5

Inland Transport, 1700-1820

ROADS

During the eighteenth century English roads were in a bad state. A succession of writers, including Celia Fiennes, Daniel Defoe, Richard Pocock and Arthur Young, complained about them.

In the towns the roads were usually dirt tracks, though in some places cobbled streets were to be found. In 1765 the City of Westminster had pavements, raised above the road, but in most towns there were none, for in those days there was little need for a division of space between pedestrians and vehicles. Rich ladies, mindful of their fineries, business men making for the coffee-house, or doctors visiting their patients were sometimes carried about the town in sedan chairs. For longer distances horses were used. All people of any substance owned horses, and the ability to ride a horse was an essential skill. The squire visiting his tenants, the parson tending his spiritual flock, the shipbuilder seeking timber, the lawyer, salesman and doctor, all depended upon the horse for their travelling. The poor, however, had to use 'Shanks' pony'—their own legs, though they might own a mule or a donkey as a beast of burden. As a consequence, the ordinary person did very little travelling. His whole life would be lived near his home, and the limit of his journeying was the nearest market town.

Road travel was fraught with danger from highwaymen and footpads. The 'gentlemen of the road' were very active in the eighteenth century, despite the 'police' activities of the Bow Street Runners, which began in 1753. The most famous highwayman of the period was Dick Turpin (1700-39), born in Hampstead, Essex. With his partner Tom King he waylaid travellers on the Cambridge road, until, after shooting his partner accidentally, he fled to York where he was later captured and hanged.

The roads were useful for the transportation of live animals. Flocks of sheep, or herds of cattle, grazing as they went, could more easily be driven to slaughter than carried by sea. Live carriage of animals by sea entailed expensive feeding: dead meat needed preserving.

Light goods, such as wool, were carried by pack-horses, heavier commodities in carts and wagons. But vehicles were liable to sink axle-deep in mud, or to find large boulders in their path, so that this was a slow mode of transport. Timber was carted by teams of four or six horses or oxen at a very slow speed—about ten miles in five hours.

Turnpikes

The problem of the roads was partly one of administration. Today our roads are repaired and built by local or central government authorities. In 1555 roads were made the responsibility of each parish, and the J.P.s were enjoined to supervise maintenance, using unpaid compulsory labour. If we still had such a system today, then roads outside our houses would probably not be in a good state of repair. This problem was partly overcome by the establishment of turnpike trusts. These trusts, set up by Act of Parliament, were made responsible for a stretch of road, and they were empowered to erect gates and to levy tolls in order to obtain money for repair work. The first trust was set up in 1663 in order to deal with the problems of through traffic on some stretches of the Great North Road, but few were in operation before 1748. Between that year and 1760 the number rose from 160 to 530, whilst the period from 1760 to 1774 saw the passing of a further 452 turnpike Acts. Although some local traffic was exempt from the payment of tolls, the erection of the gates and the charges led to riots and disorders in some areas, especially in the south-west. Bristol was the scene of one such riot in 1749. The principle of making those who used the roads pay for them was not accepted without opposition.

The establishment of the turnpike trusts meant that the roads became the responsibility of a particular group of people. The Trustees were usually local gentry, and their powers were increased by further Acts of Parliament. In 1773 the Trustees were allowed to demand the use of horses, carts and men from landowners. By other Acts of Parliament an attempt was made to reduce the wear on the roads by regulating the width of wagon wheels. As it was believed that narrow wheels cut deeper ruts than broad wheels, an Act of 1753 stipulated that wagon and cart wheels must be at least nine inches wide. In 1773 the toll charges were reduced according to the width of wheels.

The government was also directly responsible for building roads in the west of Scotland, for military rather than economic reasons. Following the Jacobite rebellion of 1715, General Wade was sent to build metalled roads in 1724 so that an army could more rapidly reach what were regarded as potential centres of rebellion.

Two scholars approaching a toll-gate on a turnpike road just outside Oxford, c. 1780. The gate-keeper lived in the hexagonal house on the left.

Towards the end of the century circumstances combined to accelerate the rate of improvement of the roads. Before enclosures, roads were not bordered by hedges or fences. Consequently, vehicles could by-pass some of the worst quagmires or boulder-strewn stretches. The enclosure of open land with hedges, walls or fences, led to the confining of roads, so that improvements had to be made to the surfaces. At the same time the need to transport heavy goods grew, as did the need for traders to travel more easily, especially to London where there were so many potential customers. Fortunately the turnpike trusts could provide the capital whereby improvements could be made, and they could employ skilled road builders.

Three Road Builders

The improvements in the technique of road building were largely due to the activities of three men, Metcalf, Telford and McAdam. John Metcalf (1717–1810), was known as 'Blind Jack of Knaresborough'. He lost his sight as a result of smallpox, but had a varied career as musician, soldier and fish-dealer, before becoming a wagoner carrying goods between Knaresborough and York. When he was nearly fifty, he was engaged by a turnpike trust to build three miles of road. There were no 'professional' road builders in those days, so that the employment of a carrier to do such work need occasion no surprise. Metcalf was remarkable, however, in that he was able to carry out his duties despite his blindness. He used to walk along the roads he was rebuilding, using his long staff as his 'eyes'. From 1765 he built 180 miles of turnpike roads in Yorkshire, Lancashire and Derbyshire. One of his greatest feats was the building of a stretch of road through marshy moorland in the Pennines. He used bundles of heather which acted as a foundation so that the road 'floated'.

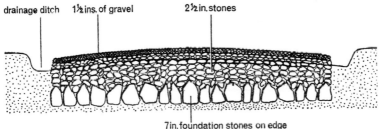

Cross-section showing Telford's method of road building.

Thomas Telford (1757–1834) is most famous as the builder of harbours, canals and bridges, but he also constructed over a thousand miles of roads, including the one from London to Holyhead. Telford reduced the camber on his roads, thus decreasing the angle of tilt for vehicles. He used large stones, placed as a foundation, over which smaller stones were laid with a layer of about 1½ inches of gravel on top. Though this type of road was an improvement over methods used hitherto, especially as it drained well, it was expensive.

John Loudon McAdam (1756–1834) found a method which ensured good drainage and a reasonably hard surface at a low cost. He
reasoned that it was not necessary to lay expensive foundations, as
the 'native soil' would support 'the weight of traffic'. He used stones
of about 2 inches diameter as the foundation, with smaller stones on
the surface. No layer of gravel was added. The action of the iron
wheel-rims of the coaches and wagons ground the stones, and in wet
weather the wheels acted as rollers, creating a hard surface. These
'water bound macadamised roads', which cost about £88 per mile,

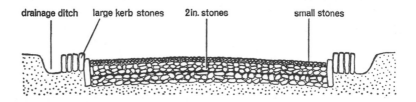

Cross-section showing McAdam's method of road building.

remained the usual method of roadmaking until the increased weight
of vehicles, the rubber tyre, and the use of tar and concrete led to the
need for and the development of new methods. Of the three great
road builders of his age, McAdam is the most important. His roads
could be built economically, and water drained off them satisfactorily.
He was not trained as an engineer. He made his fortune in business in
New York, returned to his native Scotland and began to experiment
in road building at his own cost. In 1815 he was appointed Surveyor-
General of the Bristol Road Trusts, for whom he rebuilt 180 miles of
road. McAdam was a good administrator, and also wrote several
manuals on road-making. His son James was appointed as the first
General Surveyor of the Metropolitan Roads in 1827.

Bridges

Bridge building was a necessary adjunct to road building. If large
vehicles with heavy loads were to use the roads, the crossing of water
by ford or ferry was not always possible. By using iron, larger bridges
could be built. We have already seen[1] that the 'first iron bridge in the

[1] In p. 29.

world' was built at Ironbridge in 1779. The second, built by Telford in 1796 at Buildwas, a few miles from Coalbrookdale, had a span of 180 feet. John Rennie used iron in the construction of his bridge at Boston, Lincolnshire, in 1807. But generally the new bridges built in the period were still of stone and wood, a typical example being that across the River Hamble at Bursledon, opened in 1799.

Stage-coaches

These improvements in roads and bridges increased the speed of travel. Stage-coaches, which took two weeks to travel from London to Edinburgh in 1700, were completing the journey in two days in 1820. Brighton, a whole day's journey from London in 1760, could be reached in five and a half hours in 1832. In 1790 the journey from Southampton to London by stage-coach took twelve hours, including a stop at Popham for breakfast, and at Egham for lunch. But there was not a complete network of regular stage-coach runs, so that travellers still used water transport in order to shorten a journey. This can be illustrated by the route used by the shipbuilding family of Adams, who lived at Buckler's Hard, near Beaulieu in Hampshire. When, at the end of the eighteenth century, they visited Portsmouth Dockyard, they used the following route: by horse to Fawley, across the Southampton Water by ferry to Warsash, by horse to Gosport, and then across Portsmouth Harbour by ferry.

In the period from 1800 till 1840 stage-coaches averaged 9 m.p.h. along 103 regular routes in England and Wales. Inns were used as stations where mail was collected and fresh teams of horses harnessed, while the passengers rested. Many of these old coaching inns, with their large courtyards and stables, are still standing. Descriptions of the days of the stage-coach can be found in *Felix Holt* by George Eliot, and *Pickwick Papers* by Charles Dickens. It was unfortunate for those who invested money in roads and coaches that road transport had become efficient only shortly before it was superseded by the railways, which spread throughout England in the years from 1830 to 1850.

RIVERS AND CANALS

Water transport played an important role in the carriage of both goods and passengers. In particular, very heavy goods, such as coal, iron, timber and grain, had to be carried by water wherever possible because of the great cost of road transport. England is more fortunate than many countries in having many miles of navigable rivers. But the main waterways, the Mersey, the Bristol Channel, the Thames, the Wash, the Humber and the Tyne, did not provide a complete transport system. There are few navigable rivers north of Preston, or south of the Bristol Channel. It is true that the small creeks and harbours and rivers were used wherever possible as arteries of commerce, and continued to be used until the development of motor traction. But there was a need in the eighteenth century to increase the availability of water transport. During the seventeenth century something had been done to improve the rivers, by dredging, or by cuts which eliminated some of the meanders. This improvement was continued during the eighteenth century, but many rivers had serious disadvantages, such as weirs and dams built by millers in order to increase the flow, and low bridges causing obstruction. Some stretches of river, too, were in the hands of private owners who prohibited transit or charged high dues.

Many of these limitations were removed by the construction of artificial waterways, or canals. A canal could bring water transport to a region previously without it. Tow paths could be built more easily than they could on river banks, which were often marshy or muddy. (It should be remembered that it was not possible to use sails on most stretches of inland rivers, and so barges had to be rowed or punted.) Horses, walking on firm ground, could tow a considerable weight. This is worth stressing, as in some cases canals were built *alongside* existing rivers. Also the flow of water in a canal was less than that in a river, an important consideration in non-tidal waters, where a whole journey might be upstream.

Bridgewater and Brindley

The building of canals was not a new idea in the eighteenth century, but the setting up of a complete network was. This is what was done in England between 1757 and 1840. The first canals of the 'new era' were built in order to transport coal. In 1757 the Sankey Navigation, from the St Helens coalfields to the Mersey, was opened. This canal was ten miles long, and had nine locks. Of greater importance was a canal opened in 1761 by Francis Egerton, the third Duke of

Bridgewater. The Duke, born in 1736, took over his estates near Manchester in 1757, after a 'Grand Tour' in France where he had seen canals being used. Part of the income from his estates at Worsley

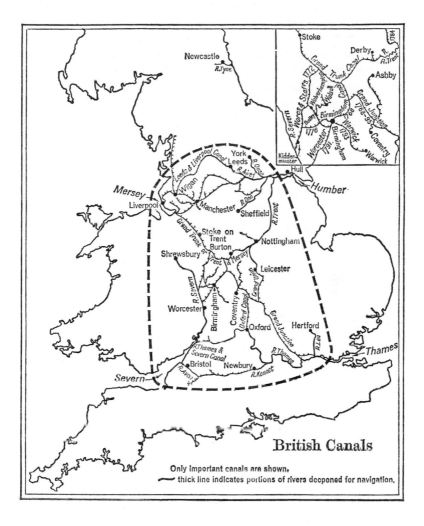

British Canals

Only important canals are shown.
— thick line indicates portions of rivers deepened for navigation.

came from coal mines, and the Duke found two problems preventing efficient working. The mines were susceptible to flooding, and the cost of transporting the coal was very high. (Road transport from Worsley to Manchester, a distance of ten miles, doubled the price of coal.) The Duke engaged John Gilbert to plan a canal to Manchester.

John Gilbert had served an apprenticeship with Matthew Boulton, and had recently had mining experience. He conceived the bold plan of building a canal leading directly from the mine. The water supply would thus be ensured, and at the same time some water would be drained out of the mine. He originally intended to link the canal with the River Irwell, which flowed from Manchester into the Mersey, but the owners of the river demanded such high fees that he decided to build a canal the whole distance to Manchester.

John Gilbert began his difficult task in 1759 with James Brindley (1716–72) as his associate. Brindley was born near Buxton, and after service as a ploughboy became a wheelwright and millwright. The three men were a perfect combination. The Duke was a born entrepreneur, able to organise the necessary capital and to lay down the broad principles. John Gilbert, the 'chief engineer', was a shrewd and steady character. James Brindley was a wayward genius, who was able to solve many seemingly insoluble problems. But he was liable to extreme moods, and often retired to bed in order to think out solutions to difficulties; he disliked writing, and preferred to do mathematical sums in his head rather than on paper. He was not, however, illiterate.

Brindley must be given the credit for overcoming one great difficulty, the crossing of the River Irwell. The Duke of Bridgewater and Gilbert had intended to run the canal into the Irwell, so that the canal traffic could cross the river, and proceed to a cut on the opposite bank. But this scheme presented two dangers: the Duke would still be in the hands of the owners of the river, and there was a possibility that the canal would lose some of its water supply. Brindley conceived the idea of building a bridge over the river to carry the canal, and demonstrated his scheme with sand, clay and a can of water. The Barton Aqueduct was a success, and inspired the lines:

> Vessels o'er vessels, water under water,
> Bridgewater triumphs, art has conquered nature.

The Duke of Bridgewater was forced to borrow a considerable amount of money in order to finance the building of the canal. There is a story that on one occasion he hid from the local vicar in order to delay paying his tithes. By 1762, a year after the opening of the canal, the Duke was over £27,000 in debt. But he was not deterred by these financial difficulties. In 1762 he began work on another enterprise designed to link the Worsley canal to the Mersey at Runcorn. This waterway, known as the Bridgewater Canal, was opened in 1776. By this time the value of canals was clearly seen by manufacturers, and work was in progress on several other schemes. In 1766 James Brindley began to build the Grand Trunk Canal to link the Mersey, Severn and Trent. Many technical problems had to be overcome and Brindley died of overwork in 1772 before the project was completed. In order to negotiate a rise and fall in altitude of 395 feet, 75 locks were built. The canal had five tunnels and five aqueducts. It was opened in 1777. Josiah Wedgwood was a principal shareholder, and by means of this canal he was able to send pottery by water to Liverpool and Hull. Other canals to be built were the Forth–Clyde (opened in 1790), the Ellesmere which linked the Dee with the Severn (1793), the Grand Junction (Birmingham to London, 1793), the Leeds to Liverpool (begun in 1770 and completed in 1816), and the Caledonian (begun in 1822 and opened in 1840).

Canal Mania

Although the Worsley and Bridgewater canals were financed largely by one man, most of the canal companies sold shares in order to raise the necessary money. Even the Duke of Bridgewater lived for thirty years on an average personal expenditure of £400 a year, though before he died his fortunes had been restored. Many of the canals which were begun in the years 1791 to 1794 (a period known as the 'canal mania') were not completed, or if they were they ran at a loss. One such was the Southampton to Salisbury canal; the company ran out of money when only a few miles had been cut. In order to continue work, the company mortgaged future tolls! In fact, the canal was never completed. Most of the 'failures' were in the south, where they ran through agricultural counties providing insufficient demand. Also, some companies began with insufficient capital and a considerable amount was required. Expenses were incurred in obtaining the Act of Parliament necessary to form the company, in acquiring land and in surveying before work could begin. Then the building took several years, during which time there would be much expenditure and no income. The gangs of labourers, known as 'navigators' ('navvies'), had to be paid, while materials for tunnels, locks and aqueducts had to be bought.

The Importance of Canals and their Defects

The successful canals were of great importance in the development of the economy in the period 1760 to 1840. They supplied water transport to areas which had hitherto had no satisfactory form of it. Birmingham and the Black Country, and the potteries of north Staffordshire benefited greatly. The canals linked London to the main industrial regions and they provided for east-west traffic. The produce of the industrial regions could be transported to all parts of the kingdom, and it could be carried to the ports for shipment abroad. Also, canals provided a cheaper form of transportation, especially for heavy goods. Carriage by canal cost between one-quarter and one-third of road haulage fees. Also, the building of canals provided valuable experience in engineering, especially helpful to the railway builders of the next generation.

Canals, however, had severe limitations. Passage was slow (the average speed was 2 m.p.h.), so that passenger traffic did not reach great proportions. As the canals were built piecemeal by many different companies, there was no uniform depth, breadth, or scale of charges. Different methods of construction meant that whilst some canals had locks, other canals came to an abrupt end and started again at a higher level, the barges being raised by a vertical lift, or towed up an incline. In order to save money, many canals had no towpath inside the tunnels, so that the horses had to be uncoupled. The barges were then propelled through the tunnel by 'leggers', i.e. men lying on their backs and pushing their legs against the sides or roof of the tunnel. The canal companies owned only the canals while other companies provided the barges, and were the carriers. Another defect of canals was that they suffered from climatic conditions such as frost and drought. But with all these weaknesses, they were invaluable until the invention of the locomotive, which hastened their decline after 1840. Canals might, however, have had a longer period of importance had it been easier to use steam-powered barges. But the wash from a fast-moving steam barge eroded the banks, while paddles were liable to damage in the locks.

Improvements in road and water transport were simultaneous with developments in agriculture and industry discussed in previous chapters. All these phases of economic life were linked. An increase in production created a need for better transport; without better transport, production could not increase.

CHAPTER 6

Sea Transport, Trade, and the Effects of the French Wars

Although the development of canals during the second half of the eighteenth century led to a decrease in the proportion of goods carried in coastal shipping, the sea still remained important in the transport of goods from one part of Britain to another. Like all other available forms of transport at the time, sailing vessels had inherent disadvantages. Ships were storm-bound in harbour, or becalmed at sea; delays were frequent and variable, so that it was impossible to plan a time-table with any accuracy. Moreover, as there were few docks, ships had to be moored in midstream. Cargoes had to be loaded into lighters at the wharves, and then taken out to the ship. This shifting of cargo, at loading and unloading, led to a great deal of pilfering.

Eighteenth-century ships were not highly specialised as they are today. Ships could carry a variety of cargoes in hold and, apart from the small wherries which acted as ferries, there was no such thing as a passenger ship distinct from a cargo ship. Yet there were a few ships of distinctive design, built for special purposes. The Whitby colliers were sturdy, shallow-draught barks (three-masted vessels); they had a blunt bow without a figure-head, and a broad round stern. Captain Cook's vessels, *Endeavour* and *Resolution*, were colliers. Coal was also carried in smaller one- or two-masted, square-rigged ships called collier brigs. These were slow, but sturdy and reliable. Deep-sea fishing vessels were stout craft designed to withstand rough seas. The whalers ventured into the Arctic seas off Greenland, and into the South Seas; the cod-fishermen sailed across the Atlantic to Newfoundland; the herring fishermen (their ships were called 'busses') made catches in the North Sea, sending their fish to the nearest ports in fast sloops. Timber hoys were stout, bluff-bowed vessels which often had a wide port at the stern so that tree-trunks could be stowed on the main deck. Packet boats were used for carrying mails and passengers from Dover and Harwich to Europe, from Holyhead to Ireland, or from Falmouth to Spain, the West Indies, and North

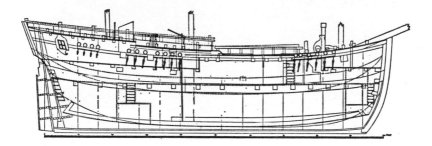

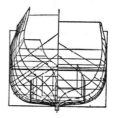

Draught of His Majesty's Bark *Endeavour*, the vessel commanded by James Cook on his first voyage (1768–71). Cook charted the coasts of New Zealand and eastern Australia. *Endeavour* was 97 feet long, and had a beam of 29 feet. The diagram on the right shows the scantlings of the frames.

America. These packets were usually two-masted ships, square-rigged and sturdy. The West Indiamen, sailing from Bristol or London, were three-masted, fully rigged ships, armed with cannon. The largest merchant ships of the period, the East Indiamen, were scarcely distinguishable from men-o'-war: they were heavily-armed, three-masted, fully rigged ships. The East Indiamen were built on the Thames, particularly at Johnson's Yard at Blackwall or at Castle's Yard at Deptford.

Shipbuilding

Though the East Indiamen and the West Indiamen were Thames-built, other smaller merchant vessels were built in many places, especially south of the Thames and the Bristol Channel. But vessels

Shipbuilders consumed a huge quantity of nails. The demand was met at first by hand forging. Up to six nailers would work at the forge shown above, which incorporates a simple mechanism for working the bellows from a distance. Typically the application of steam power, to produce the nail-cutting machine shown below, speeded up production and cut down on labour.

for local trade were usually built in the vicinity. Ships were built of wood, but towards the end of the eighteenth century fittings such as anchors, bitts and knees were made of iron. There were few important changes in design in the eighteenth century, when English shipwrights were generally conservative, if not backward. Some more advanced craftsmen were studying the mathematical implications of design, but English ships were renowned for sturdiness rather than speed.

Different types of timber were needed for different parts of the ship. For the stern and stem posts English oak (especially the *quercus robur*) was preferred. Oak was also needed for the main frames or ribs. The keel was made of oak or elm, the keelson (a kind of upper keel which locked the ribs to the keel), of elm. Beech was used for the 'thickstuff' of inside 'walls' and for underwater planking. Planking above the water line could be made from a variety of woods. Fir, spruce or pine were needed for masts and spars. Most of the oak, elm and beech were drawn from England but the mast timber had to be imported, especially from the Baltic. As masts did not usually last more than ten years, even if they escaped damage from gales or cannon-balls, a vast amount of mast timber was required. The quantity of materials required by shipbuilding was prodigious. For a ship 130 feet long, a builder needed about 2,000 tons of timber, 100 tons of wrought iron, and 30 tons of nails and copper rivets, in order to build the hull and the decks alone. Wooden ships needed frequent repairs and were often almost completely rebuilt.

Except on the Thames, ships were built on sites rather than in yards. Often a shipbuilder used a site for a few years only, and then moved to another site where there was accessible timber. Most of the work was done by shipwrights, who were highly skilled tradesmen. Other shipbuilding workers included sawyers (who worked in pairs), caulkers, carpenters and blacksmiths. Apart from the firms on the Thames, the number of men working on a shipbuilding site rarely exceeded fifty. But in addition, timber-merchants, carters, treenail-makers and sailmakers were engaged in making components and supplying materials. This scattered shipbuilding industry became concentrated in towns when later the development of iron steam ships caused radical changes in techniques, and made large shipyards necessary.

Ports

In 1700 there were, outside the royal dockyards, few tidal or dry docks. Ships usually anchored in the middle of the river or harbour, whilst lighters plied from the shore, where there were wharves, quays and jetties. If a vessel needed repair, it was beached, or moored to a quayside and allowed to list as the tide fell. One of the first docks to be built for merchantmen was at Liverpool in 1715. In 1773 John Golborne built jetties and groynes at Glasgow. The development of docks in London did not begin until the early nineteenth century, when the West India Docks were opened in 1802, followed by the London (1805), the East India (1806), and the Commercial Docks (1807). In 1700 London was by far the most important port, handling 80 per cent of the country's imports, and 74 per cent of its exports. Bristol came a poor second. Though London continued to expand as a port, so that congestion in the river became a serious problem, by 1790 its proportion of imports and exports handled had fallen to 70 per cent and 56 per cent respectively. Liverpool, which in 1700 had a population of only 500 people, expanded rapidly: by 1790 its population was 54,000 people, and it was the second largest port in the kingdom. In the period 1700 to 1790, sugar imports into Liverpool rose five-fold, rum and tobacco imports rose three-fold, and cotton imports fifty-fold. In the short period from 1770 to 1791, coal exported from Liverpool increased five-fold. This was due to the development of steam power in the cotton industry in Lancashire, and to the canal system which made Liverpool the port for many of the new industrial areas. Glasgow also developed during the second half of the eighteenth century, largely due to the importation of sugar from the West Indies, and raw cotton from the U.S.A. Its population rose from 28,000 in 1760 to 200,000 in 1830. Bristol suffered a relative decline because it was not so well placed as a port for the growing industries: it still relied largely on the slave trade.

OVERSEAS TRADE

Mercantilism

During the eighteenth century, the state regulated trade as far as it could, remembering that the enforcement of orders was not always possible. This regulation is generally known as *mercantilism* or, as

Adam Smith called it, the 'Commercial System'. The broad aims of mercantilism were to ensure that England had a favourable balance of trade, i.e. that her exports exceeded her imports. In order to achieve this, restrictions were placed upon commerce. One pillar of the mercantile system was the Navigation Act, whereby imported goods had to be carried in English ships, or in a ship of the country of origin. Laws aimed to this end were first imposed during the twelfth century, and those in operation in the eighteenth century were still based upon those passed in 1651. By another series of laws, the importation of corn from abroad was subject to the payment of duties. Tariffs were laid on many other commodities, whilst bounties were given to industries which were particularly susceptible to foreign competition.

The restrictions placed on trade came under attack towards the end of the eighteenth century, especially from Adam Smith in his book *The Wealth of Nations*, published in 1776.[1] But the removal of duties and restrictions was delayed by two main conditions. Firstly, Britain was at war for many years in the period 1700 to 1815, and even when she was not at war, relations with France and Spain could be called 'cold war'. The regulation of trade by the government is usually an essential feature of wartime. In addition, as wars cost money, successive governments were reluctant to pursue any policy which appeared to make it more difficult for them to raise revenue. Secondly, as Britain's industries were beginning to develop, it was thought essential to continue protective duties on the importation of foreign manufactured goods. The controversy between supporters of protection and of free trade became one of the burning issues of the period 1820–60. In the eighteenth century, restriction and regulation were accepted by most political thinkers.

One method of increasing trade was by the acquisition of territory overseas—an 'empire'. Such possessions were valuable as they provided markets from which other powers could be excluded. Furthermore, if the territories were in tropical or sub-tropical regions, commodities which could not be produced in England could be obtained. Colonies thus provided both markets and raw materials. During the eighteenth century, Britain laid the foundations of an empire. In 1700 she had thirteen colonies in North America, Jamaica

[1] See pp. 129 and 296–7.

in the West Indies, some small islands in the Lesser Antilles, and three or four 'factories' or depots in India. In 1815, though the North American colonies had become independent under the name of the United States of America, Britain had added to her empire Gibraltar, Newfoundland, Hudson Bay, Canada, more West Indian islands, a part of India, Australia and New Zealand, the Cape Colony in South Africa, and possessions in West Africa, as well as islands in the south Atlantic and Pacific oceans.

Trade with Europe

During the eighteenth century the value of imports (as shown in the customs accounts) rose from £5·9 million in 1700 to £28·4 million in 1800; the corresponding figures for exports are £6·9 million and £40·8 million. Despite the value of the colonial trade, Europe remained an important customer and source of supply. In 1700 Europe supplied 53 per cent of England's imports; by 1750 the proportion had fallen to 44 per cent, and to 31 per cent in 1800. In 1700 Europe took 78 per cent of our exports, 63 per cent in 1750, and 45 per cent in 1800.

Timber, corn, iron, hemp and flax were bought from the Baltic. It should be noted that most of these Baltic supplies were essential for shipbuilding and for naval stores. Raw cotton was bought from the Levant, and merino wool from Spain. Wine was imported from Portugal, whose produce was admitted at reduced rates by the Methuen Treaty signed in 1703. Some wine and corn was imported from France, but trade with France was frequently interrupted by war. However, much illicit trade, especially in French brandies, was carried on by smugglers. England sent to Europe woollen cloth, hardware and pottery, fish, lead and tin, together with re-exported colonial produce. By 1800 refined sugar, cotton goods and iron manufactured goods were the most important of England's exports to Europe. Ireland supplied England and Wales with farm produce, such as meat, butter, cheese and tallow, and imported English coal and manufactured goods.

Trade across the Oceans

British trade in the Atlantic was carried out by means of a 'triangular' system. Merchants in London, Bristol and Liverpool sent ships laden with calicoes, beads, flints and powder, knives and rum to West Africa. There these commodities were exchanged for gold, ivory and negro slaves. The slaves were supplied to the white merchants by tribal chiefs and by slave traders, and were taken across the Atlantic, where they were sold to West Indian sugar planters, who needed cheap labour able to withstand the heat. Slaves were also in demand in the plantations of the American colonies from Virginia to Georgia. This trade in 'human flesh' enabled English merchants to import sugar, tobacco, cotton, rice and indigo from America and the West Indies. Whilst some traders made a fortune, others lost heavily. The completion of one 'triangular' voyage took between nine and twelve months; and because of the nature of the 'cargo', a large crew was needed to man these West Indiamen. The development of Liverpool, Glasgow and Bristol was due, in part, to this traffic. The slave trade was at its height in Britain during the second half of the eighteenth century. It was declared illegal in 1807, and it is to Britain's credit that the Royal Navy was the biggest single force used in stopping it. Long after 1807 British naval vessels stopped ships of other countries, including America, which ignored the international agreement.

Outside the 'triangular system' other patterns of trade asserted themselves. From the middle of the seventeenth century onwards a steady flow of men and women had crossed the Atlantic to start life in the new continent. Some were taken against their will as convicts, paupers or parish orphans, while others went as free settlers or as indentured servants, working merely for their keep until their master had recouped the cost of their passage. With them from Britain went capital and manufactured goods to finance and develop the new lands. These goods and loans were financed by American trade in raw materials with the West Indies and the home country. After the American War of Independence (1776–83) the Royal Navy cut all but the American smugglers off from the West Indies, and, to the eventual disadvantage of the latter, this trade declined. At the same time the Americans were now free of the British embargo on the production of manufactured goods in the colonies and so could supply themselves with many of the items they had previously bought from Britain. Yet though the Atlantic trade in finished goods declined, the Americans still needed men and money and the British still needed cotton, sugar and tobacco.

England's trade with the Far East was carried out by the East India Company. Although the Company was able to sell some metal goods to Indians and Chinese, the greater part of its imports had to be paid for in silver. Because of this, 'John' Company was regarded by some 'experts' as harming England's economy, since bullion was exported. This, they believed, was draining the country of currency, and creating an adverse balance of trade. From the Far East the Company brought back tea, spices, silks and dye-woods. The Company argued that, by re-exporting these commodities to Europe and America, they were instrumental in bringing more bullion into the country, and that they had a favourable balance of trade. It is not possible to prove the issue one way or the other, but it is safe to say that the Company's trade did little harm to England's economy. At least they opened channels of trade which became very profitable in the nineteenth century.

THE EFFECTS OF THE FRENCH WARS 1793–1815

From 1793 to 1815 Britain was at war with France continuously, except for a short period of peace from the signing of the Treaty of Amiens in 1802 until the following year. Although by the standards of the two twentieth-century wars, the French Wars did not have a profound effect upon the economy, they had far greater effect than any previous war. At the height of the war Britain had 140,000 men in the navy, and 350,000 in the army, together with many thousands in the militia, the yeomanry, and in the East India Company's army in India. At one time as many as one in ten of the men of military age were serving in the armed forces or in the volunteers. This meant that unemployment fell, and that workers in some industries were able to demand good wages. Particularly fortunate were the hand-loom weavers, and those engaged in the iron industries. But as prices and taxation rose, in general wages lagged behind prices, and brought hardship to many of the labouring classes. Those engaged in agriculture were especially hard hit. James Carlyle, the father of Thomas Carlyle and a farm worker in Scotland, told how some of his fellows walked to a stream at the bottom of the field during the dinner break in order to drink water, as they could not afford to bring any food with them.

In 1795 the Justices of Berkshire met at the Pelican Inn in the village of Speenhamland, near Newbury, in order to consider the plight of the farm workers in their county. They decided to grant allowances from the poor rates to supplement wages which were below a specified minimum. This minimum wage varied with the price of corn, and was based on the price of 26 lb. of bread per week for each man, with the price of an additional 13 lb. for his wife and for each child. The average sum was about 3s. per week for the man, plus 1s. 6d. for his wife, so that a man with a wife and two children, whose earnings were 7s. per week, was to receive a further 6d. per week from the overseers as poor-relief. This method of supplementing wages, known as the Speenhamland System, was adopted by the authorities in most of the south and the midlands.

During the wars Britain loaned a total of £57 million to her allies. This financial drain, to which must be added the British government's own expenditure on the wars, led to a shortage of hard currency, and to recurrent financial crises. In 1797, at a time when the war was going badly and when the fleets in the Thames and Spithead were in a state of mutiny, there was a run on the banks; that is, the holders of paper currency tried to convert it into gold and silver coinage. The government was forced to suspend such transactions (specie payments), and this measure remained in force until 1819. More paper money was put into circulation, and inflation, or rising prices, resulted. In order to raise its revenue, the government increased indirect taxation (taxes on commodities), and in 1799 introduced income tax.

The effect of the wars on industry and agriculture was to stimulate production. Because of a shortage of alkali, the manufacture of vitriol grew.[1] Uniforms and blankets were needed, and this stimulated the textile industry. As one example, Benjamin Gott (1762–1840) of Leeds established a factory in 1792, and eight years later he was employing a thousand people. Iron works, such as that of Richard Crawshay of Cyfartha,[2] were busy making chains, anchors, guns and nails. Boulton and Watt were making steam engines and medals. Lintott's of Romsey were manufacturing one thousand sacks a week for the Portsmouth Dockyard Victualling Department. Shipbuilders were engaged in work on merchant and naval craft.

As well as supplying the needs of war, Britain needed to maintain

[1] See pp. 45–6.   [2] See p. 32.

her overseas trade in order to pay for necessary imports. After the battle of Trafalgar in 1805, Napoleon, unable to invade England, decided to resort to economic warfare. His plan was to prevent England from trading with Europe. Accordingly he began the 'continental system' by issuing the Milan Decrees in 1806 and the Berlin Decrees in the following year. Britain retaliated with Orders of Council, whereby she ordered a blockade of France. This economic warfare led to both gain and loss for Britain. She suffered some cutback of her trade with Europe, but Napoleon's blockade was only partially successful since he could not close all European ports to British ships. As the Royal Navy had command of the Atlantic, British trade with America grew apace. The activities of the Navy led to a war with the U.S.A. from 1812 to 1814, but British trade remained good during those years. The blackest year for British overseas trade was 1811, when Lancashire was working a three-day week. But generally the 'nation of shopkeepers' was able to continue in business as usual.

No measure to ration food or control the supply of materials was introduced. But Britain suffered from two particular shortages during the wars—corn and timber. The supply of wheat from Europe became difficult, and the shortage led to rising prices. This stimulated the production of corn at home, and more land was put under the plough. Often this land was marginal or waste land, and much capital had to be put into it in order to make it productive. Whilst the war lasted, farmers could get a good return for their investment, but when the war ended, some found themselves in dire straits.

The timber shortage was due to the increased demands of shipbuilding and to periods when the Baltic trade was interrupted. This in turn caused a housing shortage, for timber was the basic building material. The housing shortage was further aggravated by a rise in the population, and by a shortage of money available for mortgages. Even in those days the owners of houses had them built with borrowed money. The expenditure of capital on the war effort, and Usury Laws whereby the government pegged the interest rate, made the advance of mortgage loans difficult to obtain.[1] For a house mortgage a legal agreement was necessary, so that the lender could not evade the Usury Laws as he could in some private transaction. This

[1] See pp. 210-11 for effects of the wars on finance generally.

housing shortage resulted in the building of some poor houses during and after the war. In shipbuilding, attempts were made to find new sources of supply outside Europe, with a result that American and Eastern timber was used once more. As an example, the *Trincomalee*, a naval frigate, was laid down in Bombay in 1814, built of Malabar teak. She was launched in 1817, and is still afloat in Portsmouth Harbour today under the name of *Foudroyant*.

The French Wars caused an acceleration in the changes which were already taking place before they began. If no *permanent* harm was done to the economy, they added to the stress of the daily lives of the people of the time. In times of change, some prosper and some are harmed: change breeds restlessness and discontent.

PART TWO
The Nineteenth Century

CHAPTER 7

The People, 1815-1914

The Size of the Population

The first census in 1801 gave the population of England and Wales as 8·8 millions. The figure is not completely accurate, as the organisers were without experience in obtaining the necessary information. Also it did not include the armed forces (England was at war at the time, and had about 470,000 men serving as soldiers and sailors). During the course of the century the population grew as follows:

	millions
1831	13·8
1851	17·9
1871	22·7
1891	29·0
1901	32·5

Put simply, the population of England and Wales was four times as great in 1901 as it was in 1801. In no previous century was the proportionate increase as large, and unless there are some exceptional developments in later decades, the twentieth-century increase will not match that of the nineteenth. Since 1901 the census has shown:

	millions	
1921	37·9	
1931	39·9	
1951	43·6	
1961	46·0	
1965	47·6	(estimated)[1]

The general factors which cause a rise or fall in population were discussed in Chapter 1. It will be sufficient here to state that on balance England and Wales lost more people by emigration than

[1] See p. 300 for U.K. population.

were gained by immigration. The increase in population was due to a lower death-rate rather than to a higher birth-rate. The great improvement in medicine and personal hygiene, and the development of public health control, led to people living longer; this more

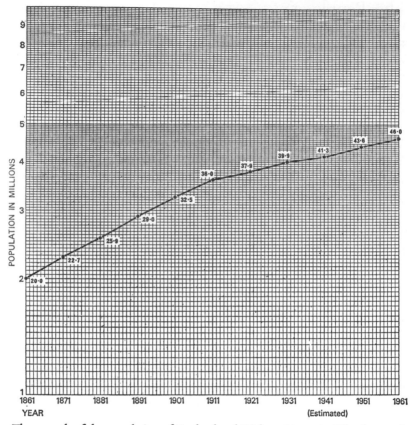

The growth of the population of England and Wales, 1861–1961. Like the graph on p. 4, this is logarithmic on the vertical axis.

than counter-balanced a slight fall in the birth-rate, a fall which became more marked during the last two decades of the nineteenth century. The decline in the *rate* of growth (though not a decline in numerical growth) after 1901 was due to a lower birth-rate. Whereas during the first half of the nineteenth century a child could be a wage-earner at a tender age, the second half of the century saw the institution of compulsory education. This is not to say that at any time parents had children because they needed their earning potential. But after 1880 another child meant another mouth to feed, and not another pair of hands. By the end of the nineteenth century many people were aware that large families could lead to poverty, and this awareness grew as the standard of living rose. Some had begun to advocate the deliberate limitation of the size of families. In 1877 Charles Bradlaugh and Annie Besant were prosecuted for publishing an American pamphlet on birth-control, and the trial led to great publicity. The subject of family limitation aroused (and still arouses) great differences of opinion, but undoubtedly the practice had some effect. In 1867 two out of every three families comprised four or more children; in 1925 the usual family was one or two children only. In the 1870's births averaged 860,000 per annum: in 1934, although the population was much larger, the number of births was only 600,000.

The effects on the economy of the variations in the growth of population were great. For instance, in the early part of the nineteenth century a great proportion of the population was young ($27\frac{1}{2}$ per cent were under ten years of age in 1821). This meant that there was child labour in plenty for the factories. The increase in population, which provided a labour force for industry, led to a greater demand for food, some of which was imported. To pay for the food, the country needed to export more goods, and this stimulated more industrialisation. It led to the rapid development of towns. As these developed there was a need for greater control of housing, transport, sewage, water supplies and power. If she was to sustain her growing population, with its rising standard of living, England needed to become an industrial nation. This meant that her people had to be skilled, educated and disciplined.

Geographical Distribution

During the nineteenth century the centre of gravity of the population shifted from the south and east to the midlands and the north. Apart from London, the most densely populated areas were Birmingham, South Wales, southern Lancashire, the West Riding of Yorkshire, and Northumberland and Durham. The reason for this was the

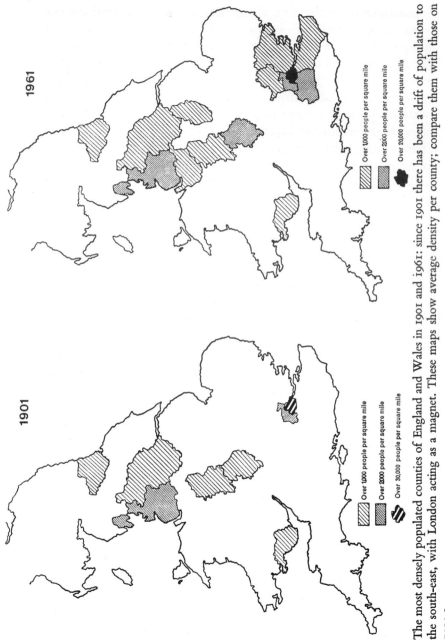

1961

Over 1,000 people per square mile
Over 2,000 people per square mile
Over 20,000 people per square mile

1901

Over 1,000 people per square mile
Over 2,000 people per square mile
Over 30,000 people per square mile

The most densely populated counties of England and Wales in 1901 and 1961: since 1901 there has been a drift of population to the south-east, with London acting as a magnet. These maps show average density per county; compare them with those on page 9.

development of industries which needed coal. Birmingham and towns to the north, such as Wolverhampton, Walsall and Wednesbury, expanded with the growth of the metal industries; Swansea, Cardiff and Newport developed as ports for the coal and iron industries of the valleys behind them; Leeds, Huddersfield and Bradford grew with the application of steam power to the woollen industries; Newcastle grew as coal production and export increased. But whilst the population in those regions grew, the density of population in other areas did not decrease. Growth in the south was simply not as rapid as in the 'new' industrial areas.

In 1801 over three-quarters of the people of England and Wales still lived in rural surroundings. In 1851, the year of the Great Exhibition, half the population lived in urban surroundings and half in rural. Since 1851 the proportion of town dwellers has increased so that today over four-fifths live in towns. Towns developed in the nineteenth century by taking the surplus population from the surrounding countryside. A typical pattern of family migration would have been as follows: of six sons born to a farm worker in Warwickshire, one remained in the village, whilst five sought employment in, say, Birmingham, Stourbridge or Dudley. Young people moved, rather than entire families, and they usually moved to a nearby town, rather than from one part of the country to another. There were, however, certain areas which were exceptional. Irishmen crossed the sea to seek work in Liverpool, Manchester, Glasgow or South Wales; Scots from the Highlands moved to the Lowlands. In 1851 there were 500,000 Irish-born people living in Britain. Skilled men, such as engineers or boiler-makers, were induced to move for higher wages. The towns offered the chance of higher wages, and acted as a magnet.

Towns

Many towns grew spectacularly during the nineteenth century, as the figures overleaf show.

London remained England's biggest 'town' by far. In spite of the national trend of population, London's proportion of the total population grew from 11·75 per cent in 1841 to 14·52 per cent in 1891. Early in the nineteenth century some men were disturbed about London's growth. London was referred to as a polypus or a 'wen' which would ultimately kill the country. This fear continued, and was a constant theme of writers. In 1913 Stephen Phillips wrote:

> I dreamed a dream, perhaps a prophecy!
> That London over England spread herself;
> Swallowed the green fields and the waving plain,
> Till all this island grew one hideous town.

We are today seeing this dream come true.

	1801 (thousands)	1851 (thousands)	1901 (thousands)
Manchester	84	366	866
Birmingham	71	233	523
Liverpool	82	376	704
Sheffield	46	135	407
Leeds	43	172	429
Nottingham	30	60	240
Bradford	10	93	280
Newcastle	30	90	215
Bristol	60	145	320
Southampton	8	35	104

Many agreed with Rousseau, the eighteenth-century French philosopher, that 'men are not made to be crowded into ant-hills . . . the more they are crowded together, the more corrupt they will become'. Certainly the evils of towns in the first half of the nineteenth century afforded much material for the novelist and social writer. Sanitation, water-supply and street-cleaning were primitive and inadequate; houses and accommodation did not increase as rapidly as did the population; social amenities and amusements lagged behind the demand. Cobbett, Dickens and Disraeli all wrote vehemently about city life in the first half of the nineteenth century. 'England's green and pleasant land' appeared to be threatened by the 'dark satanic mills'.

The growth of cities was viewed with alarm by others who feared 'the masses' and thought that the crowding together of large numbers of ill-educated people would lead to violence and revolution. This attitude helps to explain the ruthlessness with which some popular movements were suppressed. It certainly caused hostility between employers and workmen, and between rich and poor. Violence and disorder were the keynotes of the first half of the nineteenth century.

To many, however, the growth of towns enabled them to live fuller lives. Citizens took a pride in the growth and development of their city. The people of Manchester, for example, evolved a life and culture of their own, even though it could not be enjoyed by all. The Free Trade Hall, built on the site of Peterloo, held over 7,000 people (it was destroyed in an air raid during the 1939-45 war). Manchester had its own paper, the *Manchester Guardian*, public parks in 1846, and Hallé concerts from 1858. Birmingham had triennial musical festivals, and, under the mayoralty of Joseph Chamberlain (1873-76), public parks and other amenities. The growth of Middlesbrough as a 'steel' town, from 25 people in 1801, to 154 in 1831, 7,431 by 1851 and to 91,302 in 1901, would have been a source of wonder and excitement to the successive generations who witnessed it.

Occupational Distribution

Despite the development of towns, agriculture remained the largest single source of employment in England until well into the nineteenth century. The 1851 census showed that there were 1·5 million males (aged 10 or over) together with 227,000 females engaged in farming, a total of 1·75 million out of a working population of 15·7 million. Put in another way, in 1851 one out of every five adult males (i.e. aged 10 or over) worked on the land. This proportion had fallen to one in six in 1881, and to one in twenty in 1911.

In 1851 the second largest occupational group was domestic servants[1] (134,000 males and 905,000 females). During the nineteenth century rich families had many servants—butlers, valets, grooms, coachmen, footmen, lady's maids, chambermaids, and so on. Domestic service was not regarded as menial, and not all employers were 'slave-drivers'. Although a direct comparison is difficult, conditions in domestic service were not necessarily worse than in the factories. It was during the nineteenth century that the maid's 'uniform' came into vogue. Leigh Hunt, writing in 1820, described it as follows: 'Her ordinary dress is black stockings, a stuff gown, a cap, and a neck handkerchief pinned cornerwise. . . . On Sundays and holidays, and perhaps of afternoons, she changes her black stockings for white, puts on a gown of better texture and fine pattern.'

---

[1] Domestic service was the largest occupational group by 1881.

In 1851 cotton workers were the third largest occupational group. There were over half a million of them, with almost equal numbers of male and female workers. There were 442,000 building workers, 340,000 milliners and dressmakers, 216,000 coal miners, 145,000 washerwomen, 79,000 ironworkers, and 65,000 railway employees.

By 1911 changes were apparent in the occupational distribution. The number of coal miners doubled between 1881 and 1911; the number of cotton workers increased slowly, as did the number of those engaged in building and in iron and steel works. In 1911 there were still one and a half million servants, but this was a smaller number than in 1891. The railways employed over half a million people. By 1911 there were new occupations open to both men and women. For the former there was a career in driving cars or trams, or in the growing electrical industry. For women there were increasing opportunities in nursing and in teaching. Women also invaded commerce, obtaining jobs as shop assistants or as clerks. In 1881 there were 7,000 women clerks; in 1911 there were 150,000. This increase was due in part to the development of the telephone and the typewriter; women proved to be more deft than men in operating these new inventions.

The Classes

Although it is always dangerous to generalise on classes of people, some fundamentals may be stated. There was some truth in Disraeli's division of 'the two nations'—the rich and the poor—for there was a great gulf between the two. The rich were very rich, and the majority of the people were very poor. There was also a large and prosperous middle class, engaged in the older professions or in commerce, who might be termed 'upper middle class'. It was difficult for the poor man to better himself, although there were increasing opportunities for the skilled and clever worker, especially when compulsory education began. It is also true to say that bitter, and often ill-informed, class hatred was a feature of nineteenth-century England. The rich feared the poor, the poor hated the rich; this caused rioting and bloodshed, and a 'schism' in the English people. The 1914–18 war helped to accelerate a social revolution which is still going on today, whereby the divisions between the classes have become blurred.

CHAPTER 8

Agriculture, 1815-1914

The period can conveniently be divided into three: from the end of the French Wars in 1815 until about 1837 farming was not as prosperous as it had been during the Wars; from about 1837 until 1874 farming was relatively prosperous; from 1874 to 1914 farming was in a depressed and stagnant condition.

DECLINE FROM WARTIME CONDITIONS

In time of war farming usually prospers, for an increased demand for food coincides with a decrease in foreign competition. The long wars against the French (1793-1815) had the effect of stimulating agriculture, and landowners either put money into farming their land themselves or leased it to tenant farmers at high rents. Farming was a 'good speculation'; it was worthwhile to farm poor land, for even if the crop was poor, the harvest would bring in a fair reward. But marginal land, which needed draining or fertilising, needed capital before it could be used for the growing of corn. Therefore the cost of corn production rose, but during the war prices remained high also; in the period 1804-12 wheat prices doubled, reaching a record of 126s. 6d. per quarter. Prices in those eight years were also inflated because of a series of poor harvests between 1809 and 1812. If the harvest was poor the price rose, if the harvest was good then the price fell. In 1813 and 1814 the harvests were good, and the price fell sharply; the effects on the farmers would have been greater had not the demand for grain to feed the army remained great. When the war ended in 1815, a Corn Law was imposed in order to protect the British farmer from foreign competition. The Corn Law prohibited the importation of wheat when the price of home-produced wheat was 80s. or less per quarter. The price of 80s. a quarter was one which

Richard Hornsby's Agricultural Implement Factory at Grantham in the mid-nineteenth century. Several steam-engines, used for threshing, and ploughs stand in the yard. As farm machinery was made of wood and iron, stocks of timber fill the foreground, outside the forges.

was considered to allow a fair margin of profit to the producer. The Corn Law was modified in 1828, when a 'sliding scale' duty was imposed. Under the sliding scale, the duty on imported corn fell from 23s. to 1s. per quarter as the price of home-grown corn rose from 64s. to 73s. per quarter.

Distress and its Causes

This attempt to bolster up English farming by protective duties was not altogether successful; it could not be, for there were other factors which were causing anxiety to both employers and their men. In the 1820's there was a depression in industry, and this in turn led to a fall in prices of agricultural produce. Tenant farmers, in many cases still paying high rents arranged on a long lease during the profitable war years, found their profits declining. At the same time, the tenant found that he had to pay high taxation; the ending of income tax in 1816 meant that the land tax remained high. Further, the Speenhamland System, whereby wages of agricultural labourers were subsidised from the poor rate, meant that rates payable by holders of land were high. For example, in 1816 one farmer holding 300 acres was paying a total of £380 per annum in rates and taxes. In addition, farmers paid tithes to the Church of England; these tithes, a tenth of their produce, were either in money or in produce, and were payable to the local incumbent or 'parson'. Farmers gained relief from this burden in 1836 when the Tithe Commutation Act was passed. By 1840 the tithe barn was, in J. H. Clapham's words, 'a matter for antiquarians instead of a centre of rather indecent clerical activity'. The Game Laws, passed in the reign of Charles II, pressed heavily upon tenant farmers. They were strict on poachers, who were liable to transportation if caught, and this was a harsh retribution for dishonesty. But the real injustice was that the landlord owned the game—the rabbits, hares, partridges, pheasants, etc.—so that the tenant farmer could not legally destroy game which despoiled his crops. The Game Laws were modified in 1831, so that the tenant could kill game eating his produce, but the Laws were not changed radically until 1880.

The burdens on the farm worker were also great. His wages were about £26 per annum. Women farm workers received about 9d. per day, and children 6d. Some farm workers had a cottage with a vegetable garden supplied by the employer, but not all were so fortunate. In some parts of England farm labour was obtained by the Gang System, whereby a foreman contracted to supply a gang where needed. This method had advantages for the employer, for he could ignore the welfare of the men (or women and children) in such matters as housing and care during illness and old-age; for the employee there was a serious disadvantage, as the work was casual. The Gang System was declared illegal by an Act of Parliament in 1868. Low wages were coincidental with high taxation: up to 1828 malt, beer, leather, hops, soap, candles, salt, tobacco, windows, tea and sugar were all taxed. The farm labourer could no more afford the produce of the countryside, such as meat, butter, cheese and milk, than could the townsman. Further, the Corn Laws kept the price of bread high.

These economic grievances were accentuated by the changes which were taking place in agriculture during the first decades of the nineteenth century. In some places there was a change of landlord, from an employer who had a personal relationship with his men, to an absentee landlord who regarded farming as a commercial venture. The farm labourers, by and large ignorant and illiterate, were disturbed by the introduction of new machinery and methods; they saw them not as labour-saving devices which would increase productivity, but as infernal machines which would lead to unemployment. They were especially disturbed by the introduction of threshing machines, which they thought would bring an end to overtime in the autumn.

In the autumn of 1830 there was widespread rioting throughout the southern counties. These outbreaks have been called the 'Swing Riots' and the 'Last Labourers' Revolt'. Ricks were burnt, farmers threatened, and overseers whipped. The authorities, alarmed by the recent revolution in France (1830), called out the yeomanry, and tried the ringleaders. Nine men or boys were hanged, and 450 were transported. But the outbreak did provoke some heart-searching, and some farmers agreed to raise the wages of their men.

During the 1830's and 1840's there was a slight improvement in the lot of the agricultural worker. The Poor Law Amendment Act of 1834[1] ended the Speenhamland System; industry began a slow and

[1] See p. 188.

uncertain recovery; and there were new opportunities abroad, especially in Australia and New Zealand, for the farm worker with the courage to emigrate. In 1846 the Corn Laws were repealed by the Prime Minister, Robert Peel.[1]

RETURN TO PROSPERITY

When the Corn Laws were repealed, many farmers prophesied the ruination of English farming. In fact the recovery continued, so that the period from 1850 to 1874 has been called 'the Golden Age' of English farming. This prosperity was due to several factors. First, the expected flood of imported foreign corn did not occur, for no new source of grain appeared until later in the century. Most imported grain still came from Europe, as the great farming areas of Australia and the U.S.A. still lacked railways for easy transit to the coasts, and the grain from there had to be brought in sailing ships. Wars in Europe stimulated the demand in Britain for home-produced grain; the Crimean War (1854–56) prevented the importation of Russian corn; the Franco-Prussian War (1870–71) meant an interruption of French supplies. The American Civil War (1861–65) also helped the English farmer. Secondly, there was a trade boom in England, with an increased demand for manufactured goods at home and abroad. Thirdly, the development of railways in England enabled the farmer to sell his produce to the growing towns; this speedy method of transport was particularly important in the carriage of perishable foodstuffs, such as dairy produce. In these middle years of the nineteenth century, the Englishman was provided with most of his dairy produce and half of his wheat from English farms.

High Farming

Another important reason for prosperity was the impact of the more efficient methods of farming which had been foreshadowed in the previous century. In 1848 James Caird published a pamphlet called *High Farming, the Best Substitute for Protection.* The title explained the author's theme—that farmers could survive the repeal of the Corn Laws by becoming more efficient. It was by the use of

[1] See p. 133.

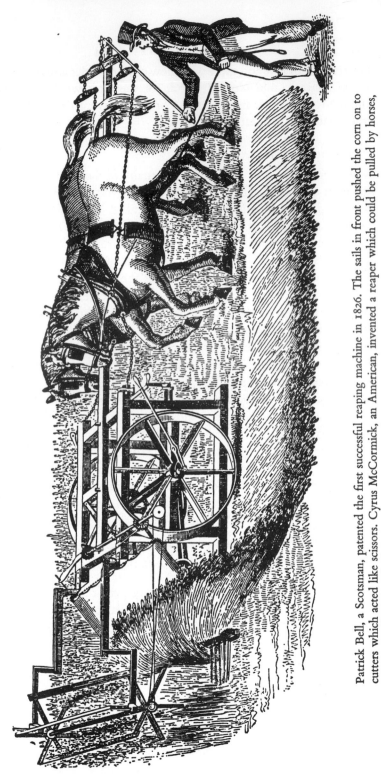

Patrick Bell, a Scotsman, patented the first successful reaping machine in 1826. The sails in front pushed the corn on to cutters which acted like scissors. Cyrus McCormick, an American, invented a reaper which could be pulled by horses, whereas Bell's was pushed.

better techniques that the English farmer was able to increase production without enlarging the labour force. Further enclosures were made, so that by about 1850 most of the arable lands were enclosed. Today some open field farming is still done on Portland Bill, whilst the village of Laxton, in Nottinghamshire, has been deliberately preserved as an example of open field agriculture.

Improvements were made in methods of draining land which was prone to water-logging. In the 1820's Smith, of Deanston, Perthshire, successfully used shallow drains, made by digging trenches and lining the bottom with pebbles. In 1843, Parkes and others began the manufacture of cylindrical clay drain-pipes, thus providing a cheap method of land-drainage.

There were few important mechanical inventions. Iron gradually replaced wood in the manufacture of ploughs and harrows. In 1837 chaff-cutters and turnip-slicers appeared on the market. In 1841 Crosskill of Beverley patented a clod-crusher. Between 1850 and 1870 steam power became more common in threshing (Ransome's had won a prize for a steam threshing machine in 1842). But attempts to mechanise the cutting of corn at first met with little success. Patrick Bell invented a reaping machine in 1826, but it was heavy and clumsy and had to be pushed by a pair of horses. More practicable reaping machines were being made in the U.S.A. in the 1830's and 1840's, notably by Obed Hussey and Cyrus McCormick. In England, Crosskill patented a reaping machine in 1853, which could be pulled by horses (and not pushed), and which laid the cut corn in sheaves. When, in 1879, Appleby invented a string binder, the reaping machine came into more general use. Where machines were not used, the scythe replaced the sickle and the hook. A man with a scythe could cut considerably more than one using a hook; also the scythe, which can be used by a skilled man standing upright, is not so hard on the back.

Great strides were made in the application of science to farming ('agricultural chemistry'). The Royal Agricultural Society, founded in 1838, was instrumental in spreading knowledge of soil chemistry amongst farmers. Much was also done by individuals. John Bennet Lawes began experiments on his estates at Rothamsted, Hertfordshire, in 1834; he was particularly concerned with the development of artificial fertilisers. The age-old practice of farmers was to add animal manure, soot, bones, salt, saltpetre, horns and hooves, marl, or chalk to the soil. The need was for greater quantities of super-phosphates and nitrates. The scientific study of plant growth was given some impetus by the publication, in 1840, of a book entitled *Organic Chemistry in its Applications to Agriculture and Physiology*, written by Liebig of Giessen, Germany. Three years later Lawes was joined at Rothamsted by J. H. Gilbert, when the Board of Agriculture established an experimental station there. Lawes opened a superphosphate factory at Deptford in the same year, using first bones and then mineral phosphates. Other chemists developed nitrate of soda, muriate of potash, and sulphate of ammonia. Important deposits of mineral sodium nitrate were discovered in Chile, and of guano in Peru; many 'nitrate' clippers were engaged in carrying these valuable fertilisers to England and Europe.

Although no new crops were introduced, some were grown more commonly, especially turnips, swedes and mangolds for winter cattle feed. However, many farmers used oil-cake made from linseed, and imported maize (or Indian corn) for fodder. Pedigree herds, such as the Shorthorns, Herefords and Devons, were improved, whilst the Sussex, Ayrshire and Channel Island breeds became more common. In sheep-farming, Lincolns, Oxford Downs and Shropshires became popular breeds.

The general prosperity in farming was shared by the farm worker, although his wages were lower than those of the town worker. The National Agricultural Labourers' Union was founded by Joseph Arch in 1872, but this organisation was unable to do much that was significant for its members. It is always difficult to compare the lot of the town worker with that of the countryman—for both have certain advantages over the other which do not appear in statistics of wages. At least, for those who found life on the farm too hard, there were opportunities of other employment, for instance on the railways.

DEPRESSION, 1874–1914

The depression which affected farming in the 1870's was accompanied by a similar movement in industry. The summer of 1873 was unusually wet, and was followed by five more wet summers between then and 1879. In 1879, a harsh winter was succeeded by a bleak spring and another wet summer, which led to mildewed grain and the loss of three million sheep through sheep-rot. A Royal Commission, which sat in 1881-82, blamed the new ill-fortunes of English farming on the weather. But the reasons were more fundamental.

The main reason was foreign competition. The development of steamships led to a decrease in freight charges; this trend was accentuated as the sailing ship companies, faced with competition, began to build faster sailing ships. With the building of railways in North and South America, and in Australia, the economic shipment of grain to Europe became a possibility. The English farmer found that he could not produce grain as cheaply as his foreign competitors. He suffered a further blow when it became possible to send meat into England from countries far distant. This was made possible by developments in the canning of meat, so that Argentinian 'corned beef' could be bought by the Englishman. Then, in 1882, the sailing-vessel *Dunedin* left New Zealand with the first cargo of refrigerated meat. This technical development also made it possible to send butter and cheese from the antipodes. At the same time there was a fall in wool prices, which had been high in the late 1860's because of the 'cotton famine' caused by the American Civil War. This fall coincided with an increase in wool production in Australia, brought to England in the fast clippers.

By the 1880's landlords had to accustom themselves to lower rents, and tenant farmers to lower profits. Farmers had to change the pattern of their production. There was still a market for fresh meat (which was generally preferred to frozen meat), and for milk, butter and eggs. Some farmers concentrated on the growing of fruit, water-cress and vegetables for the towns. In general, there was a swing away from arable farming to pastoral farming.

When the Corn Laws were repealed in 1846, many farmers had prophesied ruin. As we have seen, it did not happen—but thirty years later their fears appeared to be justified. But there was little support for a return to protection. Very little was done by successive governments to aid the plight of farmers. The legal position of tenants was improved by the Agricultural Holdings Act, 1875; an Act of 1896 partially derated agricultural land; the Smallholdings Act of 1907 gave local authorities permission to loan capital to intending tenants. But none of these Acts was of more than minor importance. From about 1896 to 1914 English farming made a slow recovery from the 'great depression'. Farms tended to become smaller; pastoral farming increased; marginal land was left 'in the rough'. The real wages (i.e. actual wages relative to prices) of the farm labourer improved slightly as prices fell. But, by and large, English farming was a depressed industry at the time of the outbreak of war in 1914. By then only 20 per cent of the cereals used by the population, and 60 per cent of the meat, were produced in England.

CHAPTER 9

Land Transport, 1815–1914

Railways, as we use the term today, are a means of transporting goods and people by locomotive traction on a permanent track. The first railway, in the modern sense, was opened in England in 1825, between Stockton and Darlington. Before that date, engineers had been grappling with two main problems—rails, and locomotives.

For many centuries men had used beams of wood to enable horses to pull wagons more easily. Sometimes wooden rails were added in order to guide the wheels. In 1767 cast-iron or wrought-iron plates, placed on wooden beams, were in use at Coalbrookdale, to form 'plate-ways'. The iron plates had a flange, and guided the iron wheels of the wagons without wearing so rapidly as wooden ones. With the development of these iron rails, some horse-drawn rail-roads were opened in the early years of the nineteenth century, in order to act as feeders to ports. The Surrey Iron Railway, the first *public* railway, using horse traction on a four-foot track, opened in 1801 and ran from Wandsworth to Croydon. It was used at first for the carriage of corn. Another, opened in 1804, was used to carry passengers between Swansea and Mumbles. After much experiment with the shape of rails (for example James Watt made a hexagonal rail in 1802), the Bedlington Rail was patented in 1820. This rail was invented by John Birkinshaw, foreman at the Bedlington ironworks; it was made of wrought iron, and had no flange (the flange was to be put on the wheels of the locomotives and rolling stock).

Meanwhile attempts were being made to produce an effective locomotive. In 1801, a Cornishman, Richard Trevithick, tested a road locomotive at Camborne. Three years later he ran a locomotive on rails in South Wales for a wager. In 1808 he built a small circular track in London, near the site of the present Euston Station, and the public were thrilled to pay 6d. for a ride. Trevithick then turned his attentions to different engineering schemes, and others were able to utilise his ideas. Many contemporary engineers considered that it was impracticable to attempt to run an engine with smooth wheels on a smooth track; they therefore experimented with rack propulsion. In 1811 John Blenkinsop made such a railway. But others continued with smooth track and wheels. In 1813 William Hedley, the engineer at Wylam Colliery, built his famous 'Wylam Dilly' (or 'Puffing Billy'). George Stephenson (1788–1848), at the Killingworth Colliery, built his first locomotive, the 'Blucher', in 1814.

Stockton to Darlington, 1825

George Stephenson has been called the 'father of the railways'. He had no formal education, began work at the age of eight, and for the next six years was employed successively in watching cows, hoeing, picking stones out of coal, and in charge of a horse gin. At the age of fourteen he became an assistant fireman, then a fireman, then a brakesman. In 1812 he obtained the post of engine-wright at the Killingworth Colliery. In 1821 he was invited to superintend the building of a railway from Stockton to Darlington. This project, the 'brain-child' of Edward Pease, a Darlington Quaker, sprang from the need to transport coal from the mines near Darlington to the river Tees, a distance of twelve miles. George Stephenson surveyed the line of the new railway with the aid of his son Robert (1803–59). He used wrought-iron rails, without sleepers, as the promoters of the railway originally intended to use horse traction. George Stephenson persuaded Pease that steam locomotives could be used, and Robert began the construction of these at Newcastle. George Stephenson built the track on a gauge of 4 feet 8½ inches, because that was the average width of the tramroads in the district, and thus new coal wagons would not have to be built. The Stockton to Darlington line was opened in September 1825. Two engines, 'Locomotion No. 1' (driven by George Stephenson), and 'Experiment', were coupled together, and the two engines pulled 21 coal-wagons, temporarily fitted with seating to accommodate the shareholders, at an average speed of 8 m.p.h. A horserider, with a red warning flag, preceded the train, which was greeted by a crowd of 40,000 at

Stockton. The Stockton to Darlington railway is important because it was the first steam railway in the world. But as an effective means of transport it is not important. It was used only for the carriage of coal (passengers were conveyed in their own coaches drawn by horses). It was a private railway, and not a public transport.

The Development of the Railway Network

In 1826 an Act of Parliament was passed authorising the building of a railway from Liverpool to Manchester. Although these two cities were linked by a canal, there was need for a better means of transport. The canal company, with a monopoly in the carriage of goods, was charging high dues, and because of the volume of traffic, there were often long delays. George Stephenson was appointed as engineer of the new railway, and he had many technical engineering problems to solve. A tunnel $1\frac{1}{4}$ miles long, was constructed at the Liverpool end of the line (Edgehill); a cutting was made through rock at Olive Mount; a bridge was constructed to carry the line over the old Sankey Brook canal; at the Manchester end the line had to cross a bog, Chat Moss. Despite these difficulties, and the opposition of local landlords, the 30 miles of track were completed in four years. The owners of the railway were undecided as to the best means of traction; the locomotive was still distrusted, and horses and stationary engines both had their champions. In 1829 the Rainhill trials were held to decide the best locomotive; the trial, and the £500 prize, were won by Robert Stephenson's 'Rocket', with an average speed of 14 m.p.h. The line was opened in December 1830, when eight special trains completed the journey from Liverpool to Manchester and back. The 700 guests included the Prime Minister, the Duke of Wellington, but the occasion was spoiled by a fatal accident to one of the guests, William Huskisson, M.P. for Liverpool and a former President of the Board of Trade. During a halt at a station, Huskisson alighted from the train to greet the Prime Minister, and he was struck by another train.

The opponents of railways were quick to point the moral of the first railway accident. Many arguments were put forward against the building of railways. It was said that the smoke would kill the birds, sparks would set fire to the countryside and passengers, cows would be frightened and cease to yield milk, horses would bolt at the sight

of a steam-engine, and foxes and pheasants would leave the neighbourhood. Besides these imagined horrors, others held more rational
fears. The owners of stage-coaches, canals and road trusts were
alarmed that the new forms of transport would lead to their ruin.
These fears proved to be well-grounded.

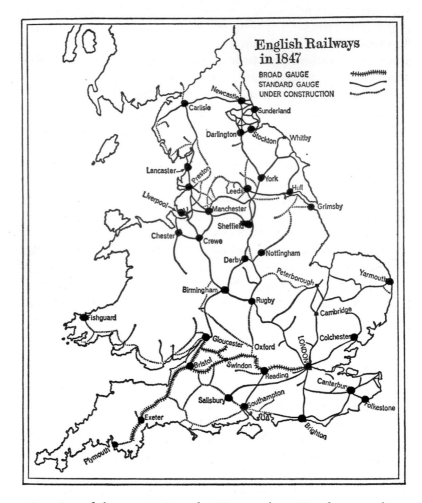

In spite of the opposition, the Liverpool to Manchester railway
proved a success as a transporter of goods and passengers, especially
the latter. But in the first half of the 1830's it was still not clear to
contemporaries that the new means of transport was to be railways.

Some inventors were still busy with steam locomotives to run on the roads. Between 1833 and 1836 Walter Hancock carried passengers between Paddington and City Road in steam omnibuses. In Southampton, William Summers made several steam carriages, one of which completed a journey from London to Birmingham. Whilst experiments were being made with these, the Stephensons were engaged in building a railway line from London to Birmingham. This was begun in 1833 and completed in 1838; its building involved a huge chalk cutting near Tring, and the Kilsby tunnel near Rugby. The years 1836–37 saw the first 'railway boom', and a number of railway Acts were passed. In 1842 there were 1,857 miles of steam railways in operation; London was linked with Bristol, Southampton, Dover, Birmingham and York. A much larger boom occurred from 1844 to 1847 (the 'railway mania'). Many companies began work on new lines, and though work was interrupted by a financial crisis in 1847, most were eventually completed in the 1850's, by which time most of the large towns were linked by rail with one another and with London. In 1848 there were 5,100 miles of track in operation; in 1850, 6,600; in 1854, 8,900.

Robert Stephenson was responsible for the building of the line from Darlington to Newcastle, and the famous high-level bridge over the Tyne. He also built the London to Holyhead line, with the Britannia Bridge over the Menai Straits. Joseph Locke, who used cuttings and embankments instead of tunnels wherever possible, completed the London to Southampton line.

I. K. Brunel

Most of the railways in south-west England were the work of Isambard Kingdom Brunel (1806–59). In 1833 he was appointed as engineer to build a line from London to Bristol by a company which became the Great Western Railway. Brunel adopted a 7-foot gauge to obtain greater speed and smoothness with larger and heavier locomotives and rolling stock. This gauge was used on all Great Western lines, which were therefore different from those of all other companies, who had adopted Stephenson's gauge. The London–Bristol line was opened in 1841, after many difficulties. The Box tunnel, two miles long, took two and a half years to bore, and one hundred workmen were killed during its construction. Brunel later built railways in Devon and Cornwall. The famous Royal Albert Bridge across the River Tamar, opened in 1859 a few months after his death, still bears witness to Brunel's genius. The Clifton Suspension Bridge, completed in 1864, was designed and partly built by Brunel.

Brunel was in many ways unfortunate. Whereas George Stephenson died a very wealthy man, famous as the first President of the Institution of Mechanical Engineers, Brunel died at a time when his failures obscured his true greatness. Three of his schemes had caused the Great Western Railway to lose a considerable amount of money. He designed an atmospheric railway, which could travel at 70 m.p.h. These trains, without engines, were worked by air pipes along the track. Unfortunately rats destroyed the leather flaps, and the scheme had to be abandoned after a few months in operation. His ship, the *Great Eastern*, a technical success, was a commercial failure.[1] His plans for Milford Haven, where he built a harbour, did not materialise. Brunel was an original thinker (unlike George Stephenson), and as such he was bound to have some failures.

The railway network was virtually completed by 1900, when there were 18,680 miles of track in England and Wales. (In 1913 the figure was 20,081.) It had developed in a haphazard way, leaving problems which remain unsolved even now.

The Government and the Railways

English railways developed without aid from the state, but suffered government interference. It could be said that they had the worst of two systems; they lacked complete freedom, and yet had no central plan. Every railway company had to obtain an Act of Parliament, and the legal costs of this were great. The Railway Act of 1844 (usually known as Gladstone's Act), authorised the purchase by the state of all lines opened from that time after twenty-one years of private operation. This power was never used, for it was not until 1948 that the railways were brought under public ownership. This same Act compelled every company to run at least one train every day in each direction, stopping at every station, at a fare not exceeding one penny a mile. These were called 'parliamentary trains', and were the object of some derision.

In the 1840's there was a movement towards amalgamation—a

[1] See p. 121.

15 George Stephenson's own drawing of a locomotive for Killingworth Colliery, 1814. Note the flanges on the wheels, and the 'steam springs' attached vertically to the boiler. The springs were operated by a piston attached to the axle and acted as a cushion. (p. 104)

16 The opening of the Stockton to Darlington railway, 1825. (p. 104)

17 Making a cutting on the Great Western Railway (broad gauge) in 1841. Railway construction required an enormous amount of sheer labour. (p. 107)

18 A broad gauge G.W.R. train in 1880, with the narrow gauge line inside. The last broad gauge train ran in 1892. (p. 109)

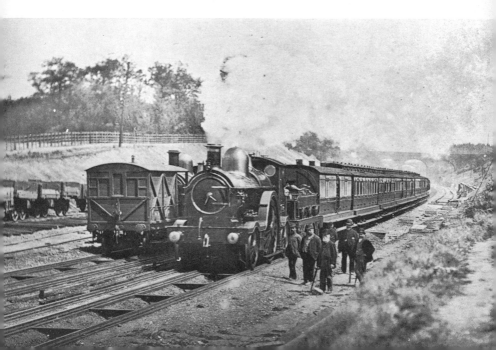

19 Bristol, 1895. Two additional horses are being harnessed to the normal pair in order to haul the bus up a steep hill. (p. 112)

20 Bristol, 1936. A tram driver seen from the top deck—such drivers needed gloves! (pp. 112, 246)

21 Clifton Bicycle Club in 'mod gear', 1886, going to Sports at Clifton Zoo. (p. 113)

22 'A tricycle made for two', c. 1900. Note the solid wheels, the absence of mudguards, and the picnic basket. (p. 113)

sensible evolution as many companies controlled only short stretches of line. George Hudson, 'the Railway King', a linen-draper in York, was active in promoting amalgamations centred on York, which eventually led to the formation of the North Eastern Railway. Hudson paid dividends out of capital, and he was disgraced in 1849. Every amalgamation caused some anxiety in Parliament, where some M.P.s feared the establishment of monopolies. Many committees of inquiry were appointed, and it was not until the turn of the century that public opinion changed to the view that amalgamations were in the best interests of both railways and the public.

The government Acts did something to aid through traffic. An Act of 1846 laid down that all lines built after that date were to use Stephenson's gauge, and the already existing broad gauge lines were eventually converted by 1892. Cardwell's Act of 1854 stated the principle that companies were to provide for through traffic from the lines of other companies.

In general, successive governments laid restrictions on the railway companies. Safety regulations were imposed, and in 1893 a scale of maximum fares was laid down. These measures added to the difficulties the railway companies were experiencing by 1914.

Some Problems

Because Britain's railways were pioneering, they inevitably suffered certain disadvantages. Firstly, because of the haphazard character of construction, often arising out of local demand, the main lines were not always laid down along the best routes. Even today, it is difficult to travel by a direct route from city to city—often it is necessary to go to London and change lines. Before a standard gauge was adopted, over 2,000 miles of track had been laid. Secondly, the early companies had to overcome great opposition. Because the people of Northampton refused to allow the railway into their town, the Kilsby tunnel had to be constructed. Some landowners refused to have a railway cut through their property, so that expensive detours had to be made. Thirdly, the cost of building was prodigious. The average cost per mile of building railways in England was £64,453 (as compared with £13,000 in the U.S.A.). An Act had to be obtained, land bought, canal and turnpike-trust companies taken over or compensated. This saddled the railways with an enormous initial debt.

Finally, as English railways were the first, there was a lack of experience in their engineers. We have noticed some of Brunel's expensive failures above. But it was difficult for the first railway engineers to envisage the need for gradual curves which would take larger engines, or for stronger bridges to carry heavier rolling stock.

The Economic and Social Results of Railways

The development of railways was a major factor of the economy of Victorian England. First, large numbers of men were employed in building them. As many as 20,000 men at one time were working on Stephenson's London to Birmingham line. The construction of one tunnel in the midlands needed 23 million bricks and 8,000 tons of cement. If one considers the men engaged in providing the materials, added to those actively engaged in construction, the numbers must have been great. In the period 1847–48 one million men were employed directly or indirectly in railway construction. When the railways were built, men were needed to man them. Later, when railways were being built overseas, many British engineers and workmen helped to build them; Brassey built railways in five continents, whilst Brunton planned railways in India. Secondly, they provided a cheap means of transport for goods and passengers. For the poor people, they afforded the first opportunity for travel. Thomas Cook began to organise excursion trains at special cheap fares, and thousands visited London for the first time to see the Great Exhibition of 1851.[1] In 1872 the Midland Railway decided to put third-class carriages on all trains, charging the 'parliamentary' fare of one penny a mile. Other companies followed suit.

Railways stimulated industry, agriculture and fisheries. They afforded a cheap and quick means of transporting raw materials and finished products. Also, railways needed coal and iron, and some firms such as Guest of Dowlais in South Wales specialised in railway iron. To a certain extent the demands of railways for iron led to the improvements in steel-making in the third quarter of the nineteenth century.[2] Farmers were able to send their milk to town, and fish landed in the east coast ports, from Grimsby to Aberdeen, could be sent to London.

Railways had some effect on the development of towns. With the

[1] See p. 137.   [2] See pp. 146–7.

coming of local railways, people could leave the centre of towns and live in suburban areas, travelling to work daily. Previously the place of work had to be within walking distance of the home. Railways also affected individual towns. Some declined in importance, if only temporarily, because they refused to have the line within their boundaries, or because the main lines did not pass through them. Northampton and Abingdon are examples of this. New towns developed

Casting the nave of a railway carriage wheel. The development of railways stimulated the iron and engineering industries.

as 'railway towns' where there were important junctions, marshalling yards, or locomotive and rolling-stock repair shops. Crewe, Darlington, Rugby, Swindon and Eastleigh all developed rapidly because of this. As the railways made holidays possible, or at least daily excurcursions, new seaside resorts, such as Bournemouth, Southend, Blackpool and Scarborough developed. Southampton became a major port as a result of the railway link with London, opened in 1840.

Three other effects are worth mentioning. Railways aided the efficiency and growth of the postal services, by providing a quick means of sending the mail. A new system of postage came into operation in 1840 which was largely the work of Rowland Hill. He made three reforms—a uniform rate of charges, a reduction in charges, and prepayment of postage. In 1839 a letter cost 4d. for 15 miles, and 9d. for up to 120 miles. Rowland Hill instituted penny postage, payable by means of adhesive stamps. Although the Post Office lost money for a few years, the volume of letters sent grew apace, from 76 million in 1839 to 169 million in 1840, and 322 million in 1847. Business men could now afford to send circulars; workmen could write for jobs. These letters were carried by the railways. Railways also aided the growth of boarding schools, many of which were founded after 1840. Finally, because the railways were so effective, the development of road transport was retarded.

OTHER DEVELOPMENTS IN TRANSPORT

Tramways and Underground Railways

The railways were most effective for long distance journeys. As towns and cities grew, there was a need for other forms of transport from one part of the town to another. Hansom and other horse cabs were expensive, and beyond the purse of ordinary people. The trams, a 'lower class ride', provided the solution. Steel rails were laid in the roads, and single-deck carriages were drawn, first by horses, then by steam traction, and finally by electric motors. From about 1860 to 1890 horse trams ran in a few urban areas, but the 1890's saw a rapid extension of them. In 1891 Leeds began to run electric trams, with overhead wires. Other towns quickly followed suit so that by 1911 there were 2,530 miles of electric tramways in Britain. The 1920's were the 'golden age' of tramcars, when an average of five million passengers were carried each year. From their inception, opponents advanced three arguments against this form of transport: the overhead wires were ugly, the trams obstructed other road traffic (passengers boarded and alighted from trams in the middle of the road!), and too much noise was made by the wheels and the clanging alarm bell. But they served a useful purpose for nearly fifty years.

Motor buses developed in the first decade of the twentieth century. The word 'omnibus' means (in Latin) 'for everyone'; like the trams, they were an important form of transport for the poor. The first motor buses in London began in 1903. Ten years later there were over 3,500 motor buses in London compared with 142 horse buses.

But generally in the provincial towns the tramcar was not replaced by buses until the 1930's.

Because of congested streets, underground railways were built in London and Glasgow. The first was the Metropolitan line, which passed through central London, and linked Liverpool Street, Euston and Paddington stations by a covered cutting just below street level. Deeper railways did not develop until electrification became possible; the first 'tube' line (the City and South London) was opened in London in 1890, passing under the river Thames. In 1898 Waterloo station, on the south bank, was linked by underground with the City and the termini north of the river. The Central London line was opened in 1900.

Bicycles and Motor Road Vehicles

The railways had caused the decline of canal and road traffic. By 1914, although the railways were still the most important means of transport, the roads were beginning to revive.

The bicycle evolved from the hobby or dandy horse, which was propelled by the rider touching the ground with his feet. In 1839 Macmillan made a cycle with pedals which turned the back wheels by rods. The 'modern' bicycle dates from the invention of the steel chain by Lawson in 1879. This type of cycle rapidly replaced the 'Penny Farthing', so called because of the appearance of its large front wheel and small rear wheel. Its pedals were connected directly to the front wheel. The development of the chain-driven cycle coincided with the invention of pneumatic tyres by John Dunlop in 1888. These machines had smaller wheels (though larger than those of today), so that they could be mounted easily, and the danger of injury from falling was minimised. The chain drive meant that the feet were immediately beneath the saddle, and as the driving mechanism was no longer attached to the front wheel, they could be steered easily. Cycling became a popular pastime for both men and women. The Cyclists Touring Club, founded in 1878 with a membership of 142, had over 60,000 members in 1899. Elderly people were able to ride tricycles, with two rear wheels (the riders did not have to learn to 'balance', but they had to be very careful at corners). The tricycle was also used to carry light goods, such as meat, groceries, milk and newspapers.

The problem of power-driven road vehicles was solved towards the end of the nineteenth century. Steam traction on roads had been used for heavy vehicles such as rollers, but such engines were heavy, slow, and expensive to run. The motor car, driven by an internal combustion engine, fuelled by petrol, was first developed in Germany by Benz and Daimler in the 1880's. English engineers were quick to experiment with similar motors, among them Edward Butler, who built a motor cycle in 1884, and Herbert Austin, who designed a three-wheeled vehicle at the works of the Wolseley Sheep Shearing Machine Company in Birmingham. The most important English motor engineer was F. W. Lanchester (1868–1946). Lanchester was educated at a Brighton preparatory school, at the Hartley College, Southampton, and at London University. After experimenting with gas engines, he turned his attention to the motor car. Benz, Daimler and Austin had, in effect, put engines into carriages (i.e. horseless carriages), which ran at low speeds of about 8 m.p.h. Lanchester began in 1894 to build a motor car to his own design. It was completed in 1896 and had new features, including a steel frame, an epicyclic gearbox with high, low and reverse gears, electrical ignition and tiller steering. The engine, of 5 h.p., proved to be too low powered. He remodelled his motor car, fitted an 8 h.p. twin-cylinder engine, accelerator pedals, and improved the chassis by using cantilever springs. This car was first tested in 1897, and reached a speed of 20 m.p.h. By 1914 the motor car was no longer a novelty in England.

The development of the motor car was hampered at first by the Locomotives Act of 1865, which stated that mechanically propelled vehicles could only run on the roads if they were preceded by a man carrying a red warning flag, and did not exceed 4 m.p.h. The red flag was dispensed with in 1878, and in 1896 the speed limit was raised to 14 m.p.h. Pioneer motorists celebrated the latter event in November 1896, by driving from London to Brighton.

The Roads

The coming of the motor car also meant that the roads, long neglected since the decline of the turnpike trusts, had to be put in order. The Highways Act of 1835 had abolished the compulsory unpaid labour of parishioners on the roads, so that the burden of repair fell upon the turnpike trusts, where they existed, or on the rate-payers of the parish. Opinion gradually moved towards the conception that main roads should be controlled by the government, and that toll charges should be abolished. Tolls ended in London in 1871, and the last main road toll (in the Isle of Anglesey) was abolished in 1895. From 1882 some state aid was given towards road repairs, but although some improvements were made, so that main roads were generally smooth and free from ruts, they were not good enough for an increasing volume of road traffic. In 1909 motor taxation was begun, and a Road Board was established to use the money obtained (the Road Fund) for the building of new roads and for the improvement of existing ones.

These improvements in land transport increased the mobility of people and goods; for the people of the nineteenth century, the size of Britain 'shrank', just as the world has grown smaller in our time.

CHAPTER 10

Sea Transport, 1815–1914

During the eighteenth century there had been no far-reaching changes in the design and building of ships. In the nineteenth century there were changes which, although they took place gradually, might fairly be called 'revolutionary'. The main developments were the use of iron, and later of steel, in the construction of both sailing and steamships; the use of steam power for propulsion; the replacement of the paddle by the screw; and, later in the century, the economical steam turbine engine, and the use of oil instead of coal as fuel. These developments led to a shift in the main locations of the shipbuilding industry. Change came gradually; each new idea had to be thoroughly tried and tested before shipowners committed themselves. A ship is an expensive piece of capital equipment, and men's lives depend upon her soundness. The building of new types of ships also demanded new skills from both craftsmen and seamen.

The Development of Sailing Ships

Britain was not the paramount shipbuilding (or shipowning) power in 1815. She had 'sea power' in the naval sense, but not in the mercantile. British shipbuilders were conservative, and resistant to new ideas. Changes in the sailing ship in the first half of the nineteenth century came about through the initiative of the new American nation. The North Americans had timber in abundance, good sites on the Atlantic seaboard, and builders and sailing masters skilled in mathematics and hydrostatics. They began to build sailing ships, designed for speed, which sailed faster than those of other countries. Further, the sailing masters, by a ruthless application to their duty

23 *East India Docks, London, in 1808, two years after their opening.* (p. 74)

24 *J. S. White's yard, Cowes, in 1853. The owner lived in the house, bottom left. The paddle-steamer is the P. and O. Vectis, which carried Florence Nightingale to the Crimea.*

25 Bell's Comet, built 1812. She was 40 feet 3 inches long, and her engine was 4 h.p.—hence the need for the sail! (p. 119)

26 Great Eastern, launched 1858, designed by I. K. Brunel. She was 680 feet long, and her engines developed 7,675 h.p. (p. 121)

and with an often inhuman attitude to their crew, tried to complete voyages in as short a time as possible. *Two Years Before the Mast*, written by the American R. H. Dana, published in 1840, gives a first-hand account of such a voyage. It was high time that the sailing ship was made to hurry. The Pilgrim Fathers had crossed the Atlantic in 66 days in 1620; in the 1790's three sailing vessels took 46, 63 and 68 days respectively for the westbound voyage. (It should be noted that, because of the trade winds, sailing ships could complete the eastbound voyage across the Atlantic in a shorter time.) In the first thirty years of the nineteenth century, the Americans evolved a faster sailing ship, with a length in proportion to beam of 5:1, compared with the 3:1 or 4:1 of European shipbuilders. These vessels, the forerunners of the clippers, cut many days off ocean voyages. In 1825 American ships of the Black Ball Line were able to travel from Liverpool to New York in 40 days, and to complete the eastward trip in 23 days. English yards began to emulate the Americans in the following decade. In 1837 the *Seringapatam*, the first 'Blackwall frigate', i.e. a fast cargo and passenger sailing ship, was launched at Green's yard at Blackwall on the Thames. In the 1840's the Americans began to build clippers, the first of which, *Rainbow*, was launched in New York in 1845. In the following twenty years clippers were breaking records for ocean voyages. In the 1850's, *Lightning*, built in Boston, Massachussetts, for British owners, sailed from Boston to Liverpool in 14 days, and from Melbourne to Liverpool in 77 days. One of the first English-built clipper ships was *Challenger*, launched in 1850 by Green of Blackwall. In the following decade several famous clippers were in the hey-day of their career. They were particularly useful on the Australian run, where they could use the prevailing westerly winds in the southern hemisphere, by sailing outward via the Cape of Good Hope, and returning past Cape Horn. They were also used extensively for the China run. In 1866 *Ariel* and *Taeping*, both tea clippers, left China on the same day, raced each other up the English Channel at 14 knots, and docked in the Thames almost together after a voyage of 99 days. By this time the Americans, who had hitherto had the lion's share of sailing ship passenger traffic, were falling behind their English rivals owing to the American Civil War (1861–65). The only English clipper which has survived from the great era of sail is the comparatively small *Cutty Sark* (built by

Denny of Dumbarton in 1869), now berthed in a dry dock near the National Maritime Museum at Greenwich.

The Introduction of Iron

Meanwhile iron was being used in the construction of sailing ships. The supply of timber was an increasing problem for English builders. Also, the wooden ships had certain defects. The maximum possible length for a wooden ship was about 300 feet, as too many scarf joints in a wooden keel weakened the structure. The underwater planking was susceptible to worm and to rot, and needed frequent renewal. Iron was the answer, and iron England had in plenty. But its use in the construction of sailing ships in England came comparatively slowly. We have already seen how John Wilkinson built an iron barge in 1787, and how iron was used for fittings in the early years of the nineteenth century.[1] Two main factors held back the development of the iron sailing ship: the effects of the magnetic field on compasses (Sir William Thomson, later Lord Kelvin, invented the dry card compass to solve this problem), and the conservatism of owners who believed that certain cargoes, such as tea, would be tainted by iron. The *Ironside*, launched in Liverpool in 1830, was probably the first British iron sailing ship. But iron ships did not immediately become common. The next general development was the composite ship, with iron frames and wooden planking (*Cutty Sark* is a composite ship). The first composite built in England was *Tubal Cain*, launched in 1851. The real revolution came about when three new British steel-making processes were perfected in the period 1859 to 1880.[2] The first British steel sailing ship was *Formby*, launched in Liverpool in 1863. In 1880 there was a boom, short-lived, in the demand for steel sailing clippers owing to the need to transport wool from Australia, grain from San Francisco, and rice and jute from India. As late as 1875 a new shipyard was opened at Woolston, Southampton, by T. R. Oswald, especially for the construction of sailing ships, and many were built there in the boom days of the 1880's. But the end of the large sailing ship was in sight—the last steel clipper was launched in England in 1907. The sailing ship was giving way to the steamship. There are those who still look back

[1] See p. 33.   [2] See pp. 146–9.

nostalgically at the days of sail. But sail was not a perfect means of transport. Sailing times could not be forecast with accuracy—tide, wind, or the whim of the master were all variable factors. The noise of wind in shrouds, the creaking of the masts, the buffeting in tacking, the rolling in a following sea—all made the sailing ship uncomfortable for passengers. The new power source, steam, had to be harnessed to the ship.

Steam Power

The development of steam power came slowly. The first steam vessel was launched in 1798; by 1850 the steamship had captured most of the short distance traffic; by 1890 it was clearly the master of the oceans. This slow development was caused by technical problems. But if the Americans had taught the Old World how to build sailing ships, they were not the pioneers of steam.

The steamship was a natural development from Watt's steam-pumps. The first steamship in the world was built in 1798 by William Symington, and it had a trial run on the Forth–Clyde canal at 5½ knots. Four years later Symington built an improved model, *Charlotte Dundas*, a wooden vessel propelled by a single stern-paddle. Viewers were not impressed, as the wash from the little steamer was thought to be too great a strain on the canal bank. In 1803 Symington demonstrated the ship to a visiting American, Robert Fulton. Fulton made copious notes and drawings, returned to the U.S.A., and in 1807 launched the *Clermont*, a twin paddle steamboat. This vessel, powered by an engine made in Birmingham, England, steamed up the Hudson River for 150 miles in 32 hours. She then began a successful career as the world's first commercial steamship. In 1812 Henry Bell of Glasgow launched the *Comet*, which began a regular service between Glasgow, Greenock and Helensburgh. Bell's *Comet* was 40 feet long, and had a beam of 10 feet 6 inches, and a burthen of 28 tons. It was quickly realised that small steamships could be of great value in estuaries and sheltered rivers, for they could sail at a regular time, without regard to tide and wind. Although the 4 or 5 knots at which they went seems slow to us, it did not seem so to the people of the time. The alternative was a long wait, or a strong pull at the oars. In 1815 steamboats were active in the Thames, where they did the voyage from London to Margate in 12 hours. In the same year a steamship entered the Southampton Water from Plymouth, having completed the trip in 23 hours. In 1820 there were 17 steamships registered with Lloyd's, and by that date some were venturing outside estuarial waters. Regular journeys were made from Belfast to the Clyde, and from Southampton to the Isle of Wight. These early steamships, however, had two major defects: their coal consumption was 10 lb. per h.p. per hour, and their boilers could not contain a pressure above 5 lb. per square inch. So they were not economical to run, and they were slow. They all had masts and sails, so that the engine could be used as an auxiliary if there was a favourable wind.

In 1830 there were 203 steamships registered in Britain, and by that date steam packets were sailing regularly to the Channel Islands and France. In England, for the short journey, the steamship was able to provide a most useful service to passengers who needed to know when they would depart, and when they would arrive. These early steamers were wooden, but in 1823 Aaron Manby built an iron steamship in sections in the Black Country, and assembled it on the Thames. This ship, named after her builder, sailed on her maiden voyage to France, where she remained.

Transatlantic Steamers

The conquest of the Atlantic by steamships came in the 1830's. Although an American ship named *Savannah* had crossed the Atlantic in 1819, this voyage cannot count as a 'steam' trip. *Savannah* had sails and retractable paddles; her engines were used for only 80 hours out of a 30 day run. The Americans were using steamships for journeys up their long rivers where there was plenty of wood for fuel, but were concentrating on sail for ocean voyages. The first steam crossings were made by British ships, and the impetus came from I. K. Brunel, the famous engineer of the Great Western Railway. He persuaded his company to consider the building of a steamship to extend the passenger service from Bristol to New York. He designed the *Great Western*, a composite vessel of iron and oak, 236 feet long, with a beam of 35 feet. On her maiden voyage in 1838 she sailed from Bristol to New York in 15 days. But another English steamship had arrived in New York a few hours before. A London company had also been building a steamship for the Atlantic crossing, but unfortunately the vessel was not completed in time owing to the financial difficulties of the builders. In order to beat the *Great Western* they chartered the *Sirius*, a small ship built for the London to Cork service. *Sirius* left Cork two days before the *Great Western* sailed from Bristol, and completed the ocean voyage in 17 days. Later in the same year, 1838, the *Royal William* did the crossing in 19 days, and the *Liverpool* in 16½ days.

From 1840 steamships began regular long-distance trips. In that year the first Cunard steamship, *Britannia*, made her maiden voyage from Liverpool to Halifax and Boston, with a contract for mail. Also in 1840 the Peninsular and Orient Line was founded, to carry mail, passengers and goods to India; and the Royal Mail Steam Packet Company began regular service to the West Indies. All three companies had obtained government contracts for carrying mail, and these contracts helped to pay the high costs of running steamships at that time. For in those days, largely because of its fuel consumption, and the 'cargo' space which fuel occupied, the steamship cost much more to run than the sailing ship; also, the capital investment in building a steamer was about three times as much as that for a sailing ship.

The Great Eastern

The classic example of a steamship which was a commercial failure, despite her technical soundness, was the *Great Eastern*, designed by I. K. Brunel. Brunel had already designed an iron steam vessel using propeller screw instead of paddle. This ship, the *Great Britain*, was launched in 1843 by Paterson's of Bristol. Although the Admiralty had held a series of trials in 1845 between *Alecto* (paddle) and *Rattler* (screw), two ships of equal tonnage and power, in which the latter had proved superior, the adoption of the screw came slowly. Shipowners were worried lest the propeller shaft should break, thus leaving the ship helpless. Brunel decided to build a vessel using both paddles and propellers, and to build the largest vessel the world had seen. The size was not a whim, for in order to get the power to drive the engines, a great deal of bunkering space was needed. The *Great Eastern*, launched in 1858, was built at Millwall on the Thames. She was an iron vessel of 19,000 tons, 700 feet long, with an 83 feet beam. She had two paddles as well as screws, and was capable of 14 knots;

she accommodated 4,000 passengers on five decks. She had one major defect—a great coal consumption. From the sailor's point of view, she had another—she was an 'unlucky ship'. By tradition, ships which 'stick' at their launching are ill-fated. Because of her huge size, *Great Eastern* had to be launched sideways (ships are usually launched stern first because the stern has the greatest buoyancy, and it acts as a brake). On the day of launching, 3rd November 1857, before three thousand people, the giant ship moved only four feet, yet one man was killed and four were injured. It was not until 31st January 1858, after weeks of gradual movement by hydraulic presses, that the ship was finally launched; but by then the owners were bankrupt. The ship made four voyages across the Atlantic, but there was insufficient demand for so large and expensive a vessel. She was later used to lay the transatlantic cables, and after service all over the world in like tasks, she was moored in the river Mersey in 1876 as a 'floating shop' for a Liverpool grocery firm; she was broken up in 1888.

Developments in Marine Engines

At the time of the launching of the *Great Eastern*, engineers were groping towards the solution of the fuel problem. In 1856 John Elder fitted a compound engine in two Pacific Steam Navigation Company ships. Put simply, in a compound engine the steam was passed first into a small cylinder, and then into a larger cylinder. The same steam was thus used to 'push' two pistons and additional power was obtained without any more coal being used. In 1881 the compound engine was made even more effective when a 'triple expansion' engine was built. This development meant that steam could now vie with sail economically, and was particularly important as the Suez Canal, opened in 1869, afforded a short cut to the east suitable for steam but not for sail.

The compound engine reduced fuel consumption. The invention of the steam turbine by Sir Charles Parsons (1854–1931) made high speeds possible. Parsons, the son of the Earl of Rosse, was educated at the University of Dublin, and then served an apprenticeship with Armstrong's at Elnwick. He moved on to the Tyne, where he became interested in the possibilities of steam turbines, i.e. engines in which high-pressure steam is directed through a nozzle onto the blades of a wheel attached to the propeller shaft. He used this system in 1884 for steam dynamos, which rotated at 18,000 r.p.m. In 1894 he built the *Turbinia*, a small 100-foot vessel, with three propellers attached to a single shaft driven by a steam turbine. In a trial run the *Turbinia* achieved nearly 20 knots. Parsons made modifications, and in 1897 his ship did 31 knots. Later in that year the *Turbinia* disturbed the review of the Fleet at Spithead, drawn up in honour of Queen Victoria's Diamond Jubilee, by travelling along the line of the Fleet at 34½ knots. The fastest naval vessels afloat, sent to catch *Turbinia*, were unable to do so. This flamboyant action was Parsons' method of showing the Admiralty the superiority of the turbine for achieving high speeds.

By 1914, two other technical inventions were beginning to make some impact on British merchant shipping. In 1912 the first diesel ship was brought into service; by that date, some ships were beginning to use oil as fuel for steam turbines. Oil fuel had advantages for the shipowner. Coal was an unwieldy commodity, and 'coaling ship' was an unpopular and lengthy operation. Oil fuel took less space, and could be put aboard by a small labour force. But, for a country rich in coal, the use of any other fuel had some dangers. It was not until after the 1914–18 war that oil made a serious challenge to coal as the fuel for powered ships.

ECONOMIC EFFECTS OF THE STEAMSHIP

These developments in ships had profound effects on the economy of the country. First, Britain became the most important shipbuilding country in the world, and shipbuilding became a major industry. The centres of the industry moved from the Thames and the south coast to the north-east coast, Glasgow, Belfast, and the north-west coast. At the same time the industry became concentrated in towns situated on wide estuaries. In the days of 'wooden' shipbuilding, the industry could be carried out in small rural sites; the coming of the steel steamship entailed large yards, with thousands of specialist craftsmen. Some shipbuilding firms started as ironworks. The classic example is that of John Brown's Atlas Ironworks, Sheffield, which at first made components for Clyde shipbuilders, and eventually began to build ships on the Clyde in 1899. Cammel, of Sheffield, who controlled hematite mines in Cumberland, joined with the shipbuilders Laird of Birkenhead in 1903. Vickers and Sons were manufacturing guns in Sheffield in the late eighteenth century, whilst in Southampton the Northam Ironworks began shipbuilding in about 1840.

The development of the steamship led to the growth of ports which were unsuitable for sail. Steam tugs were used to tow sailing vessels up long estuaries; steam dredgers deepened the fairway of such stretches of water as the rivers Test and Itchen at Southampton. There the first dock was opened in 1842, others in 1851 and 1890. Plymouth Harbour developed at the same time as Cherbourg (in the period 1811–48). Liverpool, Glasgow, Belfast and Hull all grew in importance as sea-ports. Vast extensions were made to London's dockland area; Victoria Docks were opened in 1854, Millwall in 1864, and the Albert Dock in 1875. Tilbury, opened in 1886, proved a commercial failure until after the 1914–18 war.

The coal industry was stimulated by the development of the steamship, and especially in those areas where 'steam' coal was abundant, i.e. in South Wales, Tyneside and Wigan. The demand for Welsh steam coal was one reason for the foundation of the docks at Cardiff (1835), Newport (1836) and Swansea (1859). Port Talbot, where a new dock was opened in 1897, grew in importance as the shipbuilding industry needed more steel, as did other iron and steel towns (it should be noted that steel steamships also had steel engines). Coal was taken from British ports to stations such as Gibraltar, Suez, Aden and Singapore.

If industry was stimulated by the growth of shipbuilding, agriculture suffered. The steamship led to a fall in freight charges, so that imported food was able to come into the country speedily and cheaply. The new ships became specialist ships—not 'tramps' seeking mixed cargoes. Steamships were built for particular purposes. Passenger ships were fast and comfortable. Cargo ships had steel decks with derricks and winches. Other specialised ships were built to transport oil, timber or dairy produce.

This dominant era of British ships and shipping can be illustrated by statistics. In the 1840's, half the tonnage of wooden sailing ships was built in North America: in the years 1892–94, Great Britain built 81·6 per cent of the world's merchant tonnage launched. In 1900, the British merchant fleet, totalling 9·3 million tons, was twice the size of those of the the U.S.A. and Germany combined. In 1912, a 'record' year for British shipbuilding, 1·9 million tons of merchant shipping was launched; in the same year Germany, Britain's rival, launched 0·37 million tons. British yards were, in the words of a contemporary journal, 'full of work'. Fortunately, the writer could not see into the future, and the slump of the 1920's.

CHAPTER 11

Overseas Trade, 1815-1914

THE PATTERNS OF TRADE

Although the greater part of British products were made for and used by the home market, overseas trade became an essential part of the country's economy, and grew as the century progressed, especially after 1840. For this reason, if for no other, a larger mercantile marine was essential; Britain had to export in order to live, and in so doing earned the title of 'the workshop of the world'.

Exports and Customers

In the 1820's Britain's most important exports were manufactured textiles, which comprised about 75 per cent of the total. Cotton alone accounted for 50 per cent, and woollen goods a further 15 per cent. Other important exports included bar iron, china clay, coal and non-ferrous metals. After 1850 the export of coal, machinery and iron and steel goods rose spectacularly. The export of glassware, cutlery and pottery increased steadily. In the 1880's textiles made up 50 per cent of Britain's total exports, with cotton alone accounting for $33\frac{1}{3}$ per cent. By 1913 cotton goods were not occupying so important a position; machinery, railway rolling stock, ships, motor vehicles, electrical engineering equipment and chemicals were rapidly growing export commodities. Throughout the period there was a trend towards the manufacture of quality goods, especially as other countries began to manufacture for themselves. Britain's markets were world-wide, but trade with Europe and the Empire was the most important. In 1913 about 30 per cent of Britain's exports went to Europe; India, Britain's largest single customer, took about 12 per cent; the U.S.A. took 9·4 per cent, or about the same as Germany, and Australia 6 per cent. From about 1860 valuable markets were

The Holyrood Glass Works in Edinburgh. Above, the glass is being blown.
Below, steam-driven wheels are being used for grinding and polishing.

cultivated in Africa and in Asia—coincidental with the development of British power on those continents. In the Far East, Hong Kong and Singapore became useful trading centres, whilst in Africa Britain obtained Sierra Leone, Nigeria, the Gambia, and the Gold Coast (Ghana) by the so-called 'partition of Africa' (1884). The rebirth of 'Imperialism', with Disraeli as its spokesman, Joseph Chamberlain as its advocate, Seeley as its historian, and Kipling as its muse, was not unconnected with the fear of the loss of markets.

Imports

These exports enabled Britain to pay for the imports of raw materials and food she needed. Raw cotton remained a most vital material import; after 1815 most of Britain's cotton came from the U.S.A. By 1860 British cotton mills were taking about 75 per cent of their raw material from the U.S.A., with the result that the American Civil War (1861–65) led to the 'Lancashire Cotton Famine'. Wool imports rose, though the source changed. Until about 1830 most came from Spain and Silesia, but later Australia, and to a small extent New Zealand and South Africa, became the source of supply. Sugar from the West Indies was an important item until 1833, when the ending of slavery in the British Empire increased the labour costs, with the result that German and Austrian sugar beet was used by British refiners instead. Timber was imported throughout the period; from 1815–40 much of it came from Canada and the Far East, but then a reduction in import duties enabled Baltic suppliers to capture a larger share of the English market. Flax, hemp, tea, coffee and tobacco were other important imports, but the volume of rum and dyes decreased. The amount of imported foodstuffs grew. By about 1850 approximately 25 per cent of the corn consumed in Britain was imported, mainly from France, Germany and Russia. In 1880 this proportion had risen to $66\frac{2}{3}$ per cent, and in 1914 to 75 per cent. The source was no longer Europe, but North and South America, and Australia. From the 1880's chilled meat came into the country in increasing quantity, especially from Argentina, Australia and New Zealand. Cold storage and transport also enabled Denmark, Holland and Australia to send to Britain their bacon, eggs, butter and cheese. Britain imported commodities such as lead, tin and copper (which she had exported in earlier centuries) from Spain and Scandinavia. New commodities included jute from India (for making food and sand bags), rubber from Malaya, and oil from the U.S.A.

Invisible Exports

From 1815 Britain began to lend money to developing countries, and this 'exporting' of capital increased in the second half of the nineteenth century, when North and South America, Australia and South Africa needed money to build railways, etc. The effect of this investment overseas was that the interest became what the economists call an 'invisible export'. In other words, Britain could have a seemingly unfavourable balance of trade, importing more than she exported in goods value, and yet balancing her economy. And by 1913, because British ships were carrying goods for other countries, and therefore earning an income from freight-charges, Britain had another invisible export. Britain's trade figures for 1913 can be shown as follows:[1]

		£ millions
Imports		731
Exports	Goods	597
	Interest	210
	Shipping	94
	Other services	35
		936

Since 1913, due largely to the two world wars, Britain has lost some of her sources of invisible exports.

FREE TRADE

During the eighteenth century, and before, government restrictions were placed on trade. These included *customs duties* on goods entering or leaving the country, and an *excise* on goods made in Britain for the home market. Adam Smith,[2] a Glasgow university professor, wrote a book called *The Wealth of Nations*, published in 1776, in which he

[1] Figures from E. V. Morgan, *A First Approach to Economics*, London, 1963, p. 73.
[2] See Appendix IV, pp. 296–7.

criticised the prevailing commercial policy, and advocated that trade and commerce should be freed from governmental interference. He argued that individuals would be more successful than governments. He denied the value of tariffs, and of state regulation of trade. By the time of his death in 1790, some statesmen and manufacturers had been persuaded that Adam Smith was right. By a slow process, Britain became a 'free-trade' country by 1860; she remained a free-trade country until 1932, since when tariffs have been imposed on certain commodities.

Pitt the Younger

The first statesman to start Britain on the road to free trade was William Pitt the Younger, who became Prime Minister in 1783. In 1784 he reduced the duties on tea (from 119 per cent to 12 per cent) and on brandy; in 1787 he issued a new Book of Rates (i.e. a list of duties payable), simplifying the system so that a single duty was paid on each commodity, instead of the complicated method involving percentages used before. By means of bonded warehouses other articles, such as tobacco, were brought under excise instead of customs, in order to prevent smuggling. In 1786, under the Pitt-Vergennes Treaty, Britain reduced the duties on French wines and brandy, whilst France allowed British textiles and ironware to be imported at reduced rates. This treaty was soon ruined by the outbreak of the French Revolution, and the wars against France (1793–1815) delayed further measures leading towards free trade.

The Corn Laws

Soon after the conclusion of the wars, free trade came under discussion once more. Those who supported the reduction of duties were disturbed by the re-imposition of the Corn Laws in 1815. As we have already seen,[1] these laws, designed to protect the English farmer, forbade the importation of foreign wheat whilst the price of English corn was 80s. a quarter or less—to give a fair profit to English farmers in any normal year. In times of scarcity the price would rise above this figure, and imported grain would supplement the harvest. In practice these laws kept the price of bread high; if the price of corn rose above 80s. a quarter (in fact it rarely reached that

[1] In pp. 93–5.

figure, and was generally between 50s. and 60s.) then the quartern loaf cost 1s. 4d. (The wages of many artisans were 10s. per week, or less.) The Corn Laws became a major target for the free traders.

William Huskisson

In 1820 a petition, written by the economist Thomas Tooke, signed by an influential group of London manufacturers, asked the government to consider the reduction of tariffs, including the Corn Laws. Three years later William Huskisson became President of the Board of Trade, and he initiated a series of important measures. He was thwarted in an attempt to abolish the Corn Laws because they were supported in the House of Commons by both Whigs and Tories ('a solid, ignorant, gentlemanly vote'[1]). But Wellington's government managed to modify the Corn Laws. In 1828 a sliding scale of duties on imported corn was devised, whereby the duty fell as the price rose. For example, if the price was 50s., the duty was 34s. 8d. per quarter; if the price was 73s., the duty was 1s. In 1823 Huskisson passed the Reciprocity of Duties Act, which got around the Navigation Acts by allowing the mutual admittance of shipping with those countries willing to sign such an agreement. Britain had had such an agreement with the U.S.A. since 1814 by the Treaty of Ghent; by 1829 she had similar treaties with fifteen other countries. Huskisson also lowered the duties on imported pig iron, wool and raw silk (all needed by manufacturers); he made a free-trade treaty with Ireland; and reduced duties on some imported colonial goods ('colonial preference'). The results of these measures were that English manufacturing increased, her shipping flourished, the Exchequer gained in revenue, and smuggling became no longer a profitable occupation.

Further Developments

Two other restrictions were removed in the third decade of the nineteenth century. In 1825 the emigration of skilled artisans was permitted, and the lifting of this embargo was one factor in the increased settlement of Australia. Also, the chartered trading companies, which were founded in the late sixteenth and early seventeenth centuries, lost their monopoly of trading rights with certain parts of the world. For example, in 1813 trade with India was opened to

[1] J. H. Clapham, *An Economic History of Britain*, Cambridge, 1950, Vol. I.

organisations other than the East India Company, whilst the Royal Africa Company and the Levant Company lost their exclusive rights in 1821.

The free-trade issue came to the fore once more in the 1840's. From 1837 to 1841 there was an industrial and commercial depression. The movement for free trade was particularly strong in Manchester (the free traders were referred to as the 'Manchester School'), since the cotton interests were badly hit by the slump. In 1838 a group of Manchester business men formed the Anti-Corn Law Association; in the following year, after a meeting in London, the Association became the Anti-Corn Law League. Its leaders were George Wilson (the President), John Smith (Treasurer), John Bright (a Rochdale manufacturer), Thomas Potter (Manchester's first Mayor), and Richard Cobden (a cotton merchant). The Leaguers saw the Corn Laws as a major reason for the depression in trade, and they started a well-organised agitation for repeal. They were not successful until 1846, but other free trade measures were taken meanwhile.

In 1840 a Select Committee of the House of Commons was appointed to inquire into import duties. This Committee examined the duties levied on 862 articles, and reported that the revenue from some each year was nil, and from others very small, whilst 94·5 per cent was collected from 17 commodities. These 'profitable' articles included, however, necessities, 'viz. sugar, tea, tobacco, spirits, wine, timber, coffee, butter, tallow, seeds, raisins, cheese, cotton wool, sheep's wool, and silk manufactures'. This report has been called 'a free-trade manifesto'.

Sir Robert Peel

Such was the economic climate of the country when Sir Robert Peel became Prime Minister in 1841. When he took office he avowed that he had not read the report of 1840; but he was influenced by Gladstone, Vice-President of the Board of Trade, and was convinced that a reform of the tariff was needed. Peel stated that his object was 'to revive commerce and effect such an improvement in the manufacturing interest as would react on every interest in the country'. In the 1842 budget, duties were reduced on 750 articles including many foodstuffs, and those on exported manufactured goods were withdrawn. Though many duties remained, they were graduated in

27 *A nitrate clipper, used for bringing farm fertiliser from Chile.* (pp. 100, 117)

28 *Dunedin* brought the first cargo of frozen meat from New Zealand to Britain in 1882, in a voyage of 98 days during which sparks from the steam refrigerating plant several times set light to the sails. Her cargo was 4,300 carcasses of mutton, and 598 of lamb, carried 12,000 miles at a freight charge of 2¾d. a mile. She was lost with all hands in 1885.

(p. 101)

29 Turbinia, *the first vessel powered by steam turbines, at speed in 1894.* (p. 123)

30 *An S.R.N.6 Hovercraft, travelling from the Isle of Wight to the mainland.* (p. 250)

order to stimulate Britain's industries. A duty of 5 per cent was levied on imported raw materials, 12½ per cent on semi-manufactured materials, and 20 per cent on imported manufactured goods. Opponents of the budget foretold ruin in the Treasury through a decline in government revenue. To meet a possible deficiency, Peel re-imposed income tax at 7d. in the pound for incomes over £150 per annum. (Income tax had first been used by Pitt in 1799, but it was discontinued in 1816.) The gloomy prophets were wrong, for the reduced tariffs brought in more revenue because of increased trade. After continuing his general plan in the budgets of 1843 and 1844, Peel made greater changes in 1845. Duties on 430 articles were abolished, as were all remaining export duties. Such duties as remained were on articles which were regarded as luxuries, or were left solely for the purpose of adding to the government's income.

Peel's budgets, which helped to make good his aim to 'make the country a cheap country for living', did not please everyone. Many of his own Conservative party (and of his opponents) were against free trade as a principle. The Anti-Corn Law Leaguers were displeased because their object had not been attained. Throughout the 1840's the League had carried out a well-organised campaign. Cobden and Bright were its spokesmen in the House of Commons; paid lecturers were sent all over the country; pamphlets were printed and distributed through the new cheap postal system; well-directed propaganda was diffused both nationally and regionally. Peel had further modified the Corn Laws in 1842, but a crisis came in the winter of 1845–46. Bad harvests of corn coincided with potato blight in Ireland. There was an urgent need for cheap grain to be sent to the Irish. Although Peel resigned office, as he was unable to carry all of his party with him, he returned very soon, and with Whig support, repealed the Corn Laws in June 1846. Under the new measure, an import duty of 4s. a quarter was levied, and this was reduced by stages to 1s. by 1849.

The Aftermath of Repeal

The repeal of the Corn Laws led to the end of Peel's political career. He was defeated in the House later in 1846, and retired from politics. Although political parties in the modern sense did not then exist, political alliances were radically changed by the events of 1846.

Some of Peel's Conservative opponents, led by Disraeli and Bentinck, supported 'protection'; 'Peelites', including Gladstone, were determined to further free trade; the influence of the Radicals, such as Cobden and Bright, was increased. The economic effects were not as marked as supporters and opponents of the Corn Laws had imagined. Farmers were not ruined; indeed farming entered a prosperous era. Industry was not noticeably stimulated. But the country was enjoying boom conditions by 1846, so that the immediate results of repeal were obscured. Thirty years later, English agriculture was to begin to feel the effects of the lack of restrictions on imported food. But, on the other hand, it can be argued that a nation should find its food from the cheapest source, and concentrate its own endeavours on what it can do best. For England, this was manufacturing.

Further reductions of tariffs were made in the 1850's by Gladstone, when he was Chancellor of the Exchequer. In the 1853 budget, duties were abolished on 123 articles, including those on soap (a 'tax on cleanliness'). Duties on 133 articles were reduced, including food-stuffs such as tea, fruit and dairy produce. In the 1860 budget a further 371 duties were abolished, including those on foodstuffs. Only 48 protective duties remained, as opposed to over 1,200 in 1841. Also in 1860, a free-trade treaty was negotiated with France (the Cobden-Chevalier Treaty). By this Britain agreed to reduce duties on French wines and brandies, and France lowered her tariffs on British textiles, machinery, coal and iron.

To all intents and purposes, Britain was a free-trade country by 1860. As she had an industrial lead over other countries, she could pursue such a commercial policy. But Cobden and the Manchester School had imagined that other countries would follow Britain's lead, and that world trade would flow freely without restriction. Their lofty vision imagined that 'universal and permanent peace' would result. But other countries were not commercially strong enough to follow Britain's lead.

The Navigation Laws

The Navigation Laws, passed in 1651, and re-enacted in 1660 on the restoration of Charles II, were designed to stimulate English shipping. They laid down that goods leaving England had to be carried in English ships, whilst goods coming to England had to be carried in

English ships or those of the country of origin. Originally they were aimed at the Dutch, who had captured much of the carrying trade in the middle of the seventeenth century. By the nineteenth century circumstances had changed. The Dutch were no longer the para-mount maritime power, nor were they Britain's enemy. British trade and shipping was strengthening. An attack on the Navigation Laws was a natural corollary to the movement for free trade. They had been modified by Huskisson in the 1820's; they were repealed in 1849 for ocean shipments, leaving restrictions on coastal shipping which were abolished in 1853. Manufacturers, freed from export duties, were now free to employ ships of any country to carry their wares to all parts of the world. Because of the strength of the British mercantile marine, British interests were not harmed by the abolition of the Navigation Laws.

Tariff Reform

It is possible that Britain should have become a free-trade country earlier than she did. It is also possible that she remained a free-trade country longer than she should have. By about 1873, Britain's in-dustrial supremacy was being challenged, particularly by Germany and the U.S.A. In 1873 Germany and other countries had tariffs on imported goods. They could export their produce to Britain without payment of duty, whilst British manufacturers found that their products were subject to duties. In 1881 a group of British manu-facturers founded the Fair Trade League, to persuade Parliament to impose duties on goods from those countries which taxed British goods. But this idea was contrary to majority opinion. By then most influential statesmen believed in free trade.

In 1890 the U.S.A., which had been a free-trade country for a short period, returned to protection with the McKinley Duties. France followed suit in 1892. In Britain, protectionists began a re-newed agitation. Foremost in the campaign was Joseph Chamberlain, a former Radical, who had become Colonial Secretary in the Con-servative ministry of Lord Salisbury in 1895. In 1903 Chamberlain initiated a campaign for 'Tariff Reform', in which he advocated a return to protection, with lower rates of duties on goods from the Empire ('imperial preference'). Chamberlain believed that Britain's livelihood and her future were firmly linked with her Empire. He resigned from the Colonial Office in 1903, and stepped up the campaign. But he gained little support, and the election of 1906 resulted in a sweeping victory for the Liberals, who supported free trade. At the outbreak of war in 1914, Britain was still a free-trade country, and, apart from war-time restrictions, did not impose tariffs until 1932.

CHAPTER 12

Industrial Development, 1815–1914

During the nineteenth century Britain became the workshop of the world. She had an industrial lead over other nations, she had the coal and iron, the skilled manpower, the capital, and the sources of raw materials. The basis of the country's economy lay in the 'heavy industries'—coal, iron and steel, and machinery—together with textiles. Britain kept this lead until the last quarter of the nineteenth century, when the U.S.A. and Germany, amongst others, were overhauling her as industrial producers. The U.S.A. and Germany had by then learned the techniques, they had rapidly rising populations and tariff barriers. However, in the middle of the century, there were few clouds on the industrial horizon.

The Great Exhibition of 1851

The Great Exhibition can be taken as a symbol of Britain's industrial might. The idea of a trade exhibition was not new; the medieval trade fairs, and the national exhibitions staged by France and Britain during the first half of the nineteenth century are examples. But in Britain, no exhibition held before or since (the 1951 Exhibition is already fading into obscurity) captured the imagination as did that of 1851. Much of the credit was due to Queen Victoria's husband, Albert, the Prince Consort (1819–61), and to Henry Cole (1802–82). The Prince was the President of the Royal Society of Arts, and Cole its chairman. This Society organised annual industrial exhibitions; the one held in 1847 attracted 20,000 visitors; in 1848 70,000 attended, and in 1849 100,000. The dynamic Cole then persuaded the Prince to agree to the staging of an international trade exhibition in 1851. For the next two years these two men worked indefatigably at the project. A site of 26 acres in Hyde Park was chosen, a contribution fund launched and exhibitors were approached. The project aroused violent opposition from some quarters, notably from the then radical newspaper *The Times,* and from Colonel Charles Sibthorp, M.P. for Lincoln.

By a stroke of a pen our pleasant Park . . . is to be turned into something between Wolverhampton and Greenwich Fair.[1]

Attacks in the press and in Parliament led Prince Albert to write:

the whole public, led on by *The Times,* has all at once made a set against me and the Exhibition. . . . We are to pack out of London with our nuisance to the Isle of Dogs.

Critics were later to eat their words.

The original intention was to erect a brick building, but neither the promoters nor opponents of the Exhibition liked the designs which had been submitted. Fortunately a designer of imaginative genius came to their rescue. Joseph Paxton, formerly a gardener in the employ of the Duke of Devonshire and in 1850 a director of the Midland Railway, promised to submit a design within *nine days.* He had already built a large conservatory at Chatsworth, the Duke of Devonshire's home in Derbyshire. Paxton 'doodled' his original design, an enlarged 'greenhouse', during a boring board meeting. Within nine days detailed plans were submitted for a building which *Punch* later called 'The Crystal Palace'. Paxton took the unprecedented step of publishing his design in the *Illustrated London News,* and it was so well received that opposition to the Exhibition became less virulent. However, due to the insistence of Colonel Sibthorp, the design had to be modified so that an elm tree, destined for felling, was left standing inside the building.

The building work began in August 1850, when concrete foundations were laid. The various sections were prefabricated, brought to the site, and erected. The work was completed by 1st May 1851, when the Exhibition was opened by Queen Victoria. *The Times'* leader on the following day was full of praise:

They who were so fortunate as to see it hardly knew what most to admire. . . . The edifice, the treasures of art collected therein, the assemblage and the solemnity of the occasion, all conspired to suggest something even more than sense could scan, or imagination attain.

[1] *The Times:* quoted in *The Great Exhibition of 1851,* H.M.S.O., 1950.

The building was 1,848 feet long, and 408 feet broad; the height of the roof of the transept was 108 feet, and that of the nave 63 feet. At one time over 2,000 men were employed in its construction, which used 293,655 panes of glass, 4,500 tons of iron, 600,000 cubic feet of timber, and 24 miles of guttering. Inside the building were 100,000 exhibits from all over the world. The exhibits included raw materials,

The location of industry, c. 1850: only the most important centres are shown. Agriculture was still the main source of employment, but the manufacturing industries had become concentrated near the coalfields with the growing importance of steam power. Compare this with the map on p. 26.

machinery, manufactured items and sculpture. The value of the contents (excluding the Koh-i-Noor diamond) was £2 million.

The Exhibition was a success. By 15th October, the official closing date, over six million visitors had paid entrance. The largest attendance on any one day was 109,915. These attendances were achieved without opening on Sundays, and despite the prohibition of alcohol, smoking and dogs. Many English people visited London for the first time in order to go to the Exhibition, brought to the capital in Thomas Cook's 'excursion' trains. The Exhibition cost approximately £335,000 to mount, and receipts were £522,000.

The Crystal Palace was taken down in 1852, and re-erected in a smaller and modified form at Sydenham in 1854. From then until 1936, when it was destroyed by fire, it was used for various exhibitions. In the grounds at Sydenham various sporting activities took place (there is still a soccer team called Crystal Palace). The two towers which survived the fire were demolished in 1939 as they would have been useful landmarks for enemy bombers.

Textiles

During the nineteenth century the manufacture of textiles was Britain's most important industry, with cotton in particular growing steadily. Cotton goods were also important to the British people, for they provided cheap and hygienic clothing. When Friedrich Engels, in his book *The Condition of the English Working Classes in 1844,* used the ousting of woollen garments by cotton as evidence of a deterioration of living standards, he was somewhat wide of the mark. Wool was dearer, and woollen clothes are not improved by frequent washing; cotton goods were a boon. There are no dramatic headlines in the story of cotton in the nineteenth century—there were no Arkwrights or Hargreaves—but its importance in the British economy must be realised.

A self-acting mule was invented in 1825, but its adoption in Britain was slow. Manufacturers were still installing Crompton's mules, or Horrocks' looms, though complete mechanisation did not take place overnight. In 1833, in all forms of textiles, there were 100,000 power looms and 250,000 hand looms in operation. Towards the end of the century American ideas were beginning to be adopted by English cotton masters. Ring spinning, patented by J. Thorpe in the U.S.A.

The cotton printing room of Messrs. Black of Glasgow, c. 1860. The firm had 25 machines, and produced 25 million yards of printed cotton goods per year.

as early as 1828, did not become widely adopted in Lancashire until the present century. Ring spinning made it possible for continuous thread to be made at high speed. Weaving was made continuous by the Northrop Loom, patented in the U.S.A. in 1892.

The production figures were impressive. Cotton imports, valued at £164 million in 1818, had risen to £826 million in 1850, and £1,714 million in 1880. The one temporary setback was the period of the Lancashire Cotton Famine (1862–64) when the American Civil War interrupted supplies. The raw material became so scarce that manufacturers, who were paying 9d. per lb. in 1861, were having to offer 1s. 6½d. in 1862, and over 2s. in 1863. But this was a temporary difficulty. With mechanisation, whilst the labour force grew by 50 per cent between 1830 and 1890, output per person rose by 400 per cent. In the period 1894–1914 output rose by a further 25 per cent. The cotton industry was at its peak in 1914, with India, the largest single customer, buying 3,000 million yards of cotton cloth.

The woollen industry also expanded, though not as far or as fast as cotton. Mechanisation came more slowly because wool is more liable to break, and its texture is not so uniform. In general there was little mechanisation in the woollen industry before about 1830, though by 1850 hand looms and hand-spinning machines were becoming less common. This period also saw the importation of raw wool from Australia, which supplied 50 per cent of British wool imports in 1850. The huge flocks from the large ranches supplied in quantity raw wool of similar texture and size, making mechanisation easier. By 1900 four-fifths of the wool used in British industry was imported. The last processes of woollen manufacture to be mechanised were those of combing or carding, and slubbing, both processes preparatory to spinning. No efficient carding machine (for wool) was available until the 1840's, whilst machines for slubbing did not come into general use until the next decade, when a 'condenser' invented by Goulding, an American, in 1832, found its way into English mills.

Three other branches of the textile industry are worthy of notice. Linen manufacture was carried on in Ulster, east Scotland, and in Yorkshire. Linen is made from flax, which has a hard, stubby stalk. Mechanisation came slowly in this industry; in general spinning was done by hand until about 1825, and weaving until 1850. Jute was a new fibre introduced into Britain in the 1830's, when the price of raw hemp from the Baltic rose. Jute from India was used as a cheaper substitute in the manufacture of sandbags and food bags. The third branch of the textile industry was also new, and depended on a man-made fibre. This was rayon, an artificial silk, made by chemists instead of by silk-worms. In 1906 the old-established firm of Cour-tauld's of Coventry began the manufacture of viscose rayon, made from wood pulp and sulphuric acid. By 1909 Courtauld's were employing over 2,000 people, but by 1914 the man-made fibre was used in only a small fragment of the textile industry. Cotton was still king.

Coal

Coal was the chief source of energy in Britain in the nineteenth century and the very foundation of the nation's industrial strength. The demand for it rose with the development of steam engines for industry, locomotives and ships. Its use as a domestic fuel grew with the increased size of towns, and better transport facilities. There was also an increased foreign demand as other European countries in-dustrialised. Countries with no or little coal, such as Portugal and Switzerland, or countries with coal that was as yet unexploited, were an important market. In Britain, the development of gas lighting, and the use of coal by-products, such as aniline dyes, led to an in-creased demand. Further, the growth of the iron and steel industry meant that more coal was needed for furnaces. The following pro-duction figures show the growth of output in millions of tons.

	total production	exports
1816	16	
1836	30	
1846	44	
1854	64·6	11
1874	125	
1891	185	
1913	287	98

Like the cotton industry, coal had reached its peak at the outbreak of the 1914–18 war. The 1913 output, produced by a labour force of 1,127,000 men, is a record figure—not because that quantity could not now be hewn, but because of a decline in demand.

The increased demand led to the further development of mining in the 'old' areas, the north-east, South Wales, Scotland and the midlands, and of new mines in south Yorkshire and in Kent (near Dover). Also, it led to deeper mining. Eighteenth-century pits were normally less than 1,000 feet deep; during the first half of the nineteenth century mining was carried on at a depth of over 1,000 feet, whilst after 1850 some pits were over 2,000 feet deep. This greater depth was possible because of the invention of safety lamps by Davy,

Wire was made by 'drawing' or pulling thin iron rods through holes. This illustration shows wire-drawing in Birmingham, c. 1840.

George Stephenson, and others. There were, however, few revolutionary changes in techniques. A safety fuse for use with gunpowder charges was introduced in 1831. Wire rope for hauling came into use in 1834, and an endless rope ten years later. Some improvement was made in ventilation with the invention of an exhaust fan by William Fourness of Leeds in 1837, and of the centrifugal fan by W. P. Struve in 1849. But hewing and coal-face haulage continued to be done in the main by manual means. Although a compressed-air cutter was developed in 1855, it was little used in British coal mines, partly because of the thin layers of coal. Only a fraction of British coal was cut by machine before 1914. Coal-face conveyors developed after 1902, but very slowly. Unfortunately for Britain, this great industry was lagging behind in technique at a time when German and American coal mines were becoming mechanised. The Royal School of Mines, established in 1851, was unable to inspire mine-owners to spend money on the introduction of new methods.

Iron and Steel

The production of pig iron rose during the middle part of the nineteenth century, as follows:

	million tons
1830	·65
1835	1·0
1854	3·0
1859	3·7
1870	5·9

This development was due to the increased use of iron for machinery,

An iron foundry, *c.* 1850, showing molten pig iron being poured into moulds.

locomotives and railway lines; in the building industry, wrought-iron roof trusses replaced wood, as in Euston station, built in 1839, or the Reading Room of the British Museum, built 1854–57.

Two technical improvements aided the production of iron. In 1828 James Neilson invented the hot-blast furnace. Neilson, the manager of the Glasgow Gas Works, realised that cold air blast led to a loss of furnace heat. The use of hot air reduced fuel consumption from

Blast furnaces at an ironworks, c. 1850. Earlier blast furnaces were square. The bridge-like structure is a loading ramp.

161 cwt. of coal per ton of cast iron to 103 cwt. By 1833, using raw coal (instead of coke), the consumption was cut to 45 cwt. The hot-blast furnace also led to the use of anthracite in furnaces. The invention of the steam hammer in 1840 by James Nasmyth (1808–90) was of great value in forging iron.

The great need was for the mass production of steel. This became possible because of three inventions between 1859 and 1878. Before 1859 steel was produced in small quantities for springs, cutting tools, drills and screws. But steel was dear. The first advance was made by Sir Henry Bessemer (1813–98). Bessemer, born in Hitchin, Hertfordshire, had already made a fortune by patenting a process for making gold leaf cheaply; then he invented a roller for extracting sugar from cane, and a method of casting sheets of glass. He became interested in the problems of steel manufacture during the Crimean War (1854–1856), when there was a need for new methods of casting cannon. Steel was wanted, but could not be obtained in sufficient quantities. Wrought iron, produced by puddling, a slow and laborious process,

The casting shop at the Cyclops Iron and Steel Works of Cammel and Co., Sheffield, c. 1860. The crucible method (see p. 34) was still the standard.

was used instead. Bessemer found the solution by accident. To produce steel it was necessary to get rid of the carbon, silicon and manganese impurities, and then to add small quantities of carbon. One day Bessemer found by chance that air blown across the molten iron decarbonised it. He built a 'converter', shaped like a pear; it was tested in Sheffield in 1859, and steel was produced. But when Bessemer's process was tried by other iron-masters, it failed; later it was found that Bessemer's converter could be used only for non-phosphoric ores. Most of the iron in Britain is phosphoric, and it was necessary to import non-phosphoric ore from Sweden in order to use the Bessemer process.

In 1867 the Siemens–Martin 'open hearth' process was patented. William Siemens (1823–83) was born in Hanover, but spent most of his adult life in England. Siemens invented a gas furnace (the 'open hearth'), which reached a temperature of 1650°C. Using such a furnace a Frenchman, Pierre Martin, succeeded in making steel. Because of the high temperature, pig iron and scrap iron could be refined into steel. The production of steel in Britain by these means began in 1869 at the Siemens Steelworks in Swansea.

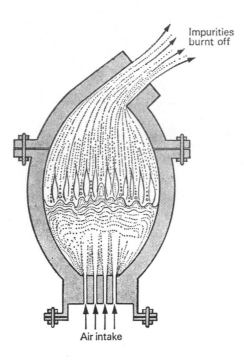

Impurities burnt off

Air intake

Diagram of a Bessemer converter. The converter was first tipped into a horizontal position, and molten iron was poured in. Then the converter was turned upright, and high-pressure heated air was forced through the holes in the base for about twenty minutes. This removed carbon and other impurities, except phosphorus and sulphur. Then the converter was turned on its side, and iron containing carbon was added. When this was 'mixed', the converter was tipped downwards and the molten steel was poured into a ladle. See Plate 32 opposite.

But a method of making steel from phosphoric ores had still to be found. In 1879 it was discovered by two cousins, Gilchrist and Thomas. Sidney Gilchrist Thomas (1850–85) was a magistrate's clerk in London. His cousin Gilchrist was a chemist in an ironworks at Blaenavon in Monmouthshire. Experiments were carried out by means of Thomas writing to his cousin, who conducted them 'after hours' where he worked. Put simply, the Gilchrist–Thomas, or 'Basic', process meant lining the converter with lime-stone, so that the lime absorbed the phosphorus. The method was tested at

31 *A painting by James Nasmyth of his steam hammer in action at Patricroft, near Manchester.* (p. 146)

32 *A Bessemer steel plant at Ebbw Vale, c. 1860. Molten steel is being poured from the converter on the right into a ladle. Air under pressure is being blown through the converter on the left.* (p. 148)

33 A pair of mule spinning machines, c. 1844. A 'scavenger' can be seen sweeping, bottom right. (p. 140)

34 A steam-powered cotton weaving shed, c. 1844. Note that the looms are minded by women. (pp. 140, 163)

Middlesbrough in 1879, and was successful. It meant that British iron ore from the Jurassic scarp could be used. This caused a change in the relative importance of iron-working locations. The Cleveland ironfields (near Middlesbrough) developed rapidly, as did those in Northumberland and Durham.

Paradoxically, the Gilchrist–Thomas Basic Process also helped those countries which became Britain's rivals in steel production. Ironfields in the U.S.A., Belgium and Germany (who obtained the Lorraine ironfields from France in 1871) are phosphoric deposits. Without the Basic Process, they could not have been developed. By 1914 Britain's steel output was less than that of the U.S.A. and Germany.

The three steel inventions caused iron to be replaced by steel for ships' hulls, railway lines, machinery, bridges, buildings and armaments. One steel bridge built after the inventions was the Forth Railway Bridge (1882–89), for which 50,000 tons of steel were used. In Paris, the Eiffel Tower, erected to commemorate the centenary of the French Revolution, was completed in 1889. The inventions also coincided with developments in concrete. Joseph Ashden, of Leeds, had taken out a patent in 1824 for a process whereby chalks and clays were fused into a 'cement' powder. During the second half of the nineteenth century, the cement industry was able to produce it in large quantities, so that 'reinforced concrete', i.e. concrete casing steel girders, became an important building material.

Figures for annual steel production in Britain show clearly the sudden development in the industry:

	tons
1850	60,000
1870	250,000
1880	2,000,000
1900	5,000,000
1966	24,300,000

Engineering

The heavy industries needed machinery and power, and to produce these engineering skills had to be improved. In many cases, those who became the great names in engineering in the nineteenth century were trained for other professions, or had little formal education.

The present-day complaint of the lack of facilities for technical education was voiced by our Victorian ancestors. But the fact is that in
the nineteenth century men of rare engineering skill were produced
by practical training at the bench.

Joseph Bramah (1748–1814) was the son of a Yorkshire farmer.
After an apprenticeship as a carpenter, he turned his considerable

The cement works of Johnson and Co. of Gateshead in 1861. The waterfront site
made for easy shipping. Cement, with steel ('reinforced concrete'), was the most
important development in building since the first use of stone.

abilities to the invention of a number of useful machines. These included an improved water-closet, a hydraulic press, a suction beer-
machine, a wood-planing machine, and a device for printing the
serial numbers on banknotes. Henry Maudslay (1771–1831) was the
son of a storekeeper at Woolwich Arsenal. He served successively in
a carpenter's and a blacksmith's shop; then he worked for Joseph
Bramah, becoming his foreman. This is how engineering skills were
handed down—not through schooling, but through the influence of
particular men and their workshops. Maudslay eventually established
his own workshop, and he is chiefly remembered for his screw-cut-
ting lathe, patented in 1800. James Nasmyth (1808–90), the inventor
of the steam hammer, was a Scot, and he did receive some formal

education, first at Edinburgh High School (until he was 12), and then at the School of Arts there. Nasmyth served in Maudslay's workshop for two years. Another who learned his craft under Maudslay was Joseph Whitworth (1803–87). Whitworth was the son of a Stockport schoolmaster, and after a period in London under Maudslay, he set up in business as a toolmaker in Manchester. There

A steam-driven machine for planing metal, c. 1843.

he made his name as the maker of machine-tools which were capable of working to great precision. Some indication of the advances made is shown by the story of Matthew Boulton, who in 1776 was impressed by the accuracy of a cylinder bored by John Wilkinson that 'doth not err the thickness of an old shilling'. Whitworth invented a machine capable of *measuring* to an accuracy of one millionth of an inch. Whitworth also invented the Whitworth thread, i.e. a standardised screw thread. This simple idea did much to aid the development of standardised spare parts. Whitworth died a millionaire, and his name lives in the thirty engineering scholarships which he endowed in 1868. The firm of Sir Joseph Whitworth amalgamated with Armstrong's in 1897; in 1928 Armstrong-Whitworth joined with Vickers to form the present company of Vickers-Armstrong.

Some New Industries

Although Britain's economy rested largely on the old-established heavy industries, some comparatively new industries were increasing in importance by 1914. These included electrical engineering, gas, bicycles, motor cars, aluminium, rubber, ferro-concrete and the chemical industry.

Coal-gas was first used at Boulton and Watt's Soho factory in 1802. This illustration shows the retort-house at the Westminster Gas Works, c. 1840. Coke was used in the furnaces.

Chemistry was increasingly being called in to make up for shortages of natural products. Agricultural fertilisers, artificial silk, synthetic dyes, plastics to replace wood, and petroleum products as a substitute for whale oil were among the developments of the nineteenth-century chemists. They also found use for coal by-products, such as naphtha for oil-lamps, creosote, gas and ammonia. Gas lighting had become common in English towns by 1914. The Gas Light and Coke Company had been formed as early as 1807, whilst Westminster had gas street-lighting in 1814. The chief problem was that not all the gas was ignited, so that people were reluctant to use it as

interior lighting because of the danger and the smoke. The problem
was solved later in the century by the invention of the gas mantle.
Then gas lighting became more common in cities, and was a great
boon to those who had been accustomed to more primitive means.
But the supply of gas was limited largely to the towns; the countryman still had to read by the inadequate light of an oil-lamp, or the
flickering candle.

Gasometers at Westminster, c. 1840. Note the cast-iron standards for street lighting.

The generating of electricity was a nineteenth-century development. Since the sixteenth century men had known how to produce
static electricity by friction, and in 1749, with the invention of the
Leyden jar, were able to store it. But such supplies were of little more
than a curiosity value. In 1800 the Italian Alessandro Volta demonstrated that electricity was produced if metal plates (copper or zinc),
placed in acid, were connected by a copper wire—i.e. by a 'battery'.
It is important to notice that, unlike the harnessing of steam, the
generating of electricity came about through the work of scientists

from many different countries; the names of units, such as Volt, Ampère, and Ohm, derive from an Italian, a Frenchman and a German respectively. But British scientists played a notable part. William Sturgeon (1783–1850) produced the first practical electro-magnet in 1825. Michael Faraday (1791–1867), who had served an apprenticeship under Sir Humphry Davy, and who in 1824 became the Director of the Laboratory at the Royal Institution, produced the first electric motor in 1821. But the true ancestor of the modern dynamo was that invented by a Belgian, Gramme, in 1870. Gramme's importance was that he perfected the armature.

Once these advances in electrical engineering had been made, electricity could be put to use for the benefit of industry and commerce. Electro-plating, the incandescent lamp (Edison, 1878, and Swan, 1879), the telephone (Alexander Graham Bell), wireless (Clerk-Maxwell, Herz, and Marconi), the internal combustion engine and the electric tram were all manifestations of man's great discovery. Also, the harnessing of electricity enabled engineers to use aluminium, which in turn was of great value in the building of motor-cars and aircraft, and as a protective covering for steel. One of the first large electrical engineering firms was established in 1878 at Chelmsford by Colonel R. E. B. Crompton (1864–1940); British Thomson, Houston Company was formed in 1896; in the same year Sebastian de Ferranti (1864–1930) established a firm at Oldham. The electrical age which was dawning was to prove a mixed blessing to Britain, for whilst coal and iron were the keystones of industry she was advantageously placed. In the new age of electrical power she was less well placed.

Foreign Competition and Technical Education

During the last quarter of the nineteenth century, British statesmen and businessmen were becoming disturbed about the country's industrial output compared with that of foreign competitors. In 1886 a Royal Commission reported on 'The Depression of Trade and Industry', and from that time the phrase 'The Great Depression' has been applied to the period 1874–96. Modern research has modified the view of these years in which, although prices and profits were falling, production increased greatly, and living standards rose. What happened was that Britain no longer had an industrial lead. She had been the pioneer, and now other countries were able to compete. Britain's output was increasing, but her share of the total of the world's trade was decreasing. Countries such as Germany and the U.S.A., with greater populations than Britain, who were well-endowed with natural resources and with technical skill, were competing in the heavy industries, as the following figures show:

Pig Iron (average annual output in millions of tons)

1870–74	U.K.	6·4	1900–04	U.S.A.	16·4
	U.S.A.	2·2		Germany	8·9
	Germany	1·8		U.K.	8·6
	France	1·2		France	2·6

Steel

1870–74	U.K.	·5	1900–04	U.S.A.	13
	Germany	·3		Germany	7
	U.S.A.	·14		U.K.	5
	France	·13		France	1·7

Coal

1870–74	U.K.	120	1900–04	U.S.A.	241
	U.S.A.	43		U.K.	225
			1913	U.S.A.	509
				U.K.	287

Textiles (U.K. percentage of world's spinning capacity)

1881–84	54
1900	43
1913	40

Britain was not declining; other countries were making more rapid progress in the 'old' industries. If our forefathers must be criticised, it can be said that they were slow to adapt themselves to the new conditions, and in particular that they were backward in developing the 'new' industries which were to be important in the present century. In one respect, however, both industrialists and governments were guilty. Technical education was largely neglected, whilst industry failed to make full use of the scientific discoveries of the university researchers. Nor were the universities blameless. There was a prejudice against applied science and the various branches of engineering, which remained the poor and sometimes despised poor relations among the university departments. The schools and the universities did not produce enough men with technical training, and industry was slow to improve the position. (The first industrial research laboratory was not established in Britain until 1873.) As a result, the state tried to fill the gap. Following the report of the Devonshire Commission on technical education, the City and Guilds Institute was founded in 1880. This body assisted in the teaching of applied science in schools and evening classes, and set examinations in technical subjects. In 1889, under the Technical Instruction Act, local authorities were empowered to pay for technical education through the rates, which they did mainly by providing evening classes. Some evening institutes developed into 'Polytechnics'. This state interest in technical education, created by a fear of German industrial rivalry, stimulated others. In 1906 the University of London founded the Imperial College of Science and Technology by joining together several existing establishments. But generally little could be achieved until secondary education was extended after 1902.[1]

[1] See pp. 206–7.

CHAPTER 13

Working Conditions

THE FACTORIES

In studying history we must beware of comparing conditions in our own time with those of the past. What to us may seem to be unbearable, was not necessarily so to our forefathers. The problem in the early factories, which developed during the later years of the eighteenth century, was that neither employers nor employees had experience of organising or working in large-scale undertakings in a free society. In times past, thousands of slaves had been forced by brutal means to obey orders and to work together; soldiers and sailors had also had to adhere to a strict and often savage discipline. But the factory workers were not pressed men, or slaves; if they could find other employment, they were free to leave. The employers had no 'King's Regulations' which they could consult; they had to make their own rules. Further, although in theory there was a body of industrial law, passed in the sixteenth and seventeenth centuries, it was rarely enforced. For example, the Statute of Artificers (1563), whereby magistrates were empowered to regulate wages, and to enforce apprenticeships, was largely a dead letter. Employers had to find their own ways of running their factories, with no text-books or public relations officers to guide them. They made mistakes, and they were given a 'bad press'. Contemporaries such as Scott, Dickens, Disraeli and Carlyle, have drawn pictures of grasping, brutal, insensitive mill-owners, who had no thought other than greed; they were compared unfavourably with the slave-owners. While there is some truth in this view, a more charitable diagnosis would be to accept that they, and their workpeople, were floundering, seeking a means of living and working in a new society.

Problems of the Employers

Problems there were in plenty. The builders of the new factories, for want of a better model, often copied the gaunt workhouses, ugly brick rectangular structures with small windows. Factories were unhealthy and ill-ventilated, without washplaces or sanitation. Machines were unguarded, so that accidents were common. The coming of steam power meant that the workers had to keep regular hours, and be punctual. The dependence of groups of workers performing one operation upon other groups engaged in other processes meant that work had to be done to time. A discipline had to be imposed upon an ill-educated labour force. (An industrial society makes great demands upon personal liberty.) But the state took little part in the matter until 1833, when the first effective Factory Act was passed.

Grinding cutlery by steam power. The development of machinery meant that men had to work together in large units, instead of at home as individuals.

The enforcement of factory discipline was a difficult problem. Casual labour had been the order of the day, and the first generation of factory workers were unused to the idea of permanent employment. In some firms there was an annual turnover of labour of 100 per cent at the end of the eighteenth century. Also, attendance was irregular. Men used to the domestic system were accustomed to working in their own time—no less hard or long than in the factory —but *in their own time*. At home they might work very hard one day, and not so hard the next. In the factory they were required to attend between certain hours for six days a week, and to perform monotonous tasks without interruption. There is perhaps a parallel in the small child, used to the freedom of home, and confronted with school discipline for the first time. The early factory workers did not always keep regular hours—as one factory owner remarked, it was like 'putting a deer in the plough'. In domestic industry there was a tradidition called 'Saint Monday'; the workers would recover from the excesses of Sunday on Monday, start work with little enthusiasm on Tuesday, and work late on Thursday, and perhaps all Friday night, in order to compensate for their earlier slackness. The first factory owners found absenteeism on Mondays a serious problem. Also, during the working day, workers had to forgo their right to stop work when they pleased; the machines worked on, and the minders had to do the same. Old traditions, whereby work stopped on the occasion of a race meeting, or a prize fight, or the news of a national victory or a disaster, had to be broken down. In the north of England there was the additional problem of the 'wakes' tradition, whereby everyone in a town took a holiday at the same time.

Employers had to enforce effort as well as hours. A workman who had taken too much ale was not an efficient workman, so that bans on drinking had to be enforced. At the same time, quality of work had to be preserved, often by severe methods.

Enforcement of Discipline

The early factory owners generally enforced discipline by methods reminiscent of nineteenth-century schools—namely the 'big stick'. (It should be noted that about 70 per cent of the labour force was under eighteen.) Corporal punishment was used, especially for children. The Report of the Commissioners on the Employment of Children in Factories (1833) stated that in one establishment 'the boys are often severely strapped'; and that 'three weeks ago the overseer struck him in the eye with his clenched fist so as to force him to be absent two days'. In another, little girls were so frightened that 'they would run home and fetch their mothers'. Fines were also levied; those current in a Manchester cotton mill in 1823 were as follows:[1]

Any spinner found	with his window open	1s.
	dirty at his work	1s.
	washing himself	1s.
	putting his gas out too soon	1s.

Lateness, absenteeism, and even whistling, were subject to fines. But the chief deterrent was dismissal; in those days there was no shortage of unskilled labour, and the unreliable worker could be replaced. Other employers tried methods of 'shame'. For example, Robert Wood of Bradford made children hold up a card with the offence written on it, or, what was probably worse, publicly declare his fault. These methods did much to create a gulf between master and man, and prevent any feeling of mutual benefit.

But some employers, a minority, sought different means, and used a kinder approach. They tried to create an *esprit de corps*, and gave rewards for good work, rather than punishment for bad. The reward might be a long-term contract, or an additional payment or bonus. They tried to improve their employees by a strict supervision of their off-duty hours, using overseers to watch behaviour on Saturdays and Sundays, and by building chapels and schools. They tried to prevent absenteeism by organising works outings. Among such 'good' employers were the Arkwrights, Jedediah Strutt, Matthew Boulton, Benjamin Gott, Josiah Wedgwood, Robert Owen, the Fieldens, and the Peels. Robert Owen provides a fair example of their methods.

Robert Owen

Robert Owen (1771–1858) married the daughter of David Dale, the owner of the New Lanark Mills, Scotland. There he established what can be called the first model factory. He believed that people would improve if their environment was improved, and set out to apply this principle at New Lanark. He did not employ children under ten years of age, and the use of the strap or stick was forbidden. Prizes were given to the hardest working boy in the factory, whilst every employee was given a 'mark' for his day's work. These marks were shown by coloured boards, which were displayed at each

---

[1] Quoted in J. L. and B. Hammond, *The Town Labourer*.

machine the next day—black (the lowest), blue, yellow and white. Owen also realised that longer hours did not always lead to greater productivity. In an age when most factory owners believed that they made their profit in the last hour's work (the rest of the day paying their overheads), Owen reduced the length of the working day to twelve hours (and later to ten). Production did not fall, and the New Lanark Mills made large profits. Owen also tried to create a happy atmosphere for his workpeople by rebuilding their houses, caring for the sick and aged, and providing education for children from the age of two. The New Lanark Mills became famous, and attracted visitors from Europe and America. Owen's success was one factor in persuading Parliament to pass legislation to control factory labour.

FACTORY ACTS

The first Factory Acts were limited in aim and content, and were concerned with the employment of women and children only. The first, the Health and Morals of Apprentices Act of 1802, was introduced in Parliament by Sir Robert Peel, the father of the future Prime Minister. A few years earlier Dr Percival of Manchester had reported on the fever epidemics then prevalent in cotton mills in that town, with the result that the J.P.s who had the responsibility of finding employment for pauper children, refused to allow those under their care to work in the mills. Peel's Act was designed to regulate the conditions of employment of pauper children in any textile mill, and applied only to paupers. They were not to be employed under the age of nine, and then only for twelve hours a day, with no night work. These factories were to be properly ventilated, and were to be whitewashed once a year. Apprentices were to be properly clothed, educated, and sent to church at least once a month. Despite the intentions of the Act, it was difficult to put it into practice. There were no government officials to enforce it, and it was left to local J.P.s (who were often the employers) and visiting clergymen to see that it was carried out. It was, in fact, largely a failure. In 1819, Sir Robert Peel and Robert Owen succeeded in getting another Act passed, which again was ineffective. It applied to all children under sixteen employed in cotton mills: children were not to be apprenticed under the age of nine, and those between nine and sixteen were not to exceed 72 hours' work a week.

The 1833 Act

Lord Althorp's Factory Act of 1833 was the first effective piece of factory legislation. It applied only to the textile industry: the employment of children under nine was forbidden; those aged between nine and thirteen were not to exceed 48 hours per week, and they were to have two hours a day in school; young persons between thirteen and eighteen were not to exceed a 69 hour week; night work for all under eighteen was forbidden. Young persons were to be allowed a minimum of one and a half hours for meals per day, and eight half-holidays a year; while in the interests of safety, machines were not to be cleaned whilst in motion. In order to enforce the Act, four full-time paid inspectors were appointed. The Act is important because government officials, as opposed to local worthies, were given this responsibility. But though the four inspectors carried out their duties conscientiously and tactfully, their number was insufficient for so large a task. Also, as the compulsory registration of births did not begin until 1837, it was difficult for them to prove the illegal employment of young children.

The Ten Hour Day

The 1833 Act was brought about largely through the efforts of a heterogeneous group of agitators, including Michael Sadler, a Tory M.P. He was aided by Richard Oastler, who wrote letters in the *Leeds Mercury* on 'Yorkshire Slavery'; Robert Owen and John Fielden, both mill-owners; John Stevens; William Cobbett; John Doherty; and Anthony Ashley (later seventh Earl of Shaftesbury). Their aim was to secure a maximum ten hour day for all factory workers, and because of their agitation a Parliamentary Commission had been appointed in 1832, with Sadler as its chairman. The Report of this Commission was published in 1833, and much of the evidence, nowadays treated with some suspicion, pointed to terrible conditions in the factories. The Act of 1833 was a disappointment to the 'Ten Hours Movement' and to adult workers. They had hoped that the curtailment of hours worked by young persons would lead to a reduction in the hours of adults, but employers were able to keep the machines working by using young persons in relays. In 1844 Graham's Act was passed. This Act brought women working in textile mills under the regulations, and made the 'fencing' of machinery compulsory; the hours of the youngest children (under thirteen) were reduced to six and a half per day, together with half-a-day's schooling. But the 'ten hour' day was not achieved until three years later. An Act passed in 1847 (Fielden's Act), limited the working hours of women and young persons in textile mills to ten hours per day. Again the hopes of the promoters of the Bill that the hours of adults would be reduced were not realised. Factory owners were able to keep their mills open between 5.30 a.m. and 8.30 p.m. by employing women and children in relays. Grey's Factory Act of 1850, which extended the working day of women and young persons to ten and a half hours, stated that these hours must be worked between 6 a.m. and 6 p.m. This meant, therefore, that the hours of adult males had to be reduced as well.

Extended Legislation

These first Factory Acts applied only to textile mills. From 1850 other forms of employment were brought under government regulation. In 1860 and 1861 bleaching, dyeing and lace-making were made subject to the Acts already passed. By that time it was evident that the shorter working day had not led to a decrease in production, and mill-owners were resentful that, whilst their hours were regulated, those of workers in other industries were not. And so other industries were included in Acts passed in 1864, 1866 and 1867; in 1874 Disraeli's Factory Act made the $56\frac{1}{2}$ hour week (i.e. ten hours per day, six and a half on Saturdays) the maximum in all factories and workshops employing over fifty people. By 1914 the usual working hours were about 52 per week. By 1919 they had fallen to about 47, and by 1960 to 40 hours per week.

Other industrial legislation was concerned with the safety and health of those who worked in industry. The Collieries Act of 1842, due largely to the efforts of Anthony Ashley, forbade the employment underground of women, and of children under ten years old. An Act of 1864 laid down sixteen as the minimum age for 'climbing boys', so that in effect those eligible for the task were too large to enter chimneys. In other industries, workers were susceptible to 'occupational diseases'. Match girls, working with yellow phosphorus, contracted a disease of the jaw ('phossy jaw'); armament workers

contracted lead poisoning; potters were prone to asthma and tuberculosis. Gradually legislation was introduced enforcing minimum
standards to reduce these diseases. The Factory and Workshops Act
of 1901 codified previous regulations and, despite considerable revision since that date, remains the basis of those Acts in force today.

An illustration from the Report of a Royal Commission on Children's Employment in Mines (1842). The Report aroused such indignation that the House of
Commons passed the Collieries Act in the same year with little opposition.

WAGES

Although it is possible to state that a particular group of workers was
paid a certain amount in a given time, such figures taken by themselves are of little value, for the following reasons. Firstly, actual
wages must be related to prices, in order to determine real wages.
A man earning £1,200 a year today is not necessarily better paid than

35 *A whimsey, or rotary steam engine for raising coal at a south Staffordshire colliery, c. 1850. The loaded trolley on the far left would be lowered onto the sliding cover of the shaft and then taken on rails to the coal dump. Note the horses and carts for moving coal away from the mine. (p. 144)*

36 *Smoke pouring from the Bowling Iron Company's works at Bradford in the mid-nineteenth century. (p. 146)*

37 *An early cotton mill, built in 1783, at Darley Abbey, Derbyshire. The river is the Derwent.* (p. 42)

38 *A huge canal-side cotton mill in Union Street, Manchester, c. 1830.* (p. 158)

a man earning £400 twenty-five years ago. There is a lack of reliable statistical evidence from which real wages before 1880 can be computed. Secondly, statements of actual wages can be misleading, as in some occupations there were hidden or open benefits in addition to money payments. For example, a farm worker sometimes had the use of a cottage, rent free; railway workers obtained travel concessions; domestic servants free board and lodging. Thirdly, statements of wages do not necessarily tell us the number of hours worked (or days unemployed), or if the particular jobs carried sickness benefits, or paid holidays, or bonus rates.

These difficulties can be illustrated by taking the example of the payment of dockyard shipwrights in the eighteenth century. The simple statement is that their wages were 2s. 1d. a day. But the length of the day varied in winter and summer; they were paid an extra day for overtime or for staying on board ship overnight; they received 2½d. a week lodging allowance when living quarters in 'hulks' were not provided; 2d. per month was deducted from their pay to provide for a surgeon; they received half-pay whilst 'under cure from hurts'; and, as perquisites, until 1801 they were allowed to take away pieces of waste wood or 'chips'. (This privilege was abolished in 1801, and an allowance of 6d. per week was granted instead.)

There are two other problems in arriving at a satisfactory statement of wages. Firstly, some workers were paid under the 'Truck System', which meant payment by goods supplied from an employer's shop. This system, which developed in the late eighteenth century, arose because of a shortage of coin, and because of a lack of shops and markets in some industrial areas. Disraeli, in his novel *Sybil or the Two Nations*, writes scathingly of the corruptness of the Truck or 'Tommy' shops, and doubtless poor-quality goods were sometimes supplied. But there are few 'hard facts' on which a judgment can be made. The Truck System had disappeared by about 1870. Secondly, the distance of time between each payday could affect real wages. In many trades, the tradition was 'long pays' at intervals of three or even six months. Again, the shortage of coin was one reason for this method of payment. To use again the example of eighteenth-century shipwrights— they were paid every six months, always one quarter (three months) in arrears. Few workmen had sufficient capital to finance themselves for a long period, so that they were forced to borrow money, on which they paid interest. By 1900 'long pays' had largely disappeared, most workers then being paid either weekly, or at least fortnightly.

Did real wages rise during the nineteenth century? The following figures[1] are a guide to the general trend:

	Real Wage Index	National Income (current prices)
1780–89	100	
1790–99	94	
1800–09	92	£230 million
1810–19	96	
1820–29	133	
1830–39	126	£350 million
1840–49	136	
1850–59	135	£525 million
1860–69	146	
1870–79	180	
1880–89	207	
1890–99	253	
1914	246	

Professor Morgan gives the warning that these figures are 'a very rough approximation'. But from them we can assume that industrialisation brought a rise in the real wages of the workers. This rise was uneven; many people toiled for a pittance, in conditions which were not regulated by Act of Parliament. The general rise was not due to government action. The first state interference in wages came as a result of an exhibition mounted by the now defunct *Daily News* in 1906—'The Sweated Industries Exhibition'. The Trade Boards Act, 1909, laid down minimum wages for the four worst-paid industries, and set up a machinery for wage-negotiation in them. The Act was extended to other trades in 1913. The rise in real wages came about through the efforts of groups and individuals acting in a free society. Some of these movements are considered in the next chapter.

[1] Figures from E. V. Morgan, *A First Approach to Economics*, Pitman, 1963, and P. Deane, *British Economic Growth, 1688–1959*, Cambridge, 1962.

CHAPTER 14

The Workers in Association, 1789-1914

Benjamin Disraeli's novel *Sybil*, published in 1845, contains the now famous phrase, 'Two nations: the rich—and the poor'. If this is an over-simplification of English society of the time, it is true to say that there was a great gulf between the wealthy and the large majority of people who lived at bare subsistence level. For the working-man, unless he was exceptionally able and fortunate, there was little hope for betterment other than through higher wages. An improvement in wages could come through voluntary action by employers or by workmen combining together to force their employers into action. Though government regulation in the nineteenth century covered hours and working conditions, the state did not intervene in the matter of wages. This was considered to be a private matter, between master and man. The matter of wages was, therefore, a straight and often bitter fight. Workers' combinations developed into trade unions, defined by Sidney and Beatrice Webb as continuous associations 'of wage earners for the purpose of maintaining or improving the conditions of their working lives'. Early trade unions had to struggle for their life against government regulation and employers' hostility. From 1799 to 1824 unions were illegal; until 1871 they were allowed to exist in fact but not in law.[1] At times their future seemed so uncertain that working men joined other movements in an attempt to improve their lot. Improvements in working conditions were also brought about by individuals or by pressure groups, from a diversity of social backgrounds. Trade unions were but one of several movements which aimed at 'improvement'.

[1] See p. 178.

TRADE UNIONS UP TO 1851

The concept of concerted action by workers against their employers was not an invention of the industrial age. Grievances had often brought about strikes, especially by skilled workers who could not easily be replaced. For example, in 1665 the shipwrights of Chatham Dockyard marched to London to protest about arrears of pay (as the time lag was two years, they had a reasonable case!). In 1742 there was a strike in Portsmouth Dockyard, and a more serious one in 1775, when part of the Dockyard was set alight. In Southampton, in 1757, shipwrights went on strike when one of their number was arrested for being drunk and disorderly; in the following year these same men stopped work until a shipwright, wrongly pressed into sea service, was released by the Admiralty. Other skilled tradesmen, such as millwrights (we would call them engineers today), printers, woolcombers and carpenters had local associations or 'trade clubs' which were concerned mainly with looking after their members in times of hardship, and provided benefits in cases of sickness or death. These trade clubs were the forerunners of trade unions, but they were not trade unions according to the Webbs' definition.

The Combination Acts

The outbreak of the French Revolution in 1789, and the spread of ideas of the rights of man and of equality, coupled with the over-throw of the monarchy and the old régime in France, made the British government fearful of popular movements and associations. In 1795 public meetings demanding reform were in effect banned by the Seditious Meetings and Assemblies Act. In 1799 London mill-owners, disturbed by the strength and vigour of a combination of journeymen who usually met at the Bell Inn near the Old Bailey, petitioned Parliament to suppress the society. The Prime Minister, William Pitt, immediately introduced a Bill which was extended to include all trades. The Combination Act of 1799 declared that combinations of workmen or employers were illegal; infringements were to be punishable by imprisonment. In the following year the Act was modified in order to prevent an employer acting as a magistrate in any case brought against a workman in the same trade.

The Combination Acts were in force until 1824, but they did not prevent the formation of combinations. In some parts of the country trade unions continued openly, whilst in others they were driven underground. It is important to remember that until 1815 Britain was engaged in a desperate war against France; that from France emanated ideas of liberty and equality—laudable in themselves, but viewed with suspicion and fear, and regarded as treasonable and dangerous by a government acting in a panic. This explains, but does not excuse, the passing of the Combination Acts. The Acts were applied most rigorously against the factory workers of Lancashire and Yorkshire. Two Bolton weavers were imprisoned for organising an association, but such punishments did not deter their fellows from vigorous action. There were many strikes: in Portsmouth Dockyard in 1801, among the spinners of Manchester in 1810 and the Scottish weavers in 1812, and a wave of strikes in the textile areas in 1819. In each case, leaders were imprisoned for periods up to two years. In the older skilled trades, combinations continued with little inter- ference from the law. A notable exception occurred in 1810, when the compositors of *The Times* were tried before Sir John Silvester (known as 'Bloody Black Jack'), and received sentences up to two years. On the other hand, the millwrights continued to combine, and were able to obtain a minimum wage and a reduction in hours.

Repeal of the Combination Acts

The end of the Napoleonic Wars in 1815 helped to cause a severe trade depression, with unemployment and a temporary fall in real wages. This depression coincided with further repressive measures by the government. One of the 'Six Acts', passed in 1819, banned 'seditious meetings'. From 1822 the economic and political climate improved, so that the trade-union movement was able to make some headway. The first success was the repeal of the Combination Acts in 1824. Francis Place (1771-1854), a tailor with a shop in Charing Cross Road, London, was largely responsible for engineering the repeal. Place wrote propaganda articles in newspapers, and gained the support of a number of influential men, including the Radical M.P. Joseph Hume. He organised a fund which enabled workmen to travel to London to give evidence before a Committee of the House of Commons set up to investigate the Combination Acts. These men, well drilled by Place, created a good impression when they were called as witnesses. Hume persuaded the Committee to submit a resolution to the House that the Acts should be repealed and cleverly coupled this with the repeal of an Act forbidding the emigration of artisans. The resolution was carried without a division, at a time when many opponents of repeal were not present. The repeal of the Combination Acts was followed by a wave of strikes, and in the following year an Act was passed allowing combination and peaceful bargaining for better conditions, but introducing penalties for 'molesting' or 'obstructing' during a strike. The important principle remained—the right to combine in unions was upheld.

Owen and the G.N.C.T.U.

From 1825 to 1829 there was a further depression which prevented the growth of trade unions. Then unions entered a new and disastrous phase in which idealistic and impracticable schemes were launched. Some dreamers had conceived a plan whereby all the workers in Britain would combine together, and their united strength would force employers to concede better wages and conditions. (An earlier scheme, organised by John Gast, a London shipwright, in 1818, under the name of 'Philanthropic Hercules', had failed.) In 1829 the cotton spinners of Manchester, under their secretary John Doherty, attempted to form a national union to be called the Grand General Union. This did not materialise, but Doherty, in 1830, formed the National Association for the Protection of Labour, an attempt to form 'one big union'. Although this movement started brightly, with members in Manchester, Birmingham, Leeds, Glasgow and Belfast, and though at one time it is reputed to have had 100,000 members, by 1834 it had failed. In the same year the most spectacular (though not the most successful) of all unions was formed. This was the Grand National Consolidated Trades Union, and its founder was Robert Owen. This Union, formed in February 1834, was intended to bring about a new system of society through an idea that had been discussed openly during the previous two years. All the workers of the land were to cease work for a 'sacred month' or 'national holiday'; industry would be ruined, and the capitalist system destroyed; the government would collapse. Government and industrial resources would then pass into the hands of the people; industry would be re-organised on a co-operative basis, and employers, if they wished, could become managers. This idea was attractive to Owen, who believed fervently in the need for a new environment, a new political system, and the public ownership of industry. The appeal to the labouring masses was instantaneous; here was hope for an end of their misery. In 1833, before the official formation of the G.N.C.T.U., lodges were formed all over England, comprising members from all trades; there was even a Lodge of Ancient Virgins. The movement alarmed both the Home Secretary, Lord Melbourne, and local magistrates. Impatient workers, believing the millennium was at hand, staged a series of sporadic strikes, instead of a concerted 'national holiday'. The authorities were already acting swiftly. Employers answered strikes by locking their works to employees who joined the Union. Others demanded that workers should sign a document declaring that they would not join a union. At Derby 1,500 workers were locked out, as were 1,300 hosiers in Leicester, and builders, calico printers and engineers in Glasgow. The funds of the Union could not support these for long, but the employers had sufficient capital to hold out. Meanwhile the G.N.C.T.U. suffered another blow through the trial of six farm labourers at Dorchester. George and James Loveless, who lived in the small Dorset village of Tolpuddle, dismayed because their employer had reduced their wages, inquired about joining the G.N.C.T.U. They were visited by Union officials, who instructed the Loveless brothers to form a lodge. In order to stimulate interest, an initiation ceremony was devised, whereby new members were blindfolded and swore an oath of secrecy. In February 1834 George Loveless and five others were arrested, and charged with contravening an Act of 1797 forbidding 'unlawful oaths'. Despite nation-wide protests, which included a petition with 250,000 signatures and mammoth demonstrations, the 'Tolpuddle Martyrs' were tried, found guilty and sentenced to seven years' hard labour in Australia. Public opinion was such that the men were reprieved in 1836, but the slowness of communications and transport in those days prevented their return home before 1838. This episode, and other difficulties, led to the disbanding of the G.N.C.T.U. in August 1834. It had failed because poor communications and organisations led to a series of sporadic strikes instead of a concerted one: because the workers were more interested in immediate gains such as higher pay and shorter hours than in Owen's ultimate aim; because the G.N.C.T.U. lacked the funds to sustain a long strike; because one 'big union' had to come after and not before the establishment of strong separate unions; and because action by the authorities, such as lock-outs and the punishment of the Tolpuddle Martyrs, frightened the workmen. With the collapse of the G.N.C.T.U., which has been aptly called the 'South Sea Bubble of British trade unionism', trade unions went into the shadows for nearly twenty years. Some separate unions for the skilled trades remained, but their aims and activities were limited.

The early trade-union movement had failed for a variety of reasons. First, unions were restricted by law and leaders were imprisoned. Second, they had aroused the hostility of government and employers who feared revolutionary aims. Third, the labouring classes had no internal unity, but were suspicious of those in other trades and other areas. It should be remembered that the majority of factory workers were women and children, and most were ill-educated. Fourth, the leaders of the unions lacked the experience, resources and skill needed for such large-scale undertakings. Fifth, because of the uncertainties of employment, most workers were afraid that action on their part would lead to their dismissal.

CHARTISM

Direct industrial action had failed. The working class now tried political action—to reform the system of government so that the lives of the labouring poor would be improved. A Reform Act had been passed in 1832 which made the franchise less narrow, but in most boroughs the working man was not enfranchised. Because of a property qualification, he could not become an M.P.—an impractible idea anyway in those days as M.P.s were unpaid. In short, to the working class, political power was in the hands of the 'other nation'— which cared not for them, or, if it did, could not understand their problems.

> How little can the rich man know
> Of what the poor man feels,
> When Want, like some dark demon foe,
> Nearer and nearer steals.

> *He* never saw his darlings lie
> Shivering, the flags his bed;

He never heard that maddening cry
'Daddy, a bit of bread!'[1]

Political representation for the working man by the working man was the need. This opinion found expression in the foundation of the London Working Men's Association in 1836 by William Lovett (1800–77), Henry Hetherington (1792–1847) and others. Lovett, with help from Francis Place, drew up a Charter containing six points: votes for all adult males (female suffrage was considered but not included), annual general elections, voting by secret ballot, equal electoral districts, payment of M.P.s and the abolition of the property qualification for M.P.s. Lovett and the L.M.W.A. were joined by other groups who were working towards the same ends. In Birmingham, the Political Union, led by the banker Thomas Attwood, was revived. In Manchester, where in 1837 50,000 workers were unemployed or on short time, a movement for reform was led by Feargus O'Connor, a former Irish M.P. and founder of a newspaper called the *Northern Star*. These three elements joined together in 1838, when a meeting was held in Birmingham at which Lovett's Charter was adopted. In the following year another meeting took place in London. By that time Chartist groups had developed in many of the industrial towns, such as Glasgow, Leeds and Leicester, as well as in rural areas. The leaders of the Chartist movement had a common aim, but differed in method. Their aim was to better the lot of 'the industrious classes'. Lovett believed that this could come through political representation and education, obtained for the poor by peaceful means. Attwood thought that currency reform would end trade depressions which created such misery for the poor. In the north, where the effects of the New Poor Law of 1834[2] were particularly severe, a rapid mitigation of conditions was sought, and violent means were proposed if the government would not agree to the Charter. But to all groups, the reform of Parliament was a means only, and not an end. The appeal made by some Chartist leaders was to the 'stomach'. Stephens, speaking in Manchester in 1838 said, 'The question of universal suffrage is a knife-and-fork question, a bread and cheese question. . . . If any man ask what I mean by universal

[1] From *Mary Barton*, by Mrs Gaskell (quoted in A. Briggs (ed.), *Chartist Studies*, Macmillan, 1962).
[2] See p. 188.

suffrage, I mean to say that every working man in the land has a right to a good coat on his back, a good hat on his head, a good roof for the shelter of his household, a good dinner upon his table, no more work than will keep him in health while at it, and as much wages as will keep him in the enjoyment of plenty, and all the blessings of life that reasonable men could desire.'[1]

The defeat of the Chartist rising in Newport. The thirty soldiers who broke up the crowd of some 4,000 miners were hidden in the hotel.

The Chartist Petition was presented to Parliament in 1839, but was rejected in the House of Commons by 235 votes to 46. This was followed by riots in Bull Ring, Birmingham. Constables were sent from London to deal with the disorders, and Chartist leaders, including Lovett, were arrested there. In Newport, Monmouthshire, a group marching to attempt to free imprisoned Chartists was met by troops who fired on the crowd, inflicting some casualties. The leaders of this Newport Rising were arrested and transported to Australia. By the end of 1839 the Chartist movement had almost died down. It was revived in 1842, when a second Petition, with three million signatures was presented to Parliament, and rejected by 287 votes to 49. This was followed by strikes and riots in the industrial regions of Lancashire, Yorkshire, Wales, Scotland and the midlands. In Lanca-

[1] *Manchester Guardian*, quoted in A. Briggs, op. cit.

shire strikers removed the plugs from the boilers of steam engines—hence the name 'Plug Plot'. The third and last Chartist Petition was presented in 1848, when Feargus O'Connor, then M.P. for Nottingham, took a mammoth document, transported in three cabs, to the House of Commons. O'Connor claimed that it contained five and a half million signatures, but a Select Committee, appointed to examine the Petition, reported that there were just under two million. Of these, some were signed in the name of 'Victoria Rex', 'F. M. Duke of Wellington', 'Sir Robert Peel', 'No Cheese', 'Pug Nose' and 'Flat Nose'. Despite O'Connor's eloquence, it was received with scorn, and rejected by 222 votes to 17. This Petition of 1848 coincided with revolutionary movements throughout western Europe; like 1839 and 1842, 1848 was also a year when business was slackening.

Importance and Reasons for Failure

The Chartist movement is important because it was the first movement in modern British history to be led and organised by working men; because it had an influence on socialist movements in Europe and America later in the century; and because, except for annual elections, the Chartist demands later became law. The Chartist leaders must have felt their movement to have failed. But they had drawn attention to the needs for reform. The Chartists were ahead of their time. They were demanding reforms which were opposed by the government and by the large majority of the enfranchised. It was a provincial movement which had insufficient support in London; its leaders lacked unity, and the resources to carry out ambitious plans. The reforms of Peel (1841–46) and an upward turn in the trade cycle made the life of 'the army of misery' a little better. The failure of Chartism to attract middle-class support was a further reason for the movement's lack of success. The Anti-Corn Law League, which was at its height from 1838 to 1846, attracted considerable middle-class support, to the detriment of the Chartist movement. Further, those of the middle class who might have sympathised with Chartism were frightened by the violent language of some of the Chartist leaders. The forgeries in the third Petition dealt a final blow to an already dying movement, although Chartist conventions were held up to 1858. After 1850, the working classes were able to achieve some of their aims through the revival of trade unions.

TRADE UNIONS, 1851–89

Model Unions

The second half of the nineteenth century saw the establishment of a strong trade-union movement. By 1851, the year of the Great Exhibition, the second generation of factory workers, more accustomed to the discipline of industrial work and to life in towns, was better able to adjust itself to the necessity of a capitalist system. Trade-union leaders were able to persuade the rank and file that hostility towards employers was not always the best policy. The new unions which developed in the third quarter of the nineteenth century are usually called 'model' unions. These model unions, for skilled workers only, adopted a moderate approach, and attempted to obtain better conditions through co-operation with employers.

The A.S.E.

The first model union was the Amalgamated Society of Engineers, founded in 1851. This union, as its name implies, was formed by the joining together of several smaller societies, and its full title was 'The Amalgamated Society of Engineers, Machinists, Smiths, Millwrights and Pattern-Makers'. It had several new features which were copied by other unions. It was exclusive to skilled men (in 1851 membership totalled 11,000). Members paid 1s. a week subscription, which at the outset gave the union a weekly income of £550. The A.S.E. had a full-time paid secretary, with head-quarters in London. It helped members in times of trouble from a benevolent fund to which members paid 3d. a quarter. Typical benefits were 10s. a week for 12 weeks for unemployment, 12s. a week for 26 weeks for illness, a pension of 8s. a week, and a death gratuity of £12. The funds could also be used to help members to sustain a strike. But as policy was in the hands of the central office, unofficial strikes received no support from the fund. The paid officials made a practice of visiting firms where strike-action was threatened, and interviewing employers in order to try to obtain better conditions without resorting to a strike. Much tact and patience was required before employers were convinced of the right of union officials to interfere in what they regarded as a private matter between themselves and their men. Also, union officials had to persuade their members that there were other means of reaching an agreement than by costly strikes.

The Junta

In time the secretaries of the large unions, all with headquarters in London, developed the practice of conferring together in order to formulate a common policy. This 'unofficial cabinet', known as the 'Clique' or the 'Dirty Pack' by contemporary opponents, was called the 'Junta' by the Webbs, the historians of the trade-union movement. The most important members were William Allan of the Engineers, Robert Applegarth (Carpenters), Daniel Guile (Ironfounders), Edwin Coulson (London Bricklayers) and George Odger (Boot and Shoe Workers). In 1860 they formed the London Trades Council, with Odger as secretary.

The Junta set themselves limited but realistic aims, such as stamp-out 'truck', ending 'long pays' and removing legal disabilities from the working man. This approach to unionism has led historians to differ about its wisdom. Some have thought the Junta followed 'a statesmanlike policy', whilst others have called them 'the servile generation'. At least this cautious policy showed some success. In 1867 the Second Reform Bill was passed by Disraeli's Conservative government. (A similar measure introduced by Gladstone, the Liberal leader, had been defeated in the previous year.) This Act gave the vote in the towns to all male householders (i.e. 'fathers'), and to lodgers who paid at least £10 a year in rent; in the rural areas there was a narrower franchise, extending only to those who occupied premises of a ratcable value of £12 a year or more—which excluded the farm labourers. Thus in the towns, where trade-union strength lay, a large number of working men had the vote for the first time. This Act was passed partly as a result of trade-union pressure. In the same year, 1867, the Master and Servant Act was passed. This gave a measure of equality to both employer and employee in law; in particular it rescinded earlier measures whereby a workman breaking his contract was guilty of a criminal offence, punishable by imprisonment. Under the new Act, a workman could be imprisoned only for damage to property or injury to persons.

Changes in the Law, 1867–75

For some of the rank and file in the unions, progress was too slow. A conference of union delegates was held in Sheffield in 1866 to discuss means of pursuing a more vigorous policy. Later in the same year occurred the so-called 'Sheffield outrages', actions by a minority to force 'blacklegs' or non-union men to join. This militant group resorted to such measures as damaging blacklegs' tools, and in one case dropped a can of gunpowder down a non-unionist's chimney. These incidents led to the setting-up of a Royal Commission to inquire into the trade-union movement. At the same time, unions suffered another blow through the ruling of the judges in the case of *Hornby* v *Close*, 1867. The Boilermakers' Society brought an action against its Bradford secretary for the misappropriation of union funds, believing that they were protected by a clause in the Friendly Societies' Act of 1855. The judges ruled that, as unions acted 'in restraint of trade', they had no legal existence, and could not therefore sue in the courts. The subtle distinction between an existence in fact (unions were allowed to exist in fact by the Act of 1825), and an existence in law must be understood. The ruling meant that unions could not be protected from dishonest officials. Also, it gave hope to some employers who pressed for unions to be declared unlawful. Under the doubtful threat of a Royal Commission and an uncertain legality, trade-union delegates met in Manchester in 1868 at a conference which is now generally regarded as the first meeting of the Trades Union Congress (T.U.C.). The unions arranged for evidence to be laid before the Commission. As a result of the report of the Royal Commission, two Acts were passed by Gladstone's Liberal government in 1871. The Trade Unions Act gave unions an existence in law, allowed them to register under the Friendly Societies' Act, and protected their funds from dishonest officials. The Criminal Law Amendment Act imposed severe penalties for 'peaceful picketing' which had been legalised in 1859. The Act contained vague phrases such as 'molestation' and 'watching and besetting'; under it a group of women strikers was committed to prison for calling 'Bah' to a blackleg. Gladstone's government, by giving with one hand and taking with the other, led to union support for Disraeli at the 1874 election. In 1875 Disraeli repealed the Criminal Law Amendment Act, thus legalising 'peaceful' picketing. In the same year the Employers and Workmen Act, which replaced the Master and Servant Act of 1867, made breach of contract a civil offence, and therefore punishable by fine.

A Quiet Period

By 1875 the 'model' unions had established themselves, and had obtained their limited objectives. Although accurate figures for the total trade-union membership at that time are not available, the T.U.C. claimed to represent 1,100,000 members, the majority of whom were skilled men. One union, the National Agricultural Labourers' Union, had a short life. It was founded in 1872 by Joseph Arch, a Warwickshire labourer and Primitive Methodist preacher. By the end of the year this union had 100,000 members, but employers met demands for higher wages with lock-outs. After some short-lived successes, the union foundered in 1876, when it was unable to meet large demands on its strike-fund. The 1870's saw the end of the prosperous era of farming known as 'High Farming'; prices for agricultural produce were falling, and cheap labour could be obtained from Ireland. The union was revived in the 1890's—but for the time being unions remained associations of town workers. Membership of all unions declined in the 1870's, but numbers rose again in the following decade with the development of a new type of union.

NEW UNIONISM 1889–1914

New Unionism is the name given to unions of unskilled or semi-skilled men, which used militant tactics to attain their ends. They developed at a time when socialism, dormant in Britain since the 1840's, re-appeared. The new unions were led by socialists, and the two movements are closely connected. The need for new unions came from several circumstances. The model unions were almost exclusively for skilled men and their leaders were against government regulation of industry. The falling prices of the 'Great Depression' meant that higher wages for the unskilled could not be obtained by moderate means. Socialism, the state-ownership of the means of production, had an obvious appeal to those who suffered unemployment during trade depression in a free economy. The nationalisation of the land (an old Chartist dream) and of industry appeared to offer a solution to the problems of the poor. The new unions were to question the entire structure of society; ideas were fed to them by middle-class intellectuals. The Social Democratic Federation, founded in 1881 by a London stockbroker, H. M. Hyndman, and the Fabian

Society, founded in 1884, were two organisations which helped to spread socialist ideas. The S.D.F. was a Marxist society which advocated revolution of the working class to bring about the inevitable overthrow of capitalism. The Fabians, of whom G. B. Shaw, H. G. Wells, and Sidney and Beatrice Webb were influential early leaders, believed that socialism could be brought about by peaceful evolution.

Strikes, 1888–89

The first successful strike by unskilled workers was brought about indirectly by the activities of the Fabian Society. At one of their lectures it was pointed out that the firm of Bryant and May paid high dividends, but very low wages. Annie Besant, a Fabian, and editor of a paper called *The Link*, interviewed girl workers, and published an article entitled *White Slavery in London*. This led to a strike by the match-girls in 1888, and they obtained a rise in wages. This 'victory' had been achieved with no funds other than voluntary subscriptions from sympathisers, and without an organised union (the Match-Girls' Union was formed after the strike, with Annie Besant as secretary). Their success inspired others to try like measures.

In 1887 Ben Tillett, a labourer in the tea-warehouses, had formed a union for London dockers. In 1889 he persuaded the men at the West India Docks to strike for a minimum wage of 6d. an hour (the 'dockers' tanner') and a guarantee of four hours' work each shift. Most of London's dockworkers followed Tillett's lead, and work in the port came to a standstill. Tillett was helped by two members of the S.D.F., Tom Mann and John Burns (Burns was a powerful orator who was known as 'The Man with the Red Flag'). Many Londoners sympathised with the dockers' demands, and £49,000 was subscribed by the general public to support them, while Australia sent £30,000 by telegraph. Cardinal Manning acted as mediator, and the employers granted the 'dockers' tanner'.

The success of these two strikes led to the rapid growth of unions for unskilled workers. Also, clerical workers and 'black-coated' workers organised themselves for the first time. In 1892 the trade unions had 1,500,000 members but membership fell in succeeding years. In 1893 there was another wave of strikes owing to demands by employers for a reduction of wages in view of a fall in profits.

39 New Lanark Mills, on the river Clyde, founded in 1784 by Richard Arkwright and David Dale. Robert Owen, Dale's son-in-law, built houses and schools there, and carried out social experiments. (p. 160)

40 St. Rollox Chemical Works, Glasgow, c. 1850. The chimneys were high in order to dispel dangerous waste gases. (p. 152)

41 *Railway bridge over Firth of Forth, opened 1890.* (p. 149)

42 *Road bridge over Firth of Forth, opened 1964.*

In some trades, notably coalmining, prolonged strikes did not prevent a reduction in wages.

Trade-union Interest in Politics

This adverse trend reinforced the arguments of those of the working class who advocated a working-class political party, with representation in the House of Commons. The Reform Act of 1884 enfranchised male householders in the rural areas (those in the towns had obtained the vote in 1867), and the property qualification, one of the Chartist targets, had been abolished in 1858, though M.P.s received no payment until 1911. Therefore, providing some funds for the support of M.P.s could be raised, there was nothing to prevent working men from seeking election. In 1885 and 1886 there were a handful of working-class M.P.s, but they sat with the Liberals; their election did not satisfy those who wanted a party to represent 'Labour'.

In 1888 the Scottish miners supported their own candidate, James Keir Hardie (1856-1915). Keir Hardie had started work in Glasgow at the age of seven; at ten he became a trapper in the mines; at the age of twenty he was dismissed for acting as the miners' spokesman. His mother had taught him to read, and he continued his education at evening school. On his dismissal from the mine he earned a living as a journalist. He was a non-conformist, a teetotaller and a pacifist. At the by-election at Mid-Lanark in 1888, where he stood against a Conservative and a Liberal, his election manifesto included an eight-hour day for miners, insurance and pensions for miners, and a Ministry of Mines. He finished at the bottom of the poll, with 617 votes. Later in the year the Scottish Labour Party was formed, with Keir Hardie as its first Secretary. In the 1892 election three independent Labour M.P.s were elected, Keir Hardie for West Ham, John Burns for Battersea, and Havelock Wilson for Middlesbrough. Keir Hardie shocked his fellow members by arriving in a cloth cap (instead of the then traditional top-hat), and wearing a red tie. In 1893 as a result of a conference held in Bradford, attended by representatives of the Scottish Labour Party, the S.D.F., the Fabians, and the trade unions, the Independent Labour Party was formed (the first word signified independence of the Conservative and Liberal parties). In 1895 the I.L.P. contested 27 seats, but all their candidates (including

Keir Hardie) were defeated. Keir Hardie saw that the need was for a party more closely connected with the T.U.C. In 1900 a delegate conference was held in London, at which the I.L.P., the trade unions, the S.D.F. and the Fabians were represented. From this meeting the Labour Representation Committee was formed, with James Ramsay MacDonald as its first Secretary. The S.D.F. left the party in 1901, and the L.R.C. adopted the name 'Labour Party' in 1906. In 1902 two of their candidates were successful, one of whom was Keir Hardie, who was to remain M.P. for Merthyr Tydfil until his death in 1915. In the 1906 election they won 29 seats, and John Burns was offered a seat in the Cabinet, as President of the Local Government Board, by the Liberal government. Funds were obtained from two sources: in 1903 all members of the Labour Party contributed 1d. a week, whilst all trade unionists were asked to pay a 'political levy' in addition to their union membership fee.

Taff Vale and Osborne Judgments

The political representation was useful to the unions in the first decade of the twentieth century, when two verdicts went against them in the courts. In 1901 the Taff Vale Railway Company sued the Amalgamated Society of Railway Servants for damages of £23,000 for loss of revenue during a strike. The courts found the A.S.R.S. liable for damages. This verdict meant that no union would dare to stage a strike. The Liberal government reversed the Taff Vale verdict by the Trade Disputes Act of 1906. The second case threatened the 'political levy'. W. V. Osborne, the Secretary of the Walthamstow branch of the A.S.R.S., supported by the *Daily Express*, challenged the right of trade unions to spend any part of their funds for political purposes. After protracted legal proceedings, in 1909 the House of Lords gave judgment in favour of Osborne. This verdict was reversed by the Trade Union Act of 1913, which stated that trade unions could use their funds for political purposes, providing a majority of their members agreed by ballot, and that individuals who did not wish to contribute were allowed to 'contract out'.

Syndicalism, 1910–14

The years immediately preceding the 1914–18 war were ones of great industrial unrest and bitter conflict between employers and workers. Whilst the total membership of trade unions grew from two and a half million in 1910 to over four million in 1913, the number of unions fell because of amalgamation. Trade-union leaders could therefore control larger numbers of men. Union leaders throughout the western world were advocating a policy of no compromise with the employers. The Industrial Workers of the World was founded by the American Marxist, Daniel de Leon, on the principle that 'the working class and the employing class have nothing in common'. In France, Georges Sorel was advocating Robert Owen's ideas of the overthrow of the capitalist system by a general strike. These ideas were given some publicity in England by Tom Mann who, in 1910, published a monthly journal called *Industrial Syndicalist*. In 1911 the sailing of the new White Star liner *Olympic* was delayed by a seamen's strike, which resulted in their getting higher wages. This was followed by strikes at London and Liverpool docks, and by transport workers all over the country. Tom Mann helped to organise these, whilst Ben Tillett was active in the London docks. Tempers were frayed, and in Liverpool two men were killed in a clash between troops and rioters. Later in 1911 there was a national railway strike, which ended after two days when the employers agreed to recognise the railway unions as official representatives of the employees. In 1912 there were strikes in the coal mines and the docks. By 1913 trade-union leaders were considering a 'general strike' of coal miners, railwaymen and transport workers (these three unions were known as 'the triple alliance'). Mann argued that such action would bring about the 'elimination of the employer', and that workers in each industry should combine 'to fight, to gain control of, and then to administer that industry'. These extreme views were not held by the rank and file of the trade-union movement, and the 'general strike' did not in fact take place until 1926. When the war began in 1914, both employers and men had a more dangerous enemy to fight.

Employers' Associations

The organisation of labour led to the growth of employers' associations. These were formed initially to show a common front against the unions. One of the first was the Clyde Shipbuilders' and Engineers' Association, formed in the 1860's. This was extended in 1896 into the Employers' Federation of Engineering Associations.

Builders, colliery owners and others developed similar organisations. These federations were concerned with the control of prices as well as with fighting the unions. Their development meant that both sides of the industry were represented at a national level. Industrial relations were reaching a new phase. The workman would not go cap in hand to his employer to ask for a rise for himself. National scales were negotiated, through reason or by threat. The struggle between the sides of industry was intensified rather than diminished by this development, since the division between the 'two sides' was underlined. The next generation was to try to re-orientate both management and men to a conception of 'partnership'.

CHAPTER 15

Social Problems before 1914

THE POOR LAW

However bad the conditions of the working population, those of the destitute, the 'casualties of life', were far worse. Destitution, the complete inability to provide the bare necessities of life, was the lot of several categories of people. Very young children, too young to work, either orphaned or abandoned; those who were sick; those who were aged; and those who were unable or unwilling to find employment—all needed care. The problem of the poor had always been present, but during the nineteenth century it was made more acute by industrialisation, which led to more pronounced trade cycles.

The 'Old Poor Law' before 1834

During the eighteenth century the poor were cared for under the system laid down by two statutes passed during the reign of Elizabeth I, in 1597 and 1601. This was known in the nineteenth century as the 'Old Poor Law'. The Elizabethan Poor Law made the parish the unit of administration. Each parish had to appoint two unpaid Overseers of the Poor who were to collect a compulsory poor rate from householders. These contributions were given by the Overseers to the sick, the aged, and the destitute orphans. The 'able-bodied' undeserving poor, 'sturdy rogues and vagabonds', were to be sent to 'Houses of Correction'. The two important principles to note are, first, that the Poor Law was not administered nationally but locally; secondly, that a distinction was made between the impotent and able-bodied pauper. These principles were to remain as part of the English poor relief system for three centuries. It was intended that the able-bodied should receive relief only in return for work done in a House of Correction.

In practice, there were insufficient 'workhouses' for this to be rigidly applied.

Only minor modifications were made to the Poor Law during the seventeenth and eighteenth centuries. As those parishes which treated paupers generously attracted 'outsiders', the Settlement Act was passed in 1662. This Act defined 'settlement' in a parish as applying to those who were born there, or who had served an apprenticeship there, or owned a house there, or, in the case of a woman, who had married a resident. Paupers who were not 'members' of a parish had to return to their own parish in order to gain relief. This Act had serious defects. It led to shady and inhuman practices—for instance, the removal of potential paupers, such as unmarried pregnant women —and it hindered the mobility of labour, for men were hesitant to leave their own locality in search of work. Gradually the Overseers of the Poor began to issue 'certificates' to those able-bodied paupers who wanted to travel in search of work. These certificates were legalised by the Third Settlement Act of 1697, whereby paupers who left their own parish under a certificate, and were unable to find work in another parish, were to be returned to their parish of origin, which had to pay any expenses incurred.

In 1722 an Act was passed to encourage parishes to build work-houses. In practice, not many did. They preferred to pay contractors a fixed annual sum to care for the paupers in the neighbourhood. Such institutions, which soon became 'mixed', i.e. housing men and women, old and young, sick and able-bodied, were a source of dread in the eighteenth century. Crabbe, in his poem *The Village*, wrote powerfully about the appalling conditions.

> Theirs is yon house that holds the Parish-Poor,
> Whose walls of mud scarce bear the broken door;
> There, where the putrid vapours, flagging, play;
> There Children dwell who know no Parents' care;
> Parents, who know no Children's love, dwell there!
> Heart-broken Matrons on their joyless bed,
> Forsaken Wives and Mothers never wed. . . .

Gilbert's Act, passed in 1782, allowed parishes to join together for the building and maintenance of workhouses. Hence these institutions became known as 'Unions'. Gilbert's Act stated that workhouses should be reserved for the impotent, and that the able-bodied pauper should be found work, or given relief outside the workhouse. But in fact few parishes adopted the principles laid down in Gilbert's Act.

The Speenhamland System, 1795

The principle of a more humane approach towards the able-bodied poor was, however, adopted in some parts of England in dealing with the problem of farm workers. The outbreak of war in 1793 led to rising prices, and wages did not rise as fast. We have earlier seen[1] how in 1795 the Berkshire magistrates, meeting at Speenhamland in order to deal with distress among employed farm workers, decided to use the poor-relief money to supplement wages, where these were considered to be insufficient. This Speenhamland System, intended as a local measure, was adopted by magistrates over much of southern England, and remained in force until 1834. It is probable that it was intended as 'an insurance against unrest', and it did make some contribution to that end. It restrained any tendency to violent revolution; it saved some families from starvation. It made every rate-payer contribute to those in distress, and made them aware of the problem. But the Speenhamland System also had defects. It had a depressing effect on wages, as employers realised that these would be raised to the minimum from the poor rates; those employers who were able to offer higher wages were reluctant to do so, for they were contributing, through the rates, to the support of workers employed by other farmers. Generally, the big employer gained more from the System than did the small employer. Further, the System was demoralising for the recipient, since however hard he worked, his wages remained the same: a whole class had to bear the stigma of living 'on the parish'. The rate-payers also had cause for complaint, as the amount of money needed to relieve the poor rose from £2 million in 1784, to £4 million in 1803, £6½ million in 1813, and £8 million in 1818. The rise in rates, together with the spread of Malthusian ideas—the Speenhamland System was thought to encourage the poor to have large families, and to prevent the migration of labour from an 'overpopulated' countryside to the towns—led to an attack on this method of poor relief.

[1] See pp. 78–9.

The New Poor Law, 1834

In 1832 a Royal Commission was appointed to inquire into the working of poor relief. A very talented Commission was appointed, including Nassau Senior, an economist and former Professor in the University of Oxford, and Edwin Chadwick, the Secretary of the Commission. The problem before the Commission was how to deal with the 'allowance' system, which, it was feared, would spread into all forms of employment. The Report, 8,000 pages long, was published in 1834, and its findings were embodied in the Poor Law Amendment Act of 1834. The Act dealt with the administration of poor relief by the appointment of three Commissioners, with offices in London, to supervise the work of Boards of Guardians who had responsibility for each district. The parish, too small a unit, was superseded. It was hoped that this would lead to economy, and to a uniform system. Once more a distinction was made between the impotent and the able-bodied. The impotent were to receive 'outdoor relief', that is money or goods which they could obtain whilst continuing to live in their own homes. The able-bodied poor were not to receive outdoor relief, but were to be sent to the workhouse. Conditions in the workhouses were to be made less 'eligible' or desirable than the standard of life of the worst paid workmen. The assumption underlying the principle of 'less eligibility' was that distress was due to personal defects rather than to external economic causes, and that if conditions in the workhouses were made unpleasant, people would try to avoid them.

The workhouses were soon called 'Bastilles'. Conditions were such that they deterred those who entered them. A typical diet was as follows:

Men: Breakfasts—6 oz. bread and $1\frac{1}{2}$ oz. cheese. Dinners—Sundays, 5 oz. meat and $\frac{1}{2}$ lb. potatoes. Tuesdays and Thursdays, ditto. Other days, $1\frac{1}{2}$ pints soup. Supper—days on which there was meat for dinner, 6 oz. bread and $1\frac{1}{2}$ pints broth; other days, 6 oz. bread and 2 oz. cheese.

A meagre diet was coupled with a harsh discipline. 'Disorderly' or 'refractory' paupers were made to wear 'a dress different from that of other inmates', and could be confined in a separate room for a maximum of one and two days respectively. Families were separated, meals were taken in silence, and rules and regulations made the inmates more like wrongdoers than 'casualties'. The opening chapters of Dickens' *Oliver Twist*, published in 1838, give a highly-coloured picture of life in an orphanage of the period.

Opposition to the New Poor Law was strongest in the north of England, where industrial workers who were temporarily unemployed were faced with the workhouse or no relief. This opposition was supported by men such as William Cobbett, M.P. for Oldham, and John Fielden, the factory owner. Anti-Poor Law meetings were held, at which fiery speeches against the Commissioners (the 'Three Bashaws of Somerset House') were made.

Some obvious criticisms can be levelled at the Poor Law Amendment Act. It ignored the problems of the sick and aged; it ignored temporary unemployment; in practice its principles of 'no outdoor relief' to the able-bodied could not be applied as there were not enough workhouse places in times of depression. In 1839 there were 98,000 paupers in workhouses, and 560,000 receiving outdoor relief; in 1844 the numbers were 231,000 and 1,247,000 respectively; in 1848, 306,000 and 1,877,000. In 1852 it was officially admitted that it was 'not expedient absolutely to prohibit outdoor relief even to the able-bodied'. But the Act did some good. The Speenhamland System came to an end, so that in the south of England agricultural wages were no longer made up 'on the parish'. The Act produced a more uniform system, and a more efficient administration than the parish could provide. It led to the growth of paid officials, and established the importance of central control. The authority of the Poor Law Commissioners grew largely as a result of the work of Edwin Chadwick who, disappointed at not being appointed as a Commissioner, became the Secretary. The country was divided into nine districts, each with an assistant Commissioner, and gradually, and not without much opposition, the 20,000 parishes were made to apply orders from above. The Poor Law Commissioners, whose offices were in Somerset House in London, were not part of a government department; in time they were given other duties, such as supervision of the registration of births and deaths in 1837. In 1847 they were superseded by the Poor Law Board, which became a government department under the name of the Local Government Board in 1871. (This department became the Ministry of Health in 1917.)

'Christian Charity'

The framers of the 1834 Poor Law envisaged that the poor would receive voluntary help, as well as 'official' help. Those who had plenty would give succour to the poor—this was an age-old tradition of charity. In the second half of the nineteenth century, apart from the organised Christian churches which continued what help they could, several new movements were founded. A brief description of two will serve as examples. Dr Thomas John Barnardo ('the father of nobody's children'), appalled by the fate of orphans, began in 1866 the movement which bears his name, when he rented a house in Stepney for twelve boys placed under the care of foster-parents. In 1870 he opened the first of his 'great houses', and he spent thirty years in raising money to build more homes for boys without parents. By 1906 there were 27,000 destitute children being cared for in Barnardo Homes. William Booth (1829–1912) was a Methodist minister who was shocked by the 'heathen slums' of London. In 1865 he founded the Christian Mission, which became the Salvation Army in 1876. His prime object was to 'take the gospel of love to the slums' where the shabby workman felt uncomfortable among the well-dressed congregations of the churches. Booth, who used to say, 'I like my tea as I like my religion—hot!', gathered around him a devoted band of 'soldiers', who set out to make religious devotion 'cheerful'. They sang joyful hymns, with instrumental accompaniment. They wore uniforms; that of the ladies included black princess robes and black bonnets, which were at that time fashionable wear. By the time of Booth's death, the Salvation Army had become a world-wide movement, which was helping 'casualties of life'. Homes were established for drunkards (all Salvationists were teetotallers), for destitute children, for ex-prisoners, and for the homeless.

The End of the Century

By the end of the nineteenth century the state was making an increasing but still negligible contribution towards the prevention of pauperism, as well as towards the care of the poor. Services such as education, vaccination and free libraries were being provided. Those unfortunates who still found themselves in the workhouses were treated more humanely. From 1892 married couples over 60 were not separated, and were allowed to receive visitors.

But despite these improvements, the poverty of a sizeable proportion of the population remained a sore. B. Seebohm Rowntree conducted a survey of York, and his findings were published in *Poverty: A Study of Town Life*, in 1901. Rowntree stated that 27·8 per cent of the total population of York, or 43·4 per cent of the wage-earners, had incomes insufficient for bare necessities. There was no reason to suggest that the people of York were worse placed than other town-dwellers. Other investigations, including one by Charles Booth, the sociologist, suggested that about 30 per cent of the population of London suffered similarly.

The Poor Law Commission, 1905–09

In 1905 a Royal Commission began an examination of the Poor Law. Two Reports were published in 1909 because the members were not unanimous. Both Reports agreed that the Poor Law should be administered not by the Boards of Guardians, but by County and County Borough Councils. They agreed that more should be done to prevent pauperism, by measures such as insurance schemes and labour exchanges. They agreed that 'mixed' workhouses should end, and that separate institutions should be used for the sick, the aged, and the very young. They disagreed on the causes of pauperism. The Majority Report stated that drink was 'the most potent and universal factor'. The Minority Report, largely the work of Beatrice Webb and George Lansbury, argued that pauperism was not due to personal defects, but to economic causes often beyond remedy by individuals. The Minority Report also suggested that the concept of a 'pauper' was wrong—that he was no different from his fellows, and that the Poor Law should be abandoned, its functions being taken over by other committees. Children could be looked after by Education Committees, the mentally retarded by Asylums' Committees, the sick by Health Committees.

Although no direct government action was taken on the recommendations of the Commission of 1905–09, some important reforms were made. In 1908 an Old Age Pensions Act granted 5s. a week to those over seventy with no other income; in 1909 Labour Exchanges were established; in 1911 a National Insurance scheme against unemployment and sickness came into operation for those who earned less than £160 a year. In all these schemes government money, obtained by taxation, was used to alleviate the suffering of the poor. This principle was extended later in the twentieth century when the 'Welfare State' was truly established.[1] But the recommendation of the Minority Report, that the Poor Law should be broken up, was not immediately carried out. Poor Law functions were transferred to local government in 1929, but the 'Poor Law' as an entity was not swept away until after the 1939–45 war.

HEALTH

One of the causes of pauperism was the interruption of earning power through ill-health. In the nineteenth century health problems also became important because the growth of towns made public as well as private health a matter of concern. Englishmen, and not only the poor, had to be educated to the idea that dirt bred disease, and that one man's health was the concern of all. Moral preaching alone would not suffice. It was of little use to exhort the destitute that they should be clean, when soap and water and sanitation were beyond the limits of their purse. Direction had to come from above, and proper facilities had to be provided.

Little was done in England to improve health before the nineteenth century. The Napoleonic Wars led to an increased interest in the study of medicine, but agitation for the improvement of public health developed largely after 1838 as a result of the efforts of the Poor Law Commissioners and their Secretary, Edwin Chadwick, who has been described as 'a fanatical enemy of filth'. Chadwick was unwilling to consider that death from disease was a natural consequence of life, and by forceful methods did much to convert those in power to his views. In 1840 the average age of death was 29, the expectation of life 41. One child in six died before reaching the age of one, and one in three before the age of five. During the period 1840 to 1900 a revolution in health took place, without which our cities would not be the populous places they are today.

Diseases and Epidemics

About 1840 the chief 'killer' diseases were typhoid, paratyphoid fever, typhus, smallpox, scarlet fever, diphtheria and tuberculosis. Many people died of starvation too. The impetus to reform came from the

[1] See pp. 281–4.

scourge of a 'new' disease, cholera, which struck England for the first time in 1831. It spread from Newcastle to central and southern England, and doctors, ignorant of its cause, were unable to prescribe a remedy. Cholera is a contagious disease transmitted mainly by water contaminated by a victim. In the 1830's the idea of 'germs' was not known, and it was believed that 'fever' was caught through malignant gases in the air, or *miasma*. (The word 'malaria' or 'bad airs' was coined as a result of that belief.) The medical profession, therefore, tried to persuade the authorities to get rid of noxious smells, but failed to comprehend the importance of the water supply. There were further major cholera epidemics in 1849, in 1853–54, and in 1866. The magnitude of these epidemics can be shown by the figures for cholera deaths in London during the 1849 visitation. There were 246 deaths in June, 1,952 in July, 4,251 in August, and 6,644 in September. These epidemics, dreadful though they were, were blessings in disguise, for they were spectacular enough to draw public attention to them. As the poor suffered more than the rich, and paupers most of all, they added to the expenses of the Poor Law Commissioners. In 1838 fever was prevalent among the paupers of London, of whom one-fifth contracted the disease; one in ten of the victims died. The cost of poor relief rose, and as a result Chadwick appointed a committee of inquiry. Two members of this committee were Dr Kay (afterwards known as Kay-Shuttleworth, who had already become famous for his investigation into health and housing in Manchester), and Dr Southwood Smith, a physician at the London Fever Hospital. The reports, published in 1838 and 1839, advocated the removal of rubbish and the construction of underground sewers. In 1840 accurate statistics became available on the number of deaths due to various diseases. This was due to the foresight of Chadwick who, when the registration of deaths began in 1836, insisted that the cause of death be shown. In 1842 Chadwick's *Report on the Sanitary Condition of the Labouring Classes* was published. In this report the lack of an adequate system of water-supply, and slum housing conditions, were listed among the prime causes of disease among the poor.

The Board of Health, 1848–58

The cholera epidemic of 1848 led to some consternation, so that the government established a Board of Health by the Public Health Act of 1848. Chadwick and Southwood Smith were members of the Board. The Act was cautious, and set up no effective executive power. The national board was empowered to establish local boards in those areas where ten per cent of the population asked for one, or where the death-rate exceeded 23 per 1,000. The national board was able to advise, but not enforce, action by the local boards. The Board of Health met much opposition, and led to what Palmerston later referred to as a war between the 'clean and dirty parties'. Opponents argued that the measures advised would cost property owners much money, and that they were an interference with personal liberty. In short, opponents argued that a man's, or a property owner's, hygiene was his own affair. The Board was abolished in 1858. *The Times* reported 'Mr Chadwick and Dr Southwood Smith have been deposed, and we prefer to take our chance of cholera rather than be bullied into health'. The message that 'Cleanliness is next to Godliness' had not yet been learned. But for all its apparent failure, the Board of Health had some solid achievements. It had created local sanitary boards for two million people, and it had pointed the way for public health measures which were successfully adopted in succeeding decades.

Water Supply and Sewage

The pioneers of public health had advocated improvements in the water supply and in the disposal of refuse. The two problems are connected, for water is an effective way of providing a sewage system.

Water had always been regarded as 'an article of commerce', a commodity to be bought and sold, and not a necessary article to be provided by the 'authorities'. Before the development of towns people were able to use wells, springs and rivers, but water had to be brought to the urban communities. During the eighteenth and previous centuries hollowed elm trunks were used; in the early years of the nineteenth century iron pipes became more common; from 1840 the cheaper and more efficient earthenware pipe came into use. But in the 1840's water was in short supply. In Manchester it was brought into the town by water-carts. In London, where eight water companies operated, the supply was unfiltered Thames water. Whilst the wealthy had taps in their homes, most of the citizens had to share a stand-pipe with perhaps another hundred families. These pipes had

no taps, and water was available at certain times only, usually half
an hour or an hour on alternate days (never on Sundays). When the
water was turned on, people rushed to the stand with buckets and
pails, pushing aggressively to get their water. Often the aged and the
weak were unable to obtain any in the mad scramble. Water was,
therefore, a precious commodity. It was used again and again. Children were washed (occasionally), and the same water was used for
washing clothes, the crockery, and the floors. Finally, it was thrown
out into the passage ways or the courts. Water was rarely used for
drinking (small beer was the usual beverage). Although the first
public baths were opened in 1846, they did not become popular until
fifty years later. In fact, working people rarely washed, for in addition
to the water shortage, soap was dear until Gladstone removed the
duty in 1853. In 1850 the number of public baths taken averaged one
per person in five years. Chimney sweeps washed their bodies on
average three times a year, and they were cleaner than some of their
fellow citizens. It is often said that the water consumption of a country
rises with its degree of civilisation. The following figures show the
'revolution' which took place after 1840:

average annual consumption of water per person

1844	7 gallons
1893	31 gallons
1939	40 gallons

The movement towards the public ownership of water, and its provision by municipal authorities, began in the 1830's, and by 1875 had
gained much ground. But London's water supply was in private
hands until 1905.

The period from 1830 to 1870 saw a more intelligent approach to
the problem of sewage. A practical engineering approach was necessary to ensure that the contamination of water by sewage did not
cause the spread of disease. In 1830 only the wealthy had water-
closets. Where such luxuries existed, they did not connect with 'main
drainage' systems, but usually flushed into the ground below the
basement. If the ground happened to be porous, this led to the contamination of nearby wells and underground streams. The poor
people in the towns had the use of communal privies—a crude seat
over a brick pit, emptied at night by contractors. Sometimes as many
as one hundred people had to share this open-air lavatory.

Where sewers existed, they were usually built of brick, and were large enough for men to enter them in order to clean them out. In London 64 sewers emptied themselves into the Thames: one sewer reached the Thames at Battersea close to the water-supply intake at Chelsea. The disposal of sewage became more practicable with the use, from about 1850, of the glazed earthenware pipe—cheap to manufacture and easy to keep clean by flushing with water. In London most open sewers had disappeared by 1870, by which time sewage was pumped into the Thames on the ebb tide *below* the city.

Greater care was taken in the disposal of refuse—always a problem in towns. The old habit of throwing rubbish into the centre of the courts died hard. But the townsman had to become clean or perish. A regular system of refuse collection was begun by town councils after 1875.

The Metropolitan Burials Act of 1850, passed after the second cholera epidemic, was an attempt to give the Board of Health powers to regulate the conduct of funerals. City graveyards were over-crowded; in some churches burials still took place *under* the church, in quicklime pits. Although the Act of 1850 was repealed two years later, it had the effect of drawing attention to the problem, and parishes began to look for cemeteries away from the centres of population.

State Action

The last quarter of the nineteenth century saw government legislation introduced to regulate public health. A Royal Commission of 1868 endorsed most of the beliefs of Chadwick and his contemporaries. Disraeli's Public Health Act (1875) codified and strengthened all previous legislation. Town councils were given the task of maintaining sewerage and drainage, and of collecting refuse. The supply of water was to be controlled by local authorities, who were to ensure purity. All local councils had to appoint Medical Officers of Health, who were empowered to disinfect premises where those who contracted infectious diseases lived, and to examine food. Disraeli's measures, which he dubbed 'sanitas sanitatum, omnia sanitas', and which were derided by his opponents as 'a plumber's policy', did much to accustom Englishmen to the idea of the public control of private health. In 1907 the School Medical Service was established.

43 Leeds, 1858. The town hall, not then completed, is in the centre background. (p. 89)

44 *Toad Lane, Rochdale,*
1844: the first co-operative
store. (p. 202)

45 *A furniture warehouse at*
Nottingham, c. 1860. This
was the factory showroom
and provides a good sample
of Victorian taste.

Doctors found many cases of rickets, short-sight, bad teeth, and ring-worm among the children, many of whom had not been seen by a doctor before; medical treatment was not free in those days. In the schools, teachers did their best by example and precept to instil the rudiments of hygiene into their pupils. And, as mothers often needed advice, the first Infant Welfare Service began to develop after 1906. Health had become a national concern—it is significant that in 1919 the name of the Local Government Board was changed to 'Ministry of Health'.

Medical Services

Engineering and administration alone were not enough to improve the health of the people. There was a need for better doctors and nurses, and for the development of more scientific methods of saving life and of alleviating pain.

Improvements in nursing were brought about largely by the efforts of Florence Nightingale (1820–1910). Before her time, the best nurses were those who belonged to the religious orders. Roman Catholic nursing sisters had a high reputation, as had the Anglican nursing order founded in 1845. The secular nurses were, for the most part, unskilled and ignorant, even if they were not as bad as Dickens' 'Sarey Gamp'. It should be remembered that most sick people were looked after at home, by their wives, mothers or children; indeed, during the first half of the nineteenth century relatives were probably more efficient, within the limits of their knowledge, in matters of nursing than the 'professionals'. Florence Nightingale received train-ing as a nurse at Kaiserwerth in Prussia, and at a hospital in Paris. When the prevalence of sickness in the British army reached alarm-ing heights during the Crimean War, she persuaded her friend Sid-ney Herbert, the Secretary for War, to allow her to go to the military hospital at Scutari in Turkey. She took with her thirty trained nurses, drawn from the religious orders. At Scutari they found thousands of soldiers suffering from dysentery, typhoid, scurvy and cholera. Medical requisites, such as bandages, bed clothes and even soap were in short supply. For the first time, trained nurses were able to alleviate the suffering, and to help save the lives, of soldiers on active service. The nurses arrived at the end of 1854, and despite all their efforts the death rate at the hospital in Scutari in February 1855 was 42 per cent. In June of that year, partly due to the efforts of the nurses, the rate had fallen to 2·2 per cent. 'The Lady of the Lamp' became a legend during the Crimean War. After the war, she devoted her life to effecting improvements in nursing and in hospitals, and was awarded the Order of Merit for her services. Florence Nightingale had made nursing a respectable profession. Her principles of fresh air, soap and water, and light were adopted by nurses as necessary in medical care.

Meanwhile, thanks to the discoveries of Louis Pasteur, a Frenchman, and Robert Koch, a German, the medical profession was able to combat disease. In 1876 Koch was able to prove that the disease of anthrax in sheep was caused by bacteria of a particular kind. In the following decade the bacteria which caused typhoid, tuberculosis, diphtheria and tetanus were isolated. Medical scientists were able to study the behaviour of the microbes which caused diseases, and to suggest remedies. Cholera and typhoid germs were carried by water, so that the supervision of water-supplies led to the decline of those epidemics. Others were prevented by immunisation, or the deliberate inculcation of a mild dose of a disease, so that the body created a defence against serious attacks. By 1900 tetanus and typhoid and diphtheria were being combated by vaccination. These scourges, together with smallpox, had largely disappeared by 1914, though the threat from diphtheria lingered on owing to the unwillingness of some mothers to have their children immunised. Tuberculosis was partly checked by the pasteurisation of milk, which began in about 1900, though this disease remained serious until diet and living conditions improved.

Advances in surgery and in medical instruments enabled doctors to alleviate pain. The use of chloroform as an anaesthetic, discovered by Dr Simpson of Edinburgh in 1847, enabled surgeons to operate for the removal of gallstones, internal growths, or enlarged prostate glands, and to remedy overactive thyroid glands and hernias. Surgery became safer because of the work of Sir Joseph Lister (1827–1912) and others, who used antiseptic surgical methods.

New and improved instruments helped doctors in their diagnoses. X-rays, discovered by the German Röntgen in 1897, made the examination of hidden parts of the body possible. The stethoscope, invented in 1819, the ophthalmoscope (1851) for examining the

TOOTH-ACHE IMMEDIATELY CURED BY USING

PROVOST'S CELEBRATED ELYSIAN FLUID.

'Oh, this dreadful Tooth-Ache drives me mad.'

Hurrah, I'm cured, thanks to Provost's Elysian Fluid.

This troublesome complaint (the Tooth-ache), which has hitherto been considered incurable, except by extraction, is now no longer so, as the following fact will prove:—When a Tooth is decayed, and the Nerve exposed to the atmosphere, it becomes swollen, and too large for the aperture in which it is contained, and thereby causes inflammation and pain, to ease and cure which, the Nerve requires an ASTRINGENT LIQUID to contract and destroy it; the Nerve—not the Tooth—being the seat of pain.

Agent for London, Messrs. BARCLAY AND SON, 95, Farringdon Street, and may be had of most respectable Medicine Vendors throughout the kingdom. Prepared by J. P. PROVOST, Chemist, Huntingdon, Agent for the Suffolk Alliance Assurance Office. Sold in Bottles, with full directions, at 1s. 1½d. each.

As doctors' and dentists' fees were often too great for the poor, there was a great trade in patent cures. This advertisement (c. 1860) is comparatively restrained. The manufacturers of some pills claimed that they would cure every ailment suffered by mankind.

retina of the eye, and the electrocardiograph (1881), were all important advances in medical science.

Finally, the medical profession was becoming increasingly aware that, even if a healthy mind was produced by a healthy body, sick minds needed care. Some publicity was given to the 'new' science of psychology by the publication of William James' *Principles of Psychology* in 1891. From about 1900, largely through the work of Sigmund Freud, increasing attention was paid to the treatment of abnormalities as 'neuroses'. This side of medicine developed during the 1914–18 war, when doctors were called upon to deal with thousands of 'shell-shock' cases.

Despite all these startling advances in medicine and in health before 1914, there was still much to be done in the next fifty years. The Victorians had done much to combat disease. The next battle was against inadequate feeding and poor housing conditions, which still caused death, misery and sickness.

CHAPTER 16

Self-Help and State-Help, 1800-1914

In the previous chapters we have seen how the state helped those who were unable to fend for themselves, and how governmental prompting was necessary in order to promote better hygiene. But in other ways groups of poor people tried to better their conditions by their own exertions. Two books written by Samuel Smiles, *Self-Help*, published in 1859, and *Thrift* (1875) epitomised this spirit. Smiles' theme was that the working class could better their conditions by applying their talents to their jobs, by educating themselves, and by being sober and thrifty. These comforting middle-class virtues could have little appeal to those who could not find employment, or who were sick with disease, or could not make their wages cover bare essentials. But to those who were not destitute, such precepts were a pointer towards the improvement of their lot.

FRIENDLY SOCIETIES

Friendly societies were a means of saving for a rainy day. The ancient guilds had performed such functions, but when they disappeared there was a need to create associations which could act as provident institutions, taking money from their members in the good times and looking after them in time of trouble. Friendly societies helped to fill a vacuum during the nineteenth century, and continued to thrive long after the model trade unions, assurance societies and state insurance schemes offered alternative means of security. Rose's Act of 1793 allowed the formation of friendly societies, provided their rules were approved by a J.P. The Combination Laws of 1799 and 1800 did not affect the friendly societies which grew in numbers because trade unions were banned. It has been estimated that in 1801 there were 7,000 societies, with some 700,000 members. In the early years of the nineteenth century many societies were mere Christmas clubs, many were badly run, and several failed. A series of Acts of Parliament forced the friendly societies to become more efficient, and afforded more security to members. In 1846, with the establishment of a Registrar of Friendly Societies, their supervision ceased to be the province of the J.P.'s. The various statutes were codified in 1875, by which time most of the societies were financially sound, and efficiently organised.

The two most successful friendly socieities were established in the 1830's. The first, Unity of Oddfellows, was founded in 1832 in Bolton, and the Order of Foresters began in 1834 in Rochdale. During the next forty years the small local 'slate clubs' decreased in number, as they were taken over by the larger orders. By 1875 most villages and towns had thriving lodges or courts of the Oddfellows or Foresters. By then assurance companies, giving premiums on death or other calamity, were becoming increasingly popular among the skilled artisans. Large companies, like the Prudential, sent out collectors for weekly contributions from working men. Another boon to the poor man was the establishment of the Post Office Savings Bank in 1861.

THE CO-OPERATIVE MOVEMENT

The co-operative movement was aimed at making a man's earnings go further. There had always been an inherent antagonism between producer, wholesaler, retailer, and customer. Middlemen were blamed for high prices, and a system whereby middlemen could be eliminated was one with an obvious appeal to the poor.

Robert Owen and others tried to foster producers' co-operatives, in which all members were to own the means of production, and all were to share in the results of their labours. In 1824 he founded New Harmony in the U.S.A., where 900 settlers lived on an estate of some 30,000 acres. The venture failed after three years. In the next decade Owen was persuaded to support another producers' co-operative estate in Hampshire, but this also failed. From 1815 attempts were made to form consumers' co-operative societies. In these, goods were bought at wholesale price and re-sold to members at less than the usual retail price. By 1832 there were 500 such societies, but none of them lasted more than two or three years. From 1834 to 1844 the co-operative ideal was in the shadows, but then a successful consumers' co-operative was founded.

The Rochdale Pioneers

In 1844 the Rochdale Society of Equitable Pioneers was founded by twenty-eight workmen, seven of whom were flannel-weavers. The aims of the Society were to establish a retail shop, to manufacture articles for sale, and to provide houses and employment for members. But although they aimed high, they kept their feet firmly on the ground. In fact, they were successful in the establishment of a retail shop, which became a model for other societies. The founders began by collecting 2d. a week from 'shareholders'. To do this, pioneers, such as Howarth, walked as much as twenty miles to collect from members in the Rochdale district. When they had sufficient capital, the Rochdale Pioneers rented the ground floor of a warehouse in Toad Lane (originally T'owd Lane) at £10 a year, and bought a few pounds' worth of stock. They sold goods at the normal retail price, and members were given a 'dividend' after it was known what the profit was. The Rochdale Pioneers succeeded because the 'dividend' was paid *after* the trading profit was known, so that the organisers had no need to forecast profit. Also, the receipt of, say, £1 each year had a greater appeal to the poor than the rebate of 4d. a week from their purchases. As the Pioneers confined their activities to the first of their aims, the establishment of a retail shop, only a relatively small amount of capital was required. The Rochdale model was copied by others. In 1851 there were 130 retail societies, with a total of 15,000 members. Thereafter membership grew as follows:

	no. of societies	no. of members	share capital
1862	450	90,000	£450,000
1875	1,266	437,000	£4·4 million
1936	1,107	7,500,000	£168·6 million
1945	1,070	9,400,000	£310 million

Widening Activities

In 1863 the English Co-operative Wholesale Society was established. The aim was to have a central organisation, which bought from manufacturers in bulk and which could sell to the co-operative retail societies. The C.W.S. shared its profits with the retail branches. From this the movement gravitated to manufacturing. The Crumpsall Biscuit Works (near Manchester) opened in 1872. In time a boot factory was opened in Leicester, a soap works in Durham, a tobacco factory in Manchester, and a cotton mill in Bolton.

The co-operative movement provided cheaper food at a time when the poor found it hard to make ends meet. It also sold pure food, in an age when adulteration, such as chalk in flour, or sand in sugar, was not uncommon. It helped to defeat the 'truck' system. As time went on, the co-operative trading activities became more varied. In 1876 the Co-operative Bank was established. Later the C.W.S. engaged in the sale of coal. Today the movement owns ships, and is one of the biggest trading concerns in England. The movement did not, however, overthrow the capitalist system, as early socialists such as Owen had hoped.

The co-operative movement did much to improve the lot of its members through education. Some of the profits were devoted to education, the formation of adult colleges, and libraries. The movement, with the friendly societies, helped the working class to learn self-government. It offered a training-ground for those with limited education to learn how to speak, to run meetings, and to shoulder responsibilities.

EDUCATION

The development of a national system of education for the poor was hampered by a divergence of aim and differences of opinion. Some saw schooling as a means of imparting information or practical skills, which would enable children to do a useful job and to avoid destitution. Others regarded education as a means of raising the moral standards of life, as a means of creating the self-discipline and reasonableness so essential to an industrial society. There were differing opinions as to whose responsibility it was to provide education. Should education be voluntary, and paid for by parents? Should education be provided by the Churches, by local government, or by the state? Popular education developed along no certain principles, but evolved by a series of experiments, some of which succeeded whilst others failed.

Church Schools

Before 1833 popular education, where it existed, was financed and organised by the Churches and philanthropists. In 1780 Robert Raikes of Gloucester introduced some instruction in reading, writing, and arithmetic into the Church of England Sunday schools in that city. It should be remembered that the working population, which included children, worked a six-day week, so that Sunday was their only free day. Sunday schools soon spread over many parts of England, and were attended by men and women, as well as children, anxious to learn to read and write. Hannah More, in Somerset, was particularly active in this field.

The next development was the provision of day schools by the Churches for children aged between six and ten. In 1798 Joseph Lancaster, a Quaker, opened a one-room school at Southwark. Tuition was free apart from the expense of writing books. Lancaster used a 'monitorial' system, whereby the teacher instructed the monitors, who in turn drilled the younger pupils. This method of overcoming the teacher shortage was also advocated by Andrew Bell, a Church of England clergyman. As a result of the pioneering efforts of Lancaster and Bell, two societies were formed to found elementary schools: the British and Foreign Schools Society by the Nonconformist Churches, and the National Society by the Church of England. The mechanical method of instruction to large numbers was condemned by David Stow (1793–1864) and others, who advocated the value of infant schools, and the importance of moral training. Several infant schools were founded after 1816.

In 1833 Roebuck moved a resolution in the House of Commons for a 'universal and national education of the whole people'. The measure was opposed by both Whigs and Tories, but a meagre grant of £20,000 per annum was given by the government to the two Societies. This was increased in 1839 to £30,000. The systematic training of teachers was begun by voluntary means also. Dr. Kay-Shuttleworth (1804–77) established the Battersea Training College in 1840, and the National Society (Church of England) founded St. Mark's Training College in London in the following year. By 1845 there were 22 church training colleges, with a total of 540 students.

The role of the state in the period from 1833 to 1870 was supervisory. As government grants were being given to privately owned schools, inspectors were appointed from 1839 to ensure minimum standards. But the state did not provide schools, largely through a division of opinion. The Churches opposed secular education, and were jealous of the influence of sects other than their own. Other 'parties' were opposed to the granting of taxpayers' money to the Churches. But by 1870 the need for a national system of elementary education had become more pressing. There was a need for technical training for industry, which necessitated some knowledge of the 'three R's', and England's industrial rivals, the U.S.A., Germany, France, Belgium and Switzerland had already started technical education. There was also a need to educate the poor so that they could play their part in a democracy. When the franchise was widened in 1867, Robert Lowe, an opponent of the measure, shrewdly said, 'Now we must educate our masters'.

State Schools

An Act of major importance was passed in 1870 during Gladstone's first ministry. This was Forster's Education Act, which 'filled up the gaps'. Where church schools existed, they were to continue with the aid of government grants. Where there were no elementary schools, School Boards were appointed to build and maintain schools financed partly from government sources, and partly from the rates. The 'board schools' were to provide education for children aged five to ten, and they were empowered to charge small fees (a few pence a week). As schooling was not free, and as there were insufficient places for all the child population, compulsory attendance was not enforced. Religious instruction was given in the board schools, but no denominational doctrines were to be taught. Also, parents could withdraw their children from the lessons in religion if they so desired, under the 'Cowper-Temple' clause. Thus a dual system of education developed, with some schools run by voluntary bodies, and others by local government. Schooling was made compulsory in 1880 (Mundella's Act), and free in 1891. In 1902 (Balfour's Act) the School Boards were abolished, and their powers were transferred to county and borough councils. At the same time, the councils were given greater control over the church schools, and all elementary schools came under the general supervision of a government department, the Board of Education. In 1906 local authorities were empowered to provide free school dinners for children in need, and in the following year free medical treatment was provided. By 1914, the younger generation, though not all the older, had had some elementary education. The beginnings of a revolution in education had begun, but the years after 1918 saw far-reaching changes.

Secondary Schools

Secondary education in the nineteenth century was available to those whose parents could afford the fees or to pupils of promise. In 1868 there were 37,000 pupils in 782 endowed schools. Most towns had day schools, where boys were given a grounding in the classics, and mathematics. During the second half of the nineteenth century the curriculum was widened to include a variety of subjects and skills. The boarding schools, many of them long-established, underwent a transformation during the nineteenth century, due largely to the work of great headmasters such as Arnold of Rugby, and Thring of Uppingham. Changes in the law made it possible for ancient foundations to widen their curriculum, whilst organised games also developed. There was an increased demand for places in boarding schools, owing to the greater number of people earning between £500 and £1,000 a year, who wanted their sons (not daughters) to have a good education. The development of railways made travel easier, whilst the development of the Empire, which meant that some parents spent years in India or elsewhere, made the boarding school an essential. As a result, the old schools expanded, and new ones, such as Marlborough (1843) and Wellington (1853), were founded. The first secondary school for girls was the North London Collegiate School opened by Miss Buss in 1850, to be followed by Cheltenham Ladies' College (Miss Beale) in 1858.

Generally there was little secondary education for the poor until 1907, when secondary schools receiving public money were made to allow 25 per cent of their places to non-fee-paying 'scholars' from the elementary schools. The Balfour Act of 1902 had also made the local education authorities responsible for the provision of secondary education, and in most areas new grammar schools were built but the pupils were fee-paying.

Further Education

Further education remained largely outside the sphere of the state in the nineteenth century. In 1823 the London Mechanics' Institute was founded by George Birkbeck, who had already played a major role in the establishment of a similar venture in Glasgow. By 1850 there were 622 Mechanics' Institutes in England and Wales, with 600,000 members. These Institutes gave 'evening classes' in science and useful arts, intended for the instruction of working men. They disappeared during the third quarter of the nineteenth century, largely because it was found that they were attended more by lower middle-class 'white-collar workers' than by working men. But great developments were made in adult education in the twenty years before 1914. Ruskin College, Oxford (1899) and Fircroft, Bourneville (1909) were founded for the full-time instruction of men who possessed some potential but had not had the advantage of higher education, and the Workers' Educational Association was founded in 1903.

The older universities of Oxford and Cambridge saw a 'renaissance' in the nineteenth century. The degree system was overhauled, studies were widened, and new Chairs endowed. New universities, such as Durham and London were founded, together with university colleges which eventually became universities. London admitted women to their degree courses in 1878, before which date it was impossible for any lady to receive a university education. This increase in the number of universities was remarkable in so far as there had been no new foundations in England for 500 years.[1] The present century has seen a great increase in the number of establishments for further education: this is the logical extension of the process begun in the nineteenth century—the erection of 'the ladder from the gutter to the university'.

[1] In 1901 there were 20,000 university students.

CHAPTER 17

Money and Banking, 1694-1914

Means of Exchange

In our own age we have a well-regulated and defined monetary system, whereby the amount of money in circulation is controlled by the Treasury, and the coins and notes we use are in the same form as those used in other parts of the country. During the eighteenth century matters were very different. The coins in circulation were gold guineas and half-guineas and silver coins. The guinea was first minted in 1663, and was named after the Guinea Coast of West Africa, the main source of England's gold at that time. In 1717 Sir Isaac Newton, then Master of the Mint, valued the guinea at twenty-one silver shillings. This use of two metals for legal tender is known as *bi-metallism*. Unfortunately Newton's reform left silver undervalued as compared with gold, with the result that many silver coins went out of circulation, as possessors of silver coinage tended to keep them, or melted them down. This caused a shortage of small coin, which was needed the most. Employers were forced to seek means of paying the wages of their workmen other than in coin. Some employers adopted the truck system; others, like John Wilkinson, issued their own 'coins' or 'tokens'; others adopted the 'long pay'. Bimetallism came to an official end in 1816, when gold was made the sole standard. But in practice England has been on 'the gold standard' since about 1730. Under the 1816 Act silver coins were made legal tender only for payments up to 40s., but more 'silver' coins were minted, and these contained but a fraction of their face value in metal.

In addition to coins, paper money was in circulation. The Bank of England issued notes, which were 'promises to pay' rather than legal tender. But these notes were for large denominations of £10 or more, and circulated only in London. Private banks also issued promissory notes. A man would deposit a sum of money with a bank, and was given in return a written promise to pay coin on demand. The depositor could use this note for another transaction. Another mode of monetary transaction was the 'bill of exchange'. This was, in effect, a bill written out by the supplier of goods, to the receiver of the goods. The debtor receipted the bill, i.e. signed his name on it, and returned it to the creditor. The creditor could either keep it until the debtor paid him, or he could try to find a merchant who would give him cash for the bill (less a charge for interest, or *discount*).

This means of exchange was reformed in the nineteenth century, by which time banks were sufficiently developed to be able to play an efficient role in the economy.

Banks

The Bank of England was founded in 1694, largely through the efforts of a Scot, William Paterson (1658-1719). England was fighting in the war of the League of Augsburg against the France of Louis XIV, and the Crown had to secure loans at a reasonable rate of interest. A group of London businessmen loaned to William III the sum of £1,200,000 for a yearly interest of £100,000. In return, they were granted a charter to form the Bank of England—a charter which was renewed periodically. The Bank was empowered to act as any other bank, i.e. to receive deposits and to make loans, to discount bills and to issue notes. Although the Bank of England was privately owned (it was nationalised in 1946), it worked closely with the government from the time of its foundation. In 1696 the Bank of England co-operated with the Mint in the reform of the coinage, and it is significant that, when there was a danger of rioting during the Sacheverell affair in 1711, troops were sent to protect the Bank. In 1708 an Act was passed forbidding the establishment of any bank in England (but not in Scotland) with more than six partners. The Bank of England remained the only joint stock bank in England until the law was changed in 1825.

The Act of 1708 had a profound effect on the development of banking in England in the eighteenth century. The banks which were founded had to be small private banks; often the owners were all members of the same family. These private banks, outside London, were known as 'country banks', and the first was that opened by James Wood of Bristol in 1716. By 1750 there were only about a dozen of these in existence. Then they increased rapidly in number, to 119 in 1784, nearly 400 in 1793 and 700 in 1810. Very few lasted long, as they were unable to amass the necessary reserves to avoid closure or bankruptcy in times of trouble. They did, however, perform a useful service in affording credit facilities for industrialists.

Banking during the French Wars, 1793–1815

By 1793 the Bank of England was in a special position which was to enable it to have some control over the monetary policy of the country. It loaned most of its deposits to the government, and it handled the government's accounts. It was, therefore, the government's bank. But also it was becoming the 'banker's bank', for the private banks were holding Bank of England notes as their securities instead of gold. Therefore, most of the gold reserves of England were held by the Bank of England. As bank-notes were issued as 'promises', they had to be redeemed for gold if the holders of notes so wished. But further, as gold was an international currency, gold had to be used in order to pay for imports if the country's exports did not match them. In other words, an adverse balance of trade led to a drain of gold from the Bank of England.

A financial crisis was brought about by the long wars against France. Pitt, Prime Minister at the outbreak of war in 1793, thought that the war would be a short one, and borrowed from the Bank of England to avoid large increases in taxation. At the same time, England's exports suffered, leading to a 'trade gap'. These two factors, coupled with lending to Britain's allies, led to a fall in the gold reserves held by the Bank of England. In 1796 and 1797 people began to become uneasy as the war was not proceeding well. In 1796 there was rebellion in Ireland; in the following year the fleets at Spithead and the Nore mutinied, and there was fear of an invasion of England by the French. If a régime is brought down by the invasion of a foreign power, then paper money is valueless (as were the notes issued by the Southern states during the American Civil War). Gold, however, is of value, whatever the state of politics. The English people began to demand gold coin instead of notes, causing a run on the banks. As the Bank of England's gold reserves were threatened, the government passed the Bank Restriction Act of 1797, which suspended specie payment, i.e. the redemption of notes by gold. The Bank of England began to issue notes for amounts smaller than £10, and the country banks also began to issue more paper money. As the war progressed, more and more paper money was put into circulation, and since the value of money is dependent, other things being equal, on the amount of money in circulation, the value fell, i.e. there was inflation. Towards the end of the war, the holder of a £5 note found that he could get only £3. 11s. in gold for it. In 1810 the Bullion Committee recommended that cash payments, or the exchange of notes for gold, should be resumed. The government did not act on this recommendation, and cash payments were not resumed until 1821.

Banking from 1815 to 1844

The Act of 1816 had made gold the sole monetary standard; that of 1821 had caused the resumption of cash payments. But private banks continued to issue paper money in excess of their reserves, with the result that many of them failed. It was obvious that they had insufficient capital to carry on their business with safety. The failure of a bank meant more than ruination for the owners. It also meant that depositors lost their money. An efficient banking system could only develop where depositors could have every faith in their bank. Accordingly, the Bank Act of 1826 allowed the formation of joint-stock banks, with the right to issue notes, outside a 65 mile radius of London. Several joint-stock banks were immediately formed, and in 1833 they were allowed to do business in London.

Financial crises, however, continued to occur at regular intervals. One in 1836 was followed by another in 1839, when the Bank of England was saved by a loan from the Bank of France negotiated by the international bankers, Rothschilds. Experts of the time argued fiercely about the remedy. The 'Banking' school of thought, led by Thomas Tooke, thought that banks should be free to issue notes according to the state of trade, providing notes could be converted into gold on demand. The 'Currency' school argued that, as the value of money was affected by the amount in circulation, note-issue should be tied to the gold reserves; in order to effect this, they advocated that only the Bank of England should be allowed to issue notes. The Currency school won the day, and some of their ideas were incorporated in the Bank Charter Act, passed by Peel's government in 1844.

The Bank Charter Act, 1844

The aim of the Bank Charter Act was to concentrate the note-issue in the Bank of England. Note-issue by other banks was not forbidden, but the Act stated that no *new* bank, founded after 1844, would be allowed to issue bank notes; existing banks were not to increase the number of notes in circulation. Those banks already in existence would lose their right to issue notes if they amalgamated with other banks. The framers of the Act realized that it would take time for the note-issue to become the monopoly of the Bank of England, but the process took much longer than they had envisaged. The last private note-issuing bank—Fox, Fowler and Company of Taunton—did not disappear until 1921.

The number of Bank of England notes to be issued was laid down. The Bank was to issue notes to the value of its gold coin, gold and silver bullion, so that notes could be redeemed if holders demanded it. But as the number of notes in circulation issued by all the banks exceeded the total metal reserves in 1844, the Bank of England was allowed to issue a further £14 million in notes. This excess amount, backed by government securities, was known as the *fiduciary issue* or issue on faith. As note-issue was abandoned by the other banks, the Bank of England fiduciary issue was to be increased by two-thirds of the amount of the lapsed issue. The price of gold was set at £3. 17s. 9d. per standard ounce. The Bank Charter Act also set up a new department of the Bank of England. The Bank was to consist of two sections, one dealing only with the issue of notes, the other continuing the ordinary day-to-day business of banking.

Banking after 1844

It was hoped that the Bank Charter Act would prevent the occurrence of financial crises, but it did not do so. There were particularly severe crises in 1847, 1857 and 1866. In 1866 the failure of Overend, Gurney and Co., one of London's largest merchant-banks, caused hardship in England and abroad, for its assets were world-wide. But after 1866 there were no other serious crises before 1914. The governors of the Bank of England learned by experience how to prevent them, by asking for a temporary suspension of the Bank Charter Act, and by altering the Bank Rate.[1] It can be said that 'the Old Lady of Threadneedle Street' became the guardian of the nation's finances.

The second half of the nineteenth century saw a movement towards amalgamation of the joint-stock banks. In 1873 there were 121 joint-stock banks; by 1924 the number had fallen to 13, of whom only five were large (Barclays, Lloyds, National Provincial, Midland and Westminster). This amalgamation strengthened joint-stock banks. They were able to have higher capital and larger deposits; they were able to open branches all over the country (the 13 banks had over 8,000 branches in 1924); they became safer and more stable. Today, when we pay money into a bank, we do not contemplate that the bank will 'fail'.

Britain as the World's Banker

During the eighteenth century, Britain borrowed a considerable amount of capital from abroad, notably from the Dutch. Many British businessmen sent agents to Amsterdam, then the centre of the world's money market, to borrow money for their enterprises. The Dutch had considerable holdings in the Bank of England, and in large British concerns, such as the East India Company.

But the establishment of the Bank of England in 1694 coincided with the beginning of the development of London as the financial centre of the world. This gradual evolution continued throughout the eighteenth century so that by 1815 London, not Amsterdam, was the financial centre. In 1733 the London Stock Exchange was formed by groups of business-men who had formerly met in coffee-houses. One coffee-house, opened by Edward Lloyd near the Tower of London, quickly became a meeting-place for those engaged in shipping. In 1692 Lloyd moved to Lombard Street and produced a news-sheet containing information about ships which he thought would be of interest to his customers. In 1726 the first *Lloyd's List*, which contained information on ships, tides, prices, stocks and shares, was published. By 1770 Lloyd's had become the foremost marine insurance business in the world.

[1] See p. 293.

The French Revolutionary and Napoleonic Wars (1793–1815) hastened the decline of Amsterdam and the rise of London. Large mercantile houses, accustomed to lending money internationally (they were not 'bankers'; they loaned to governments or large concerns and not to individuals), moved their headquarters to London. Henry Hope of Amsterdam transferred to London in 1794 because of the threat of a French invasion. By 1800 the Rothschilds had a branch in London, whilst the Baring Brothers had come from Bremen fifty years earlier. Mercantile houses such as these strengthened London's position.

On one famous occasion, the firm of Rothschild lent the British government £4·5 million. In 1876 the Prime Minister, Benjamin Disraeli, had to raise the money quickly in order to buy shares in the Suez Canal, which were offered for sale by the Khedive of Egypt. Disraeli was unable to obtain the consent of Parliament (and therefore draw on the Treasury), as it was not in session. Rothschilds supplied the money to effect the purchase until Parliament met and subsequently approved the action.

After 1815 Britain was a lender of capital, and not a borrower. In the 1820's the mercantile houses lent money to the United States of America and to the new independent countries of Latin America, and to Greece, which became independent of Turkey in that decade.

In the middle years of the nineteenth century, much British capital was used in the building of railways and in the provision of industrial equipment in Europe. In the same period, much was done to finance large projects in Canada and India. In the last quarter of the nineteenth century a good deal less British money was invested in Europe, whilst Australia, South Africa and North and South America were receiving a considerable amount of British capital. By 1913 a total of £3,763 million of British money was invested abroad, much of it in Canada and the Americas. Approximately half this amount was invested in countries within the Empire. The income from these overseas investments was a great help to Britain's economy, as it added to her invisible exports.

So London became the world's banker, the chief money-market, and the centre of marine insurance.

PART THREE
The Twentieth Century

CHAPTER 18

The Great War, 1914–1918

In August 1914, Great Britain joined her allies against Germany and Austria-Hungary. The war was of such magnitude as to be beyond the experience of any of the world's leaders. For the first time a total war had to be fought which required a concentration on military efforts and needs, and the subjugation of ordinary living. But in 1914 the Prime Minister, Asquith, and his Liberal government envisaged that the war would be of short duration. The slogan 'Business as Usual' typifies the government's policy. Britain lived by trade: Britain's markets could still be reached by sea, together with most of those of her enemy Germany. By continuing as a trading nation, with some diversion of her resources to the military, she could fight and win the war whilst normal business went on. The result of this 'Business as Usual' policy was that the urgent and radical measures needed were not carried out until the war had been in progress for over a year. The appointment of Lloyd George as Minister of Munitions in December 1915, and his appointment as Prime Minister in a coalition government in 1916, marked the end of 'Business as Usual', and the beginning of a more vigorous and single-minded prosecution of the war. The effects of the war on the social and industrial development of Britain were profound. The 1914–18 war saw the end of an epoch.

Finance

The outbreak of war meant an immediate increase in government expenditure. The armed forces had to be paid, fed and clothed; armaments had to be bought. Throughout the war the government relied mainly on borrowing. Government income from taxation covered only about 30 per cent of expenditure.

Year	Revenue £ million	Expenditure £ million
1914–15	226·7	560·5
1915–16	336·8	1,559·2
1916–17	573·4	2,198·1
1917–18	707·2	2,696·2
1918–19	889·0	2,579·3

The National Debt of £650 million in 1913 had risen to £7,836 million in 1918.

Taxation was raised in a supplementary budget of November 1914, prepared by the Chancellor of the Exchequer, Lloyd George. Income tax was raised from 1s. 2d. in the pound to 2s. 6d. The duty on beer was raised by a penny a glass, and that on tea from 5d. to 8d. per lb. In 1915, McKenna, who succeeded Lloyd George as Chancellor of the Exchequer, increased income tax and postal charges, and imposed new customs duties on 'luxury' goods such as cars and motor-cycles, cinematograph films, clocks and watches, and musical instruments. The aim of the new duties was more to save valuable cargo space than to raise revenue. In the same budget McKenna placed an 'excess profits' tax on firms engaged on war contracts. This tax was in answer to popular agitation against 'profiteering', but was difficult to apply. In 1916 McKenna increased the excess profits tax and income tax on earned incomes over £2,500 per annum (and unearned incomes over £2,000). By the end of the war the standard income tax rate was 6s. in the pound. The exemption limit was lowered from £160 to £130 in 1915, and as prices and wages doubled during the war, the number of income tax payers rose from 1·2 million in 1913–14 to 7·8 million in 1919–20. In addition to raising taxation, the war governments obtained money through loans. National Savings Committees were set up to organise this. Also, about 10 per cent of Britain's foreign investments were sold to help to finance the war. In 1914 these investments totalled about £4,000 million, including about £850 million in the U.S.A. and £500 million in Canada.

The war brought changes in currency. One pound and ten shilling notes were put into circulation. This paper money soon replaced sovereigns, which were worth much more than their face value by 1918. The Bank of England was empowered to issue notes in excess of the limits laid down by the Bank Charter Act.

The government's financial measures during the war have been described as 'feeble' and the failure to balance the budget during the war left great problems for the post-war statesmen.

Industry and Agriculture

The normal pattern of Britain's trade and industrial production was soon disrupted by the war. Some sectors of industry were stimulated, others suffered. The war hastened the development of the aeroplane, wireless, and motor transport. Firms which had hitherto been working separately and secretly on new projects were made to work together. The government helped to stimulate the cross-fertilisation of ideas through the Department of Scientific and Industrial Research (D.S.I.R.), established in 1916. The D.S.I.R. did much to bring together the work being done in universities and in private industries. Greater efficiency and better organisation resulted in the rapid advance of those industries which were essential to the war effort.

All branches of engineering made rapid progress. Some branches of manufacturing had to expand in order to supply what Britain had formerly bought from Germany—scientific instruments, ball bearings, laboratory glassware, tungsten. The steel industry expanded rapidly. The difficulty of obtaining high-grade imported iron ore led to the development of the British ironfields of the east midlands, which could be worked only by using the Open Hearth Process. Steel-makers had to work with greater precision, especially when they were engaged on shell contracts.

Agriculture had to become more efficient as the war progressed. In 1914 Britain was importing 80 per cent of her cereals, 40 per cent of her meat, and 75 per cent of her fruit. Little was done to increase home food production until 1916, apart from the establishment of War Agricultural Committees. After 1916 the shipping losses caused by the intensified U-boat campaign, and the poor harvests in North America in 1917, led to an intensive effort to increase the acreage of land used for arable farming. Three million acres of grassland were ploughed up during the last two years of the war. This resulted in an increase in home-grown cereals, but a decrease in the production of milk and meat. The sudden change caused a great increase in the use of tractors on farms. The government helped farmers during the war by the distribution of fertilisers, and by the direction of labour. The farming labour force was augmented by the use of prisoners-of-war, and the creation of the Women's Land Army in addition to the 300,000 women who worked part-time. Food production was increased, but at great cost.

The war led to an increased demand for coal, but the required production was not achieved. At the beginning of the war many miners volunteered to serve in the armed forces, with the result that production fell. Despite government control during most of the war, the pits were producing only 228 million tons in 1918, less than the 1913 total. As a result, coal exports suffered, and markets were lost which were never recovered. Countries unable to obtain British coal found new sources of supply, or turned to oil or electricity.

British shipyards, though they were busy throughout the war on Admiralty contracts, suffered as a result of foreign competition. The shipbuilding industry had relied to a great extent on orders from abroad in the immediate pre-war years. During the war, countries such as Norway, Sweden, Denmark, Holland, Japan and the U.S.A., unable to obtain British ships, increased their own shipbuilding capacity. Like the coal industry, shipbuilding lost markets which were never fully regained.

State Control

At the beginning of the war, the normal practice of the government was to purchase war materials from private firms under contract. As the war progressed, the tendency was for the state to direct industry and its production. In 1915 the shell shortage on the Western Front led to the creation of a new government department, the Ministry of Munitions. The Defence of the Realm Act (known as DORA and characterised by cartoonists as a ferocious busybody with an umbrella) was passed in the same year, and gave the government powers to take over factories and to requisition useful materials, such as sandbags. Railways were controlled by the government from the outset of the war, whilst the Admiralty had the right to requisition shipping. But the state was slow in dealing with the supply and distribution of food. The first rationing scheme was introduced in 1918 and affected sugar, meat, butter, margarine, bacon, ham and lard. Until then, food was 'rationed' by the price. The wealthy were able to live well, the general mass of the people were unable to afford more than bare essentials. By the end of the war the government was buying about 85 per cent of all imported foodstuffs, and distributing them fairly among the people. The extent of increased governmental activity is shown by the growth of the Army Contracts Department. With 20 clerks in August 1914, it grew into the Ministry of Munitions, which by November 1918 was employing 65,000 clerks.

Labour was also brought under state control, though belatedly. Conscription for the armed forces was not introduced until 1916. In the first two years of the war, the armed forces were brought up to strength by volunteers. This led to some disruption of industry as frequently those who enlisted were those whose skill was desperately needed at home. For example, many coal miners enlisted, whilst by June 1915 one-fifth of the male workers in the engineering industry had volunteered. And so in 1915 a list of 'starred' or 'reserved' occupations was introduced. But this system, and conscription which followed, worked badly. Generals at the front, seeking means of bringing battalions up to strength, were able to persuade the government that military needs were greater than those of industry.

Labour and the Trade Unions

In 1911 trade-union membership was 2·4 million. By 1913 it had risen to 3·9 million. This rapid increase was accompanied by a militancy of mood, in which many workers envisaged the overthrow of the capitalist system by concerted trade-union action. The outbreak of war was a dangerous moment. Would the trade unions support it, or would their members regard the war as an 'employers' war' which gave them the chance to take over the control of industry by disorganising the system? In fact, the response of trade-union leadership was immediate and unqualified patriotism. As Ben Tillett said, 'My country, right or wrong!' This was a war which concerned all the British people and, in the opinion of the trade-union leaders, internal differences of opinion had to be shelved whilst all bent to the common task. On 24 August 1914 trade-union leaders passed a resolution that an 'immediate effort be made to terminate all existing trade disputes'.

The same issue confronted the Parliamentary Labour Party, where there was a division of opinion. Some M.P.'s, led by Ramsay MacDonald, decided to oppose the war; the trade-union M.P.'s were in favour of supporting the war. On 5 August 1914 Ramsay Mac-Donald resigned as Chairman of the Parliamentary Labour Party, and was succeeded by Arthur Henderson. MacDonald, with other prominent Labour M.P.'s, maintained a consistent conscientious objection to the war, and suffered much public abuse. Among other indignities, MacDonald was expelled from Lossiemouth Golf Club.

The support of the Labour Party and the T.U.C. for the war led to the cessation of strikes and disputes in the early months of the conflict. They agreed to the national recruiting campaign, and advised workers to relax existing 'trade practices' for the duration. But the workers became disturbed by the steady rise in prices and the incidence of unemployment in some areas. Finding that the trade-union leadership supported the government, factory workers elected their own local spokesman, or 'shop stewards'. These 'officials', though not recognised by the unions, remained as part of the trade-union organisation after the war, and their authority was ultimately recognised.

In March 1915 the unions made the 'Treasury Agreements' with the government—so called because Lloyd George and Walter Runciman, Chancellor of the Exchequer and President of the Board of Trade respectively, met representatives of the Parliamentary Labour Party and the unions in the board-room of the Treasury. The unions agreed to compulsory arbitration in trade disputes, and to the relaxation of trade practices which hindered war production. In the same month employers and unions in the engineering industry made the 'Shells and Fuses Agreement'. Under this, 'diluted' or unskilled labour was to be used in the production of shells and other war materials. The principle of the 'dilution of labour' was applied to other industries, on the understanding that the agreement came to an end with the end of the war. This led to a rapid growth in the number of women engaged in occupations formerly reserved for men. Women worked as bank clerks, porters, chauffeurs, navvies; they worked on the farms, in shops, hotels, offices, cinemas and theatres. In 1918 there were 1·6 million women workers engaged on government contracts.

But if labour relations improved, 'unofficial' strikes did not cease.

In February 1915 about 9,000 engineers went on strike on Clydeside, against the orders of union officials. In July 1915, 200,000 miners of South Wales were on strike. One can perhaps have some sympathy with the skilled iron-moulders who struck in 1917 because their un-skilled labourers were earning more than they were. But the number of hours lost through strikes was considerably less during the war years than in the immediate pre- and post-war years. For this, credit can be given to the responsible attitude of trade-union leaders, and to governmental activity designed to sweeten labour relations. In 1916 the government set up 'Whitley Councils', comprising representa-tives of both trade unions and employers' association, in order to arbitrate on disputes over wages. Though these councils were unable to achieve much during the war, they became a permanent feature of the post-war years.

In general, the war saw greater attention being shown towards working conditions. Works canteens were built so that employees could obtain meals on the premises instead of taking 'sandwiches' or drinking at the nearest public house. The war also saw the relative rise of the wages of unskilled labour as opposed to skilled. This was due in part to the dilution of labour.

The Economic Results of the War

The war accelerated trends already apparent in 1914. Had the war not occurred, Britain's position as one of the leading industrial countries and as the centre of the world's money markets would still have been threatened.[1] Britain's position was certainly weakened by the war, but she was not ruined by it.

At the end of the war Britain had a net loss of about 10 per cent of her £4,000 millions of foreign investments. This reduction was com-paratively slight. However, during the war and partly as a result of it, there was a revolution in Russia (1917), which resulted in Lenin and the Bolsheviks gaining power. The new Russian government re-pudiated its foreign debts, and Britain, as the chief creditor, lost a further 5 per cent of her total foreign investments. Some states in Latin America also refused to pay their debts, and again Britain was the chief loser.

Britain's biggest loss in capital equipment was shipping. Seven

[1] See pp. 154–6

million tons, representing about 40 per cent of the merchant fleet, was lost during the war, mostly as a result of the intensive U-boat campaign. Much of this lost tonnage was replaced during or immediately after the war. The loss of machinery, plant, and property due to enemy action was very small. The few air-raids did negligible damage. But because there was no building of private dwellings during the war there was an acute housing shortage by 1919 when a further 600,000 to one million dwellings were needed.

The war hastened the amalgamation movement in banking. By 1920 the 'Big Five' (Barclays, Lloyds, Midland, National Provincial, and Westminster) controlled 83 per cent of all deposits.

The loss of manpower was greater than in any previous war, and far greater than in the 1939–45 War. British casualties were 745,000 killed, and 1,700,000 wounded.[1] The dead represented 9 per cent of the age range 20 to 45, so that in the post-war years people talked of the 'lost generation'. Many of those killed were the best of their generation, who bravely volunteered in the early months of the war. Throughout the war, casualties among junior officers remained high. Perhaps some of the 'lost generation' would have proved better leaders in state or industry than those who survived. Raymond Asquith, son of the Prime Minister Herbert Asquith, was one of the many brilliant young men who gave their lives. Many who survived were 'wounded' in spirit, and never forgot the horrors of the trenches; others were physically weakened by disease. Civilian losses through enemy action, 1,500, were small compared with the 1939–45 War. But the effects on the civilian population of grief, loneliness, boredom or frustration cannot be measured. It can be argued that the influenza epidemic of 1918–19 was caused by a lack of balance in the war diet. But, by and large, there was no serious reduction in the labour force as a result of the war. On the contrary, as so many more women had received some form of industrial training during the war, the labour force had grown. Trade-union membership also grew, from 4·5 million in 1918, to 6·5 million in 1920.

Women gained and lost by the war. Because of the heavy loss of men, many women were left to grieve the death of their sweetheart or their husband. In 1918 there were 1,068 women to every 1,000 men. The discrepancy was more pronounced in the younger age

[1] See p. 259.

range 20 to 45, so that some women were condemned to spinster-hood. Fortunately, the war had led to the further 'emancipation' of women. Many more avenues of employment were open to them, so that some were able to find a career in business. For the fortunate few, there was an opportunity to enter Parliament after 1918. The first lady M.P. was Nancy, Lady Astor, who was elected to represent Plymouth in 1919.

CHAPTER 19

Between the Wars, 1918-1939

Plans for Reconstruction

Two weeks after the end of war in 1918 the Prime Minister, Lloyd George, echoed the feelings of most Englishmen in these words: 'What is our task? To make Britain a country fit for heroes to live in.' In the following month, December 1918, Lloyd George's coalition government was confirmed in power by a general election, and held office until October 1922.

Plans for a 'better Britain' had been laid in the midst of war. As early as December 1914, the Board of Trade had asked that measures to avoid unemployment after the war should be considered. In 1916 the Reconstruction Committee was established; this became the Ministry of Reconstruction, under Dr. Addison, in the following year. This Ministry considered plans for demobilisation, employment for those in the armed forces and the munitions factories, houses, education, civil aviation, the supply of raw materials, and industrial research. The heroes of the trenches and their families were to be offered a better life. In fact, not many of the plans were put into practice.

The demobilisation scheme did not work perfectly, mainly because some servicemen were unwilling to wait their turn, and returned home without official permission. But because of the plans made by the government, most were able to find work. The transfer of labour from war industry to other employment worked well.

The Reform Act of 1918 extended the franchise to all men aged twenty-one and over, and to women over thirty. By this Act six million women and an additional two million men were added to the electoral registers.

The Education Act of 1918, largely the work of H.A.L. Fisher, the

Minister of Education, raised the school-leaving age from thirteen to fourteen. More free places were provided in the grammar schools for able pupils, chosen by a 'scholarship' examination. By 1922 about one-third of the pupils at maintained secondary schools did not pay fees. But the proportion of the total child population able to go to grammar schools was very low.

THE MAN WHO ASKED A HOUSE-AGENT IF HE HAD A HOUSE TO LET.

This cartoon, drawn in 1919, would have been just as appropriate in the decade following the 1939–45 war.

The building of 'homes for heroes' was begun in 1919. There was a shortage of between 600,000 and one million houses, mostly in the cheaper range. Dr. Addison, then Minister of Health, introduced the Housing and Town Planning Act in 1919. Local authorities were to build houses to rent, and were given government grants to assist them to do so. By 1922 a total of 155,000 houses had been built under the Act, a considerable accomplishment. But because of a shortage of building materials, and unbusinesslike methods, each house cost the then high figure of £800 to build. The Act was suspended in 1922, with the housing shortage as acute as ever. Although private builders had completed some 44,000 houses since 1918, there were by 1922 some 460,000 more families than in 1918. The continued decrease in the *size* of each family led to a great demand for small houses.

Other Housing Acts

The housing shortage was alleviated by other measures after 1922. The Chamberlain Act (1923) reduced the subsidies given to local councils by the central government, but encouraged private builders to expand their activities. This Act was repealed in 1929. In 1924 the Labour Government passed another Housing Act (Wheatley's) designed to encourage once more the building of council houses to rent. The subsidies granted under this Act were continued until 1933. By 1930 some 725,000 houses had been built under these two Acts, half of them by local government, and half by private enterprise. A further half-million homes were built between 1918 and 1930 by private builders without government subsidy. During the 1930's there was a boom in private enterprise building, so that by 1939 the housing situation, though not perfect, was better than it had been.

The Trade Cycle

The plans of the immediate post-war government for a 'better Britain' were halted by the reappearance of a slump in world trade in the winter of 1920–21. Economists use the term 'trade cycle' to denote alternation of periods in which wages, employment, prices, and industrial output rise and fall. Although there were trade cycles during the eighteenth century, they became more pronounced during the period of industrialisation. In the hundred years before 1914 the complete cycle of downward and upward trend appeared to take about ten years, and these fluctuations became regarded as a natural consequence of capitalism. The trade cycles in the inter-war years were as follows:

1918–20	boom conditions due to the replenishment of stocks
1920–22	a sharp downward movement
1922–29	a slow uneven growth

46 *Women shipyard workers during 1914–18 war.* (p. 222)

47 *Women at work in a Norfolk electronics factory, 1967.* (p. 279)

48 *R.M.S.* Queen Mary
*(no. 534), being built at
Clydebank, 1934. Work on
her had been stopped in 1931
owing to lack of funds in the
depression.* (p. 239, 247)

49 *A street scene in Wigan,
November 1939. Even the
outbreak of war did not
bring an immediate end to
unemployment.* (p. 231)

1929-33   severe depression
1933-39   a steady upward trend.

Similar cycles were felt in all other industrial countries, except Japan
and the U.S.S.R. The most severe depression, that of 1929 to 1933,
began in the U.S.A. and spread over the western world. We now
know that governments can do something to prevent the trade cycle,
and that it is not an inevitable consequence of capitalism. Since 1945
the western industrial countries have enjoyed the benefits of expanding production. But in the inter-war years the usual government
response to a depression was to cut governmental expenditure, which
added to the problem by reducing the demand for labour. From 1922
to 1939 unemployment was a great social evil.

Unemployment

Unemployment was felt the more because of the high hopes of those
who had survived the war that a new age was dawning. But within
two years of 1918, the old problem, for it was an old problem, was
there once more. Further, the standard of living and the real wages of
those in work were rising between 1922 and 1939, so that those who
were unemployed had a greater reason for bitterness. In Britain, the
incidence of unemployment was higher in some parts of the country
than in others. These parts were called 'depressed areas' and were
found where the 'old' industries, such as coal and textiles, were
situated, namely in South Wales, the north-east, Lancashire, and the
lowlands of Scotland. In 1922 14·3 per cent of the working population
of Britain was unemployed; in 1927 the figure was still high at 9·7
per cent, and in 1929 it was 10·3 per cent. In 1932 38 per cent of the
insured population in the depressed areas was unemployed, as compared with the national average of 23 per cent. Even during the upward trend of the trade cycle after 1933, unemployment was never
less than 10 per cent, and there were still one million unemployed in
April 1940, after six months of war.

Economic Crisis, 1931

The severe depression of 1929-33 began in October 1929 with a
sudden and dramatic fall of prices in Wall Street, the American stock
exchange. World trade shrank, and the number of unemployed in
the U.S.A., Europe and Britain rose alarmingly. By 1930 19·9 per

cent of the British working population was out of work. Factories closed, businesses were ruined, and the government (since 1929 a Labour administration under Ramsay MacDonald) was unable to balance the budget. In August 1931 the government received the report of a committee led by Sir George May which showed that the government deficit was £120 million. The Bank of England, worried by the drain of gold from the country, was negotiating a loan from New York bankers. The latter wanted the government to make economies a condition of the loan. The Cabinet met to consider possible cuts, and split on the issue of a proposed 10 per cent reduction in unemployment pay. Unable to carry all his colleagues with him, Ramsay MacDonald, on the advice of King George V, formed a new National government comprising Conservatives, with some Liberal and Labour support. The new government introduced a budget which increased taxation and reduced government expenditure. The wages and salaries of all government employees (which included the armed forces) were cut by 10 per cent; unemployment pay (the 'dole') was cut by the same proportion.[1] These measures, though they led to a greater confidence in sterling abroad, did not help the unemployment problem.

Another action of the National government in 1931 was to take Britain off the gold standard. British currency was no longer to be valued in gold in the international market, and could not be exchanged for a fixed amount of gold. Britain had returned to the gold standard in 1925 in order to arrest the tendency for the large finance houses to leave London for Paris and New York. The return to the gold standard had helped to restore Britain's position as the financial centre of the world, but it had meant that British exports cost more. The end of the gold standard in 1931 meant that the pound was devalued as compared with foreign currency, so that British exports were cheaper abroad.

In November 1931 the Abnormal Importations Act was passed. This allowed the Board of Trade to impose duties on imported manufactured goods, ending a policy of free trade which had been in operation for seventy years. In 1932 the Import Duties Act laid down a detailed tariff of duties on a variety of articles. The Chancellor of the Exchequer, Neville Chamberlain (son of Joseph Chamberlain,

[1] It was restored in 1934.

who had advocated Tariff Reform earlier in the century) emphasised that other countries imposed duties on British goods, and that such protection of British produce was necessary to the economy. Later in 1932, at the Ottawa Conference, agreements were reached on preferential tariffs for goods from the Commonwealth.

The unemployment situation, however, had worsened by 1932, when three million people, or 23 per cent of the insured population were without a job. Thereafter, the country gradually pulled out of the severe depression, although there were still two million unemployed in 1935, and one and a half million in 1939. As late as 1937 22 per cent of the working population in South Wales were unemployed. The slow recovery after 1933 was due to a recovery in world trade, to the Ottawa agreements which helped the new industries, to the building of houses by local government and by private investors, to a reduction in the interest rates, and, after 1935, to rearmament. But the recovery was limited to certain sectors of industry, and, apart from iron and steel, the old staple industries remained in a state of stagnation.

Life on the Dole

Bare statistics of the numbers of unemployed do not show the hardship brought to individuals. Some men, not without skill in their trade, were unemployed for several years. Their children were forced by economic circumstances to leave school at fourteen, regardless of their suitability for higher education. The school leaver had to take whatever opportunities for employment were offered, and begin a career by chance rather than by choice. There were, before 1939, too many people chasing too few jobs. For example, several local education authorities, including the London County Council, would not employ married women teachers, so that many young teachers were forced to make an invidious choice between marriage or their career. Housewives whose husbands were on the 'dole' had a hard task in trying to feed and clothe their families. Something of the mood of hopelessness and bitterness of those years can be seen in such works as *The Road to Wigan Pier* by George Orwell, Walter Greenwood's play *Love on the Dole*, or Cecil Day Lewis' parody:

> Come, live with me and be my love
> And we will all the pleasures prove

Of peace and plenty, bed and board
That chance employment can afford.

I'll handle dainties on the docks
And thou shalt read of summer frocks:
At evening by the sour canals
We'll hope to hear some madrigals. . . .

To some of the population, the inter-war years were indeed the 'Wasted Years', for Britain's productive capacity was reduced by the wastefulness of having some of its labour force idle. To have lived in Jarrow, a town almost entirely dependent on one shipbuilding firm, and in which in 1935 72·5 per cent of the insured population was unemployed, must have been demoralising.

The Standard of Living

Despite the plight of the unemployed during the inter-war years, the standard of living of those in employment, which was the majority of the population, rose. Real wages increased by some 13 per cent between 1920 and 1938 owing to a fall in prices. As interest rates were low, it was possible for the working-man to buy a new semi-detached house through a building society on a twenty-five year mortgage. In the 1930's some houses were built for about £300, whilst for £800 a superior middle-class suburban home could be bought. Food was comparatively cheap, and although there were still too many of the population living below the 'poverty line', in general the people were better fed than in earlier periods. Health improved, partly because of the provision of better services by local authorities, such as clinics and infant welfare centres. In 1934 the Milk Act led to the provision of one-third of a pint of milk for all schoolchildren for a halfpenny (or free in special cases). But these improvements seem insignificant compared with the 'social revolution' which occurred after 1945.

Trade Unions and the General Strike of 1926

During periods when labour is plentiful and jobs are scarce, trade unions must perforce be active but relatively weak. The troubles in the coal industry led to a worsening in the relations between the unions and the government, culminating in the so-called 'General

Strike' in May 1926.[1] Half a million coalminers were already on strike when the General Council of the T.U.C. called out a further million and a half workers, including those employed in transport, printing, power, textiles, and iron and steel. The aim of the strike was to obtain better conditions for coalminers. The method, the withdrawal of labour by those not directly connected with coalmining, can be viewed from two standpoints—as a corporate action by trade unionists to help their fellows in distress, or as an attempt by one section of the community to force the government to a certain course of action by disrupting the economy of the country.

The General Strike began on 4 May 1926 and followed a plan drawn up by the T.U.C. during the previous week. The withdrawal of labour meant that there were few trains, trams, or buses running; power stations were unable to continue production, and there were no newspapers. But the government had been making preparations to combat such a strike since July 1925, when Sir John Anderson, a civil servant, was asked to draw up a plan, which was completed by November. The plan was brought into action. Troops and police were used to maintain essential services and to supervise the distribution of food. Volunteers were asked to help in transport services. White-collar workers and university students undertook with more enthusiasm than skill the tasks of driving buses or even trains—but this amateur labour did not succeed in establishing an effective transport system. There is a legendary story that one train reached a London terminus with a pair of level-crossing gates on its buffers. One local strike committee reported ironically, 'We understand that luncheon cars are to be put on trains running between Westminster and Blackfriars'. There were some clashes between strikers and those whom they regarded as blacklegs, but generally there were few unpleasant incidents. At Plymouth a football match was arranged between strikers and the police. If transport services were disrupted, the dissemination of news was effected by a government publication, *The British Gazette*, a daily newspaper printed by the Stationery Office, whilst the T.U.C. issued the *British Worker*.

On 6 May, Sir John Simon, a former Liberal Attorney General, stated in the House of Commons that the action of the T.U.C. in calling the General Strike was illegal. A few days later, however, Sir

[1] See p. 238.

Henry Slesser, a former Labour Solicitor General, stated that the strike was not illegal. But the question of legality did not seriously affect the actions of the T.U.C. The strike was brought to an end by indecision among the leaders of the T.U.C. as to the precise demands they should make on the government, and through a fear that they would lose control of the trade-union movement to extremists. Accordingly, when Sir Herbert Samuel offered to act as mediator, the T.U.C. called an end to the strike on 12 May without obtaining any firm assurances from the government. Workers, except the coal-miners (who stayed out until the end of the year and then had to return with no tangible gains), returned to work with a sense of being betrayed by their leaders. Some workers who had been strike-leaders were victimised or dismissed by employers, and no one had gained. But the speed with which the T.U.C. decided to end the strike, and the loyalty and obedience of the rank and file in returning to work, showed that the trade-union movement in Britain was not aiming at the overthrow of the established order. Beatrice Webb wrote in her diary: 'The failure of the General Strike shows what a *sane* people the British are.'

The Results of the General Strike

The government was sufficiently alarmed, however, to introduce a measure to ensure that such a general strike could not be repeated. The Trade Disputes Act of 1927 declared illegal any strike aimed at coercing the government 'either directly or by inflicting hardship on the community'. Civil servants were forbidden to join any union which was affiliated to the T.U.C. The voluntary contributions of all trade unionists to the Labour party were to be paid by 'contracting-in', i.e. the additional membership fee was paid only by those who signed a declaration that they would do so. Since 1913 the political levy had been collected by means of contracting-out, i.e. objectors signed a declaration that they did not wish to contribute. As a result of the introduction of contracting-in, the Labour party's income from trade unionists was cut by one-third.

The failure of the General Strike led to a decline in the prestige of trade unions, and to a decrease in membership between 1925 and 1927 of half a million. Many of those disappointed at the 'surrender' joined the tiny Communist party of Great Britain, whose membership doubled to 12,000 by the end of 1926. However, many of the new recruits were soon disillusioned by the aims and methods of the party, and left it. Another result of the General Strike was that the T.U.C. leaders began to work more closely with the Labour party. In 1928 Transport House was opened, with offices for the Labour party and the T.U.C. in the same building. This was symptomatic of the general trend in the trade-union movement between 1926 and 1939. The improvement of the lot of the working-man was to be achieved by constitutional means, through government departments. In one way the failure of the General Strike had strengthened the trade-union movement; the old syndicalist ideas of overthrowing the established order by the withdrawal of labour lost their hold on even the minority of the rank and file. The more moderate aim was the only practicable one at a time of mass unemployment which coincided with a Labour party weakened and almost impotent because of MacDonald's National government. The outbreak of war in 1939 saw co-operation between the unions, management, and the government in the face of the common enemy. In 1940 Ernest Bevin, one of the 1926 strike leaders, was appointed Minister of Labour by Winston Churchill. When the war ended in 1945, the Labour party had a majority in the House of Commons for the first time, so that trade-union co-operation with the government continued. The return of the Conservative party to power in 1951 did not result in any radical change in the relationship between unions and government—for both political parties were by then pledged to continue a policy of full employment.

CHAPTER 20

Industry, 1918–1939

Before the 1914–18 war Britain had made a living by manufacturing and exporting heavy industrial goods, such as iron and steel, ships, and machinery; by the export of cotton manufactured goods; and by giving financial services. Britain's industries were being closely challenged by those of other countries in the decades preceding the war, and the war had further weakened Britain's position. The immediate task which faced the country was to find a new way of making a living. Britain had to reorganise and reorientate her industrial capacity. The task was made difficult because of the upward and downward turns of the trade cycle, and because of the reluctance of governments to consider a planned economy.

Britain's comparative decline as an industrial power (the word comparative is used because she was and still is a great industrial power) was due to several factors. First, although many new inventions had been perfected in Britain, they were exploited more fully in other countries. For example, much of the pioneering work in the development of the motor-car was done in Britain, but by 1919 the U.S.A. was far ahead. Secondly, Britain had not the same incentive as had countries short of coal to turn over to oil and electricity. Thirdly, British firms were smaller and less centralised than those of their rivals. The large-scale firm, necessary for greater efficiency, was regarded with some suspicion in Britain. Fourthly, British manufacturers were handicapped by the tariffs imposed by other countries, for Britain remained a free-trade country until 1932. These factors affected the old industries situated in South Wales, the Scottish lowlands, Lancashire and the north-east, more than the newer industries in the south-east near London, and in the midlands. The expansion of the new industries went on concurrently with the decline of the old.

THE OLD INDUSTRIES

Coal

The following table shows clearly the decline of the coal industry.

Year	Output (in mill. tons)	Exports (in mill. tons)
1913	287	98
1923	267	79
1929	258	77
1933	208	57
1938	227	36

The main reason for the decline in demand for coal was the fall of exports. The increase of coal production abroad, the opening of new mines in the Netherlands, Spain, and the Far East, and the more efficient use of fuel led to a decrease in demand from former customers. Also, countries which had been great consumers of coal were increasingly using other fuels or sources of power. Petroleum, lignite, and hydro-electric power were coal's chief rivals. As the price of oil fell, shipowners sought oil-fired ships—and more customers were lost for British coal. In 1914 96·6 per cent of the world's shipping was coal-burning; by 1932 it was 60 per cent, and by 1939 54 per cent. And whilst the exports of British coal declined domestic demand did not grow. More coal was wanted to produce electricity and gas, and by the householder. But this was counter-balanced by a fall in the use of coal in the iron and steel industry, which turned to other fuels. Further, the use of coal by the railways diminished as some lines were electrified.

Miners' Troubles

An obvious consequence of the lessening demand for coal was the reduction of the labour force in coalmining. In 1913 1·1 million were employed in coal production; in 1920 1·2 million, in 1929 0·97, and in 1938 0·78. The coal industry became the centre of industrial disputes. The situation was exacerbated by the taking over of the mines by the government during the war. In January 1919, the Miners' Federation demanded a six-hour day, a 30 per cent increase in wages, and the nationalisation of the mines. The government appointed a Commission under Sir John Sankey to consider the future of the mines. The Sankey Commission was unable to reach agreement, and the Chairman, as a compromise, recommended that 'the *principle* of State ownership . . . be accepted'. In 1919 the boom conditions of the immediate post-war years were still prevailing, and the miners had little inkling of the dark days ahead. As the government, which still controlled the mines, showed no sign of nationalising them, the miners staged a national strike, which lasted seven days, in September 1919. By the end of 1920 the demand for coal was beginning to slacken, and it was obvious that the mines were running at a loss. Accordingly, the government decided to speed up the return of the mines to private owners. The owners could see no alternative to a reduction in wages, which the miners refused to accept. On 31 March 1921, the day on which the mines passed out of government control, the miners were locked out by the owners, who were unable to consider running a business in which they would lose money. After two weeks the miners gave in, and accepted a cut in wages. Four years later, trouble brewed once more. Because of the government's financial policy (in 1925 Britain returned to the Gold Standard), there was some deflation, i.e. the value of money rose. The mine owners asked the men to accept a further cut in wages. The government appointed another Royal Commission, this time under Sir Herbert Samuel. The Samuel Report, issued in 1926, recommended a reduction in wages. This the Miners' Federation refused to accept. Their secretary, A. J. Cook, stated their case as 'Not a penny off the pay, not a second on the day'. This impasse caused the General Strike of May 1926.[1] After remaining on strike for several months, the miners (those who *had* work), were forced to return, and to accept longer hours and less wages.

In 1930 the Coal Mines Act was passed, under which prices and output were regulated, and amalgamations controlled. In fact little reorganisation took place, but by 1939 mine owners were working together and controlling output, marketing and prices.

Other Declining Industries

The iron and steel industry was in the doldrums throughout the 1920's and suffered a sharp decline in the slump of 1929–32. Thereafter it recovered, and by 1937 steel output reached the record level

[1] See pp. 232–5.

of 12·9 million tons. This recovery was due to two main factors. The demand for iron and steel rose with the recovery of the motor-car, shipbuilding, and engineering industries, and was further stimulated by rearmament. Secondly, in 1932 a duty was placed on imported iron and steel. Further, the government initiated a reorganisation of the industry, forming the British Iron and Steel Federation in 1934. The Federation advised firms on reorganisation schemes, controlled competition, and subsidised modernisation and development plans. The Federation for example, made the firm of Richard Thomas build new rolling mills at Ebbw Vale, where unemployment was great, instead of in Lincolnshire.

As with the coal industry, the ills of the iron and steel industry were mainly caused by a decline in exports. A feature of the industry between the wars was a shift in its geographical centre eastwards to Northamptonshire and Lincolnshire.

The cotton industry declined rapidly between the wars, largely through a fall in exports. It was hit by the development of mills in countries which had formerly been customers, especially India. Also, Japan captured many former British markets in China and the Far East. The imposition of tariffs by the U.S.A. and Brazil caused further damage to the export of British cotton goods. Generally, Britain lost much of the cheap cloth trade, and had to concentrate on higher quality goods. The woollen industry also declined, though not as spectacularly as cotton, as it relied more on the home market. The woollen industry's exports were curtailed by tariffs, but Britain still retained much of the trade in high quality woollen and worsted goods.

Shipbuilding was in a fairly healthy state until 1920, as tonnage lost in the war needed replacing. After seven lean years, from 1920–27, there was a temporary recovery between 1927 and 1930 when the average tonnage launched per year was 75 per cent that of in the period 1911–13. Then the world slump affected the industry, so that in 1933 the tonnage launched was but 7 per cent of the pre-war average. From 1933, owing to a recovery in world trade, and to state help in the completion of a new Cunard ship, the *Queen Mary*, the shipyards made a slow recovery. The troubles in this industry were due in part to conditions outside its control, but in addition British yards were slow to build the new types of vessels, such as motor-ships, for which there was the greatest foreign demand.

EXPANDING INDUSTRIES

The industries which expanded in the inter-war years were those which demanded a high level of skill from managment and men, and in which the cost of the raw material was comparatively small. Britain had to live on her brains rather than brawn, by making sophisticated goods. These 'new' industries were all based on earlier discoveries, but they were comparatively unimportant before 1914. They included electrical engineering, chemicals, man-made fibres, radio, films, aircraft, and motor manufacture. They developed mostly in the home counties, the south-east, and the midlands. Thus they afforded no relief to the unemployed in the old industrial areas.

The electrical engineering industry grew rapidly as electrical power spread over parts of the country. In 1920 there were but 730,000 consumers of electricity; by 1929 there were 2·8 million, and in 1938 8·9 million. In the homes there was a demand for electric cookers, irons, and vacuum cleaners, whilst the more wealthy purchased refrigerators. The increased use of the telephone and radio for communications also acted as a stimulus to electrical engineering. Further, electricity gradually replaced gas for lighting in homes and streets, whilst the railways began to extend their use of electric power beyond the London and suburban lines. The number employed in these industries grew from 173,000 in 1924 to 367,000 in 1937.

The chemical industries grew as they became the manufacturers of products essential to other industries. They made dyes for textiles, fertilisers for the farms, industrial gases, and plastics. Further, as the country began to rearm after 1935, there was an increased demand for explosives and other war materials. By far the most important organisation in this industry was I.C.I., formed in 1926 by the amalgamation of four companies—British Dyestuffs, Brunner-Mond, United Alkali, and Nobel Industries.

The most important man-made fibre in the period was rayon, made from vegetable matter. There are two main types of rayon, viscose and acetate. The former is made from wood pulp and sulphuric acid, the latter from cotton linters treated with acetic acid. Viscose rayon was developed by Cross, Bevan and Beadle in 1892, but its manufacture in England was mostly in the hands of Courtaulds of Coventry.

The Motor Industry and Mass-production

The motor industry was more important in producing motor-cars for home consumption than for export. During the 1914–18 war, the industry in Britain had fallen behind its American counterpart, owing to Britain's concentration on munitions. Before 1914, Britain produced hand-made quality cars. From 1918 to 1939 the industry developed the American methods of mass-production with the amalgamation of smaller firms into larger units.[1] The first British mass-produced car was the Austin 'Seven' (i.e. 7 h.p.), brought out in 1922. Austin's were followed by Morris, and by the American firm of Ford, producing cars for the British market in Manchester, and after 1931 at Dagenham, Essex. The number of vehicles produced in Britain grew from 95,000 in 1923 to 511,000 in 1939. The number employed in the motor industry grew from 220,000 in 1924 to 380,000 in 1939. The industry was heavily concentrated in Birmingham, Coventry, Oxford, and the London region. Exports comprised only about one-eighth of the total production. This was due in part to the motor-taxation system, under which the amount paid varied with horse-power. As insurance companies used a similar system, the small car was in demand in Britain, but such cars were not suitable overseas. This system of taxation, however, coupled with an import tax of $33\frac{1}{3}$ per cent on foreign cars, enabled the British car industry to capture the home market, whilst preferential tariffs led to the sale of some British cars in the Commonwealth. The industry was not greatly affected by the slump of 1929–33. As in the 1930's successive Chancellors of the Exchequer increased the duty on petrol, demand grew for small-engined cars, with a low fuel consumption.

The development of the motor industry had important effects on other industries. First, mass manufacturing was adopted in other sectors of industry. This led to cheaper goods, but at the same time created social problems among workers doing dull, repetitive tasks. However the conveyor-belt system meant that semi-skilled labour could be utilised. The motor industry also stimulated other industries

---

[1] There were 96 British car manufacturers in 1922, and 20 in 1939.

which were concerned with making components, such as lights, sparking-plugs, magnetos, and other electrical goods. Also, mechanical engineering, metallurgy, and glass-making all profited from the expansion of the motor manufacturing business, as well as firms making rubber tyres, or producing oil and petroleum.

CHAPTER 21

Transport and Communications after 1918

After 1918 there was a revolution in transport every bit as remark-able as the age that saw the coming of the railways. Particularly important were the developments in road and air transport. Today it is possible to travel round the world in a fraction of the 'eighty days' which were regarded as fanciful by Jules Verne's nineteenth-century contemporaries. During the 1920's and 1930's, however, the private motor-car was still a luxury, and air travel was enjoyed (or endured) only by a very small minority. Most people relied on public transport, or on cheaper means of travel.

Hikers and Cyclists

Between 1918 and 1939 walking for pleasure was in vogue. This was because young people in the towns were unable to afford mechanical transport, yet wished to see the countryside. These walkers were known as 'hikers', and were a common sight, dressed in khaki shirts and shorts, and carrying rucksacks on their backs. A popular song in the early 1930's was entitled 'I'm happy when I'm hiking'. The bicycle was another popular form of transport. The three-wheeled tricycle grew obsolete as wheels became smaller. Bicycles could be now mounted without a step on the rear-wheel axle, whilst the cyclist had greater control as his feet could reach the ground from the saddle. Ladies' cycles had no 'bar'. Cycling was made less laborious by the introduction of the three-speed gear, and drop handle-bars made it possible to exert more pressure on the pedals. Cycling at night was made safer by the introduction of dry-battery or dynamo electric lighting, which replaced the flickering carbide lamps. The possession of a new Raleigh, Royal Enfield, or Hercules cycle was a source of envy, and owners looked after them with great care. The bicycle was used for pleasure; it enabled the townsman to get out into the countryside. It was a useful means of conveyance for workpeople, housewives and children; and it was used for carrying light goods, such as newspapers, bread, and meat. The sale of ice-cream was widened by large firms, such as Walls and Eldorado, who used tricycles with a small refrigerated unit in the front as mobile shops.

Railways

Railways, though still important for the transportation of passengers and goods, declined in importance during the inter-war years. The 120 railway companies had been nationalised during the 1914–18 war, as they were vital to the prosecution of the war. The Railway Act of 1921 was a compromise measure. The companies were merged into four large concerns; London Midland and Scottish, London and North Eastern, Southern, and Great Western. These were returned to private ownership, but as fares were standardised, competition between the companies was eliminated. The fares were regulated by a body called the Rates Tribunal, which unwittingly contributed to the decline of railways, already being threatened by road competition. Railway fares were based on mileage: a journey of 100 miles cost twice as much as one of 50 miles. Road fares tapered off, so that long journeys were cheaper by road than by rail. Also, railway freight charges were based on the value of the goods, whilst road charges were assessed on the size and weight. Road vehicles could transport goods from door to door, whilst railway traffic entailed taking the goods to and from the nearest railway station. Further, as road vans were smaller units, they were more flexible. Faced with this competition, the railway companies extended their activities. In 1934 they took over the two largest road-haulage companies, Pickfords and Carter Patersons. But the amount of freight (particularly coal and iron) carried by rail fell, and so did profits.

Electrification of surburban services was completed in London, Manchester, Liverpool and Newcastle. The electrification of main lines was begun by the Southern Railway with the lines from London to Brighton and Worthing in 1933. Plans for further electrification were stopped by the war in 1939. Railway companies began running

50 *William Morris' motor-body shop, Oxford, in 1913. Cars were then largely hand-made, and not mass-produced by machines. Wood and metal-workers continued techniques learned in the days of horse-traffic. (p. 114)*

51 *Austin Seven, 1922—yesterday's 'mini'. It was the first car to be mass-produced in Britain. (p. 241)*

52 *A Bristol tram, July 1914. The overhead electricity supply enabled trams to run through flooded streets. Route numbers were first used in Bristol in 1913. (p. 246)*

53 *An outing to Weston-super-Mare in a 17-seater charabanc, 1911. The vehicle was chain-driven, and had solid tyres. (p. 112)*

fast non-stop named trains, such as the *Flying Scotsman* and the *Royal Wessex*, in order to attract passengers. Despite these measures, the total number of passenger miles, 19·2 billion in 1920, had only risen to 20 billion in 1939. The peak years of railway passenger mileage were between 1939 and 1945, when other forms of transport were not available at a time when the population was 'on the move'. In 1945 railway passenger mileage was 35·2 billion. After that the total declined steadily: in 1963 it was 19·6 billion. The railways were losing customers to road and air transport.

Private Motoring

The most revolutionary change in transport was the development of the motor-car and motor-bicycle. Between 1922 and 1938 the number of registered motor vehicles rose from 498,000 to 2,422,000; the number of private cars rose from 353,000 in 1922 to 1,127,000 in 1930 and to 1,846,000 in 1938. By 1939 approximately one family in eight had a car, so that the possession of one could be regarded as a status-symbol. The quality cars were the Rolls-Royce and the Armstrong-Siddeley; the middle classes bought an Austin, Morris or Hillman; young men rode motor-cycles such as the Norton, the Royal Enfield, or the Velocette; many families travelled in side-cars driven by powerful motor-cycles like the B.S.A. 7·8. Three-wheeled Morgans, chain-driven, also enjoyed some popularity. The motor-car had important social effects. Car-owners were able to live further from their work, they could shop outside their immediate neighbourhood, and were able to visit the sea-side at week-ends. The countryman was no longer as isolated as he had been. It can be argued that this period was the golden age of motoring, before English roads became too crowded for enjoyment. For despite the hazard of breakdowns (and it must be conceded that the pre-1939 motor-car was prone to them) motoring was still a relaxed pleasure.

During the 1930's the volume of road traffic, though light by our standards, was such that government regulation became necessary. Under the 1930 Road Traffic Act, motorists had to furnish evidence of physical fitness in order to obtain a driving licence. It was still not necessary to pass a driving test. Anyone over the age of 18, who was physically fit, could obtain a licence and go straight on the road, even if he did not know the brake from the accelerator! Under the same

Act, third-party insurance was made compulsory. In 1934 driving tests were made obligatory for *new* applicants for driving licences. Those already in possession of licences did not have to pass a test. There are still some motorists on our roads who have not had to pass a test. Under the same Act, a speed limit of 30 m.p.h. was imposed in built-up areas, but the English motorist, used to freedom, ignored the speed-limit whenever possible. A few years later, pedestrian crossings were instituted on the roads in congested cities in order to give pedestrians the right of way. These crossings were marked by standards with yellow globes called 'Belisha Beacons' after Leslie Hore-Belisha, the Minister responsible for their introduction.

Trams and Buses

The majority of the people were not car-owners between the wars. They relied on public transport. For the townsman, the cheapest form of transport was the electric tram, the hey-day of which was in the 1920's when an average of five million people a year travelled in them. The tram has been rightly called 'the first public transport within the pockets of the poor'. There were indeed bargains to be had; from the Dee to the Don in Aberdeen for a penny; five miles through Glasgow for the same sum; from Lewisham to Vauxhall for two-pence. As children were half-price, the trams were convenient for parents with large families. At first the trams were single-deckers, or, if two-deck, the upper-deck was open to the weather. In cold weather the drivers wore mittens and balaclava helmets—but still looked and were cold. By about 1930, the double-decker became more common, and the front of the tram was glass-covered. Trams had three major defects. The over-head wires were ugly, and spoiled the look of city streets; the vehicles monopolised the roads, as tracks were usually in the centre, so that cars could not easily pass them. Also, when the trams stopped, traffic was brought to a halt, as passengers disembarked on to the middle of the road. School children had to be taught to get off with great care. The trams were noisy, as the wheels clattered along the steel rails, and as drivers clanged the foot-operated bell. A tram ride, usually on wooden perforated seats, was rickety, jerky, yet exciting. During the 1930's many cities replaced the trams with trolley-buses. These had two main advantages. They could use the side of the road, and could pull in to the kerb at stops; and they were less noisy, as they had pneumatic tyres. The one disadvantage of the trolley-bus was that routes could not be varied, as they could only run where the overhead power-lines were. For the latter reason, the motor-bus gradually became the chief method of public transport. In London, bus transport became more reliable if less exciting by the gradual elimination of competition. In 1924 there were 500 different bus companies in London, and buses raced each other to the stopping places in order to collect passengers ahead of competitors. The London Traffic Act of 1924 laid down routes and time schedules, but the rivalry still continued. In 1927 the independent companies were amalgamated into the London Public Omnibus Co., whose black buses, commonly called 'pirate', were in even fiercer competition with the large metropolitan red buses. More orderly and efficient methods were brought about through the creation of the London Passenger Transport Board (largely the work of Herbert Morrison and Lord Ashfield), in 1933. The L.P.T.B. took over 66 bus companies, 17 tramways companies, and five underground railways. As in London, other towns learned that a unified system of public transport was to be preferred to the chaos of a large number of small concerns.

Shipping

Shipping entered a period of slump by 1921, caused by a fall in freight charges and a shrinkage of world trade. Tramp steamers, i.e. cargo carriers with no regular itinerary, were particularly badly hit. Many were laid up, and it was a common sight in the 1920's and 1930's to see rusty ships moored in the approaches of the larger ports. But world trade and freight charges recovered in 1936, and this upward trend was accelerated by the worsening of the international situation. The larger shipping companies were able to continue in business under difficulty. In 1934 two large companies who had been in competition for the trans-Atlantic trade, Cunard and White-Star, amalgamated. In the same year, the government lent the Company £9·5 million to complete a new liner, work on which had been stopped three years previously. The ship, named *Queen Mary* was launched in September 1934. She was the largest vessel the world had hitherto seen (81,000 tons), capable of travelling at over 30 knots, and could cross the Atlantic in less than five days. The giant Cunarder was fitted out luxuriously in the first-class accommodation, in order to attract wealthy people who wanted to 'be at sea and yet away from it'. She was, in effect, a first-class hotel, with cinemas, lounges, a swimming-pool, and most of the amenities one would find on land. Also, because of her size, she could still proceed at a fair speed in face of the strongest winds. This vessel was a much-needed replacement for the ageing ships of the Cunard-White-Star Fleet, which then included a former German vessel, renamed the *Majestic*, the *Aquitania*, and the *Berengaria*. These older vessels caused some passengers discomfort at sea, as they pitched and rolled badly in the Altantic swell. Work was begun on a sister-ship for the new vessel. The second ship, completed in 1940, was the *Queen Elizabeth*, twelve feet longer than the *Queen Mary*, and with a displacement of 83,000 tons. These two ships began a weekly Atlantic service in 1946, but by the 1960's airtravel had made them no longer profitable. The *Queen Mary* was taken out of service in 1967 and sold to an American syndicate as a floating museum. The two 'Queens' were to be replaced by a smaller ship, *Queen Elizabeth II*, which could combine cruising with trans-Atlantic voyages.

Air Transport

Air transport was not of great importance before 1939. In 1919 two Englishmen, Alcock and Brown, crossed the Atlantic, from west to east, in a converted bomber. Their flight showed the potential of air travel, but considerable technical advance was needed before air travel over the oceans could become a safe commercial venture. In 1924 four private companies joined together, were subsidised by the government, and formed Imperial Airways. This company started with thirteen aircraft, with a total capacity of 112 passengers. Imperial Airways opened new routes (with frequent re-fuelling stops) to India, the Far East, South Africa, and Australia. In 1939 the company owned 77 aircraft, but was still carrying no more than 300,000 passengers per annum. In 1935 the government formed British Airways for flights to European countries. The two subsidised organisations were merged in 1939 to form the British Overseas Airways Corporation (B.O.A.C.). But it was not until after 1945, with the development of jet propulsion, that air travel became important.

The invention of the jet aircraft can be credited to Sir Frank

Whittle (born 1907). His father was a gifted mechanic, and young Frank showed an early technical aptitude. After attending a grammar school in Leamington, he became an aircraft apprentice at Cranwell at the age of fifteen. He then became an officer cadet, and was later commissioned in the R.A.F. When his scheme for a turbo-jet engine was rejected by the R.A.F. in 1936, he founded Power Jets Ltd., to make a test engine. By 1937 this experimental engine was sufficiently successful for the R.A.F. to take an interest, and the Service allowed Whittle the time to continue his experiments. The first test flight of a British jet aircraft took place in May 1941. By 1944, both the British and the Germans were using jet aircraft. After the war ended, the turbo-jet engine caused a revolution in civil aviation. Aircraft became able to cross the Atlantic in six hours, flying at over 30,000 feet, i.e. above the atmospheric disturbances nearer the Earth's surface. Speed, safety, and comfort were assured, so that long-distance passengers who formerly would have travelled by sea, went by air. By 1965 it was possible to travel from Britain to New Zealand in less than two days. Jet-propelled aircraft had two main disadvantages: they were noisy, and required long runways. The noise at take-off and landing was most disturbing to those who lived near large airports, but once the planes were airborne, they flew at great heights and could not then be heard from the ground. Airports had to be extended, and in some cases built at a distance from the large cities. The time saved in a fast flight for relatively short distances was cancelled out by a long road journey to and from airports. As a generalisation, it can be said that air travel is still not necessarily better than road or rail for journeys of less than 200 miles.

Transport after 1945

The increase in air travel after 1945 coincided with a growth of road transport. Private motor-cars became more common during the 1950's; the number of private vehicles in Britain rose from 1·8 million in 1946 to 2·4 million in 1951, 4·2 million in 1957 and 9·5 million in 1966. This rapid development led to congestion on the roads of large cities, so that elaborate and not very successful schemes for limiting road traffic were introduced. In 1963 many cities installed parking meters, or forbade street parking. In 1964 the Buchanan Report recommended more stringent prohibitions on vehicular traffic in towns. The motor accident rate remained such that road transport is the least safe method of transport.

The rise in air and road transport led to a further decline in the number of passengers carried by the railways. As British Railways were losing money, Dr. Richard Beeching, an executive of I.C.I., was employed by the government to modernise the railways. The 'Beeching Plan', published in 1961, advocated the closure of many branch lines and small stations, and improvements on main lines. No more steam engines were made; they were replaced by diesel-electric engines. Fast 'liner-train' freight services were instituted, in order to attract more goods traffic. Dr. Beeching's plans caused some controversy, as some thought that railway policy could not be divorced from plans for the roads and advocated the co-ordination of rail and road traffic. Dr. Beeching resigned in 1965, and returned to I.C.I.

The development of the Hovercraft in the late 1950's pointed to the transport of the future. The first Hovercraft, invented by C. S. Cockerell, was financed by the National Research Development Council, which set up Hovercraft Development Ltd. in 1959. A successful prototype, SR–N1, was built by Saunders-Roe of Cowes in 1959, and later in that year the first Hovercraft crossed the English Channel. By 1965 Hovercraft, mainly SR–N6's, were in regular use for short journeys such as from Deal to Calais or from the Isle of Wight to the mainland. Hovercraft were capable of some 80 m.p.h., and passengers could journey at speed without the fear of air-travel or the discomfort of a sea-journey. But they were an expensive means of travel, and could not be used over very rough seas.

COMMUNICATIONS

Letters and Telephones

The revolution in transport in the twentieth century was greater than that which occurred at the beginning of the nineteenth century. Further, the rapid changes in transport were accompanied by improvements in communications. The Post Office became more efficient in the delivery of mail, and the number of letters posted each year continued to rise. In 1913 3,477·8 million letters were posted, and in 1939 8,150 million. By 1950 the postal services were handling 23 million letters *per day*. The standard letter rate, raised from 3d. to

4d. in 1965, was relatively cheap compared with 1d. in 1840. The transit of overseas mail was speeded up by the introduction of light-weight air letters; during the 1960's it took about three days for air-mail to reach a destination in the U.S.A. from England, and four days to New Zealand. The cost of such air mail letters was 9d. in 1967.

The increase in telephone services enabled people to discuss busi-ness or private affairs at a distance. Whilst before 1939 the telephone in the home was a rarity except among the upper and middle classes, after 1950 it became more commonplace. In 1967 there were 11·5 million telephone installations in Great Britain, and about two-thirds of British families had a private telephone. Subscriber Trunk Dialling (S.T.D.) was extended over a wider area during the 1960's, enabling short conversations to be held at a relatively cheap cost. Improve-ments in long-distance telephonic communication made it easier and cheaper to speak to people overseas. In 1967 a three-minute call from Britain to New Zealand cost £3. This development meant that those in responsible positions could keep in touch with their organisations from a distance, and urgent decisions could be made instantly. In the near future, the extension of radio-telephonic services will lead to further improvements in communications throughout Britain, and in Britain's links with Europe.

Broadcasting

Sound broadcasting, although invented before 1914, developed after the 1914–18 war. The U.S.A. was first in the field of broad-casting, and Americans had many small competing companies. In Britain, the Post Office favoured a monopoly, with the result that the British Broadcasting Company was formed in 1922 (the name was changed to Corporation in 1926). The B.B.C., under the directorship of J. W. C. (later Lord) Reith, soon developed distinctive features. Reith had firm ideas on the future policy of this new means of communication. The B.B.C. was not to be motivated by profit; it was to perform a social service to all sections of the community; it was to contribute to 'the intellectual and moral well-being of the community'. These ideals were upheld, with the result that the B.B.C. gained world-wide recognition for its impartiality and its tone. The first 'listeners' used earphones attached to crystal sets; then the loud-speaker became more usual. There were 3 million licence holders in 1929, and 9 million in 1939. During the war, the B.B.C. was an important instrument in the war effort. The people were informed from an authoritative source of the latest events. Sound broadcasting was at its height during and immediately after the 1939–45 war. During the 1950's, television services spread all over the country. The B.B.C. had a monopoly in the early years, but in 1955 an Independent Television Authority was established to provide an alternative. Whilst the B.B.C. relied on income from licences, the I.T.A. obtained its money from advertisers. In 1964 the B.B.C. began a second channel (B.B.C.2) and the first programmes in colour were broadcast on that channel in 1967. Television, like all new inventions, was regarded with suspicion at first. Some warned that children would no longer read, that conversation and social intercourse would decline. At first this new medium was abused. Families spent too many hours in passive 'watching'. But television proved to have a great educative and unifying effect. It enabled people to 'see' great events, such as the funeral of King George VI in 1952, or the World Cup matches in 1966. It proved a boon to the aged and the inactive, whose vision was hitherto limited to four walls. It also led to the decline in cinema attendances—as people could see 'pictures' in their own homes.

All these developments made for a rapid 'shrinking' of the world. Distance no longer prevented communication.

CHAPTER 22

The Second World War, 1939-1945

In September 1939 Great Britain and France declared war on Germany, following Hitler's invasion of Poland. By the end of June 1940, Germany had overrun most of Western Europe, including France, so that German soldiers at Calais were but twenty-one miles from Britain. Italy joined the war as Hitler's ally, making Britain's sea-lanes in the Mediterranean difficult to keep open. During the winter of 1940–41 Britain and the Commonwealth stood alone. The United Kingdom was subjected to heavy air-raids, and was like a fortress under siege. In June 1941 Germany attacked Russia. In December 1941 the Japanese assault on Pearl Harbour brought the U.S.A. into the war. By the summer of 1942 the tide was beginning to turn in favour of the Western Allies, and their landings in Italy in 1943 and in Normandy in 1944 heralded the beginning of the end. Germany surrendered in May, and Japan in August 1945.

Pre-war Planning

Britain was better prepared for war in 1939 than she had been in 1914. Since the early 1930's paper plans were being prepared by various government departments. In 1937, following the experience of the Spanish Civil War, an Air Raid Precautions Act was passed to initiate plans for civil defence. Many of those in positions of responsibility and power had been young men during the previous war, and they were able to use the experience they had gained then. Plans had also been made for the granting of wide powers to the government, to provide for the control of food supplies and industry. After the Munich Agreement in September 1938, Chamberlain's Conservative government speeded up naval building and aircraft production. An Act to begin compulsory military service (i.e. conscription), the first such to be enacted in Britain in *peace-time*, was passed in the spring of 1939. Those aged 21 were to be called up later in the year.

Chamberlain's Administration, 1939–40

As a result of these plans, it was possible for the government to take some action immediately the war began. Schoolchildren from large cities were evacuated to more remote areas in case of air-raids. Their destination was kept secret even from parents and teachers. These schoolchildren often found themselves sharing a school with the 'permanent residents', perhaps doing morning or afternoon lessons only. They were billeted with local families. Many householders had air-raid shelters in their gardens, the most popular being the 'Anderson' shelter, with a rounded roof. There was just room for three people to lie down, or for about six or seven people to squat in them. Sand-bags and other anti-blast protection were placed round public buildings, and sand and water-buckets were put ready to deal with fire. The civilian population were issued with gas-masks, in little cardboard cartons. The mood was very different from that in 1914. Business could not be as usual. The front line was to be the home. All, civilian and service man alike, were to be in the front line.

New ministries were established, including Economic Warfare, Information, Food, and Shipping. Identity cards were issued to all British citizens who had to produce them on demand. Men between 18 and 40 had to register, and the 'call-up' of those aged 21 to 25 had been completed by April 1940. To help to pay for the war, income tax was raised to 7s. 6d. in the pound, and an excess profits tax was imposed. Food rationing began in January 1940.

These measures, good though they were, were insufficient for the demands of the situation. Many plans were still 'on paper', whilst the control of industrial production, keeping it to essential supplies only, had not been brought into action. The British government was moving into war at a pace which would have been admirable in 1914, but which was too slow for 1940. Stocks of food were insufficient; the services were haggling for supplies; there were still one million unemployed in April 1940. A far greater control of production, labour, resources, and consumption was necessary.

Churchill's Administration—'Total War'

Neville Chamberlain resigned in May 1940, and Winston Churchill formed an all-party National government. The Deputy-Premier, Clement Attlee, leader of the Labour Party, set the tone when he stated that the government 'demands complete control over persons and property'. Total war was to become a reality. Action was to replace administrative activity.

The control of the labour force was accepted by the people. Some men were drafted into the armed forces; others, whose special skills were regarded as essential to the war effort, were in 'reserved occupations'. Men outside the military age were directed into essential jobs. Training schemes were organised in order to give unskilled workers special skills, or to retrain those skilled in one trade for other sectors of industry which needed labour. In 1943, young men aged 18 were given the option of joining the services or working in the mines. Those who chose to join the coalmining industry were called 'Bevin boys', after Ernest Bevin, the trade-union leader who became Minister of Labour in the Churchill government. In March 1941, women were made to register for service, and they also were liable to be drafted into essential jobs. In December 1941, for the first time in Britain's history, powers were given to the government to conscript some women into the armed forces. Those liable for conscription were single women and childless widows. Women's sections of the three services were expanded under the names the Women's Royal Naval Service, the Women's Royal Army Corps and the Women's Auxiliary Air Force. Some members of the women's forces even served on anti-aircraft sites, but the majority were engaged in non-combatant duties. Many women worked on the land in the Women's Land Army.

Many new factories were built in remote country areas, whilst some firms were dispersed or moved. The workers had to be prepared to move about the country, and to live in 'hostels'. This mobilisation of the civilian population proceeded smoothly. All felt that they had to contribute to the war effort. By June 1944, 22 out of every hundred of the labour force were in the armed forces, and a further 33 working in war production.

Strikes were made illegal, and wages were assessed by an arbitration board. There was, in fact, little unrest in industry, despite the hardships which many suffered. Air-raids on large cities often disrupted everyday life. Transport and power were interrupted; sometimes workers had to walk to work and on arrival had to use ingenious temporary devices in order to keep the wheels of industry turning. Long hours in the workshops were often followed by interrupted nights spent in an air-raid shelter. But the temper of the work-people remained good. They lived to the slogan of the Londoners at the height of the blitz—'Britain can take it'. Employers had to obey orders; they were told what to produce, and raw materials were allocated to them; they were made to provide welfare services for their labour force. These facilities included canteens, nursery schools for the young children of married women workers, and 'music while you work'—recordings broadcast to cheer those engaged in monotonous tasks.

Both management and men had to accept new methods. Trade unions allowed semi-skilled men to perform work hitherto done only by fully trained craftsmen. This led to more mass-production, for the semi-skilled could quickly be trained to do repetitive jobs. The shortage of raw materials, either because the country of origin was in enemy hands, or because shipping space could not be spared for sufficient importation, led to great developments in chemical engineering. Synthetic rubber, man-made fibres, and nylon all came into increasing use. The Department of Scientific and Industrial Research stimulated improvements in such inventions as radar and asdic, useful in war and peace. The invasion of Normandy in 1944 exemplified the alliance of industry with the armed forces: a prefabricated port, Mulberry Harbour, was towed across the Channel, and fuel oil was pumped from the English coast to France by means of Pluto (pipe line under the ocean).

Food Supplies

The nation had to be fed. In 1939 Britain was importing about 70 per cent of her food, and paid for it by exports. The coming of war meant that more had to be grown at home. The most urgent need was an increase in the production of wheat, for only about 10 per cent was home-grown in 1939. Farmers were given a subsidy of £2 per acre, and they were encouraged to use more machines and fertilisers. There were about 60,000 tractors in use in 1939, and 190,000 in 1945. An increase in arable farming meant that there was less land for pastoral use. But, because of the need for dairy products, the number of cattle had to be increased. Accordingly, severe reductions were made in the number of pigs, sheep, and poultry. Private citizens were urged to grow more food. The cry was 'Dig for Victory'. Flower-gardens were converted into vegetable patches; waste-land and unproductive land was used to grow potatoes, cabbages and lettuce.

Before the war, food was rationed by price. There was a limit to what the poor and the unemployed could afford to buy. During the war, with almost all the adult population at work, the demand for food grew and prices would have risen sharply without government control. Further, as farmers were using more tractors and fertilisers, and were farming marginal land, their costs were rising. The Chamberlain government began the subsidising of food to prevent a sharp rise in food prices, and the Churchill administration continued this policy. Whilst the farmers received double the pre-war price, the public paid only 25 per cent more, the remainder being found by taxation.

The rationing of food began in January 1940. At first only sugar, butter and bacon were affected, but gradually most foodstuffs were rationed. The weekly ration per person varied according to the available stocks, from 1s. to 2s. 2d. worth of meat, 2 to 4 oz. of tea, $\frac{1}{2}$ to 1 lb. of sugar, 1 to 8 oz. of cheese, and 4 to 8 oz. of bacon. Manual workers received a higher allocation than did clerical workers; children and expectant mothers were given extra milk and eggs, as well as free orange-juice, cod-liver oil, and malt tablets. National Dried Milk was supplied for babies at a comparatively low price. Items that were not rationed were allocated through a points system; everyone had a certain number of points per month (it varied from 16 to 24), and could use these for food of his choice. 'Personal points', used for chocolates and sweets, gave each person about 4 oz. per month. This complicated but just system ensured that the farmers' products were fairly shared. Despite rationing, the average consumption of food per head rose during the war; malnutrition was largely eliminated, and the nation was healthier than in the days of the depression.

Utility Goods

In order to control supplies, materials, and prices, in 1941 the government introduced a unique scheme for 'utility' clothing and furniture. Articles were made to certain specifications, and sold at a controlled price. To conserve material, for example, men's trousers had no 'turnups', and jackets had no inside pockets. Furniture and clothing were rationed, also by a points scheme. Newly-married couples had to plan their purchases with care, whilst young ladies had a very limited choice of fashion.

Taxation

The increase in governmental activity, and the subsidising of food and welfare, together with the cost of the war, led to the increase of direct and indirect taxation. Income tax was raised to 10s. in the pound in 1941, and those with very high incomes faced a surtax of 19s. 6d. in the pound. Death duties were raised from 50 per cent to 65 per cent. In 1944 'pay-as-you-earn' (P.A.Y.E.) was introduced. Hitherto income tax had been charged on income earned during the previous financial year; under P.A.Y.E., by a series of ingenious tables, tax was deducted from the weekly or monthly salary of the current income. This system is still used today. In 1941 an additional income tax was levied, known as 'Post-war Credits'. The extra tax was deducted, and the tax-payer was given a voucher for repayment, to be redeemed at some time in the future. Indirect taxation was also raised, especially on spirits and tobacco. A new tax, called a purchase tax, was levied on luxury or non-essential goods from 1940. Even this weight of taxation did not pay for all government expenditure, which rose from £920 million in 1937–38 to £6,179 million in 1944–45. But, whereas the government raised only 39 per cent of its expenditure in 1940, by 1944 the proportion had grown to 55 per cent.[1] The remainder was found by borrowing from private citizens through war loans or National Savings, and from the U.S.A. and Commonwealth countries. The Americans supplied Britain by a 'cash and carry' scheme until Britain's dollar resources were almost exhausted, and then from March 1941, under an arrangement known

---

[1] Compare these figures with 20 per cent in 1915–16 and 30 per cent in 1917.

as 'lend-lease', loaned Britain goods and equipment worth £7,000 million for the duration of the war.

Britain at the End of the War

During the war Britain had used £1,200 million of her foreign investments (leaving £2,800 million) in order to obtain supplies from abroad, and had had to borrow an additional £3,400 million. This meant that, whereas before 1939 Britain could pay for some of her imports with the interest from her investments, after 1945 all imports had to be paid for with exports. Further, Britain now had to pay interest to other countries, so that she had to export more than she could import in order to preserve a balance of payments. This change in fortune meant that new problems faced the country. Exports needed to rise to 150 per cent of the pre-war level in order to attain the pre-war standard of living.

But Britain had suffered other losses. Many of her export markets were lost, as her customers had found other sources of supply. Much of the country's capital equipment—machines, factories, railways, or houses had been damaged by enemy air attacks, or was in need of repair. Shipping tonnage had decreased. In 1938 Britain had about 18 million tons of merchant shipping, but such were the losses in the war that, despite an intensive shipbuilding programme, in 1945 she had only 13 million tons. Britain's losses in manpower, though much lower than the 1914–18 war casualties, were about 400,000 including those killed in the armed forces, the merchant navy, and civilians. In addition, there were many thousands who were injured, and who would be unable to play their full part in life. Other losses cannot be measured: the tiredness of the working population, and their emotional disturbance can but be surmised.

But the nation had also gained something. Agricultural production had doubled, so that by 1945 about 75 per cent of the country's food was being produced at home, for farming was more efficient and new methods were more widely used. Industry also had had to become more efficient, and management had adopted more modern methods. Factories or airfields, designed for war, could be adapted for peacetime use. The labour force had increased from 18 million to 22 million during the war, because there were no longer large numbers of unemployed and because more women were in employment. The average working week had increased from $46\frac{1}{2}$ to $48\frac{1}{2}$ hours. Many people, unskilled before the war, had received some training for specialist jobs during the war. Further, a gain which cannot be estimated statistically, the war had united the British people in a common task. Victory had been brought about by a common effort; the immediate post-war years brought the nation face to face with fresh challenges.

54 *The Short Jupiter Calcutta sea-plane at anchor in the river Medway, 1928.* (p. 248)

55 *The Gloster E 28/39, Britain's first jet aeroplane. Sir Frank Whittle's W.I. turbo-jet engine stands in front of it.* (p. 249)

56 *Southampton schoolboys being evacuated to Bournemouth, 1939. The schoolmaster leading them, Dr Horace King, later became Speaker of the House of Commons.* (p. 254)

57 *Southampton High Street the morning after a night of air-raids, 1940.* (p. 256)

CHAPTER 23

Economic Problems since 1945

The Main Problems

The years after 1945 can be divided into three distinct periods. From 1945 to 1951, when the immediate consequences of the war had to be dealt with, there was an age of 'austerity'. From 1951 to 1955 confidence grew with an obvious but slow rise in prosperity. After 1955, and throughout the 1960's there was an age of affluence, tempered in the 1970's by some doubt that this might not last for ever.

Three major problems beset successive British governments. First, there were repeated crises over the balance of payments.[1] As Britain had to import half her food and most of her raw materials she had to export goods and services in order to pay for them. During the war, Britain had spent some of her reserves of gold and foreign currency, so that she now had to pay her way in the world. Moreover, other countries had sterling balances in London, and any lack of confidence in Britain's economy led to a tendency for holders of sterling to withdraw them in favour of gold or other currencies. There were frequent crises, notably in 1955, 1960, 1964, 1966 and 1974 when Britain had to rescued by loans from foreign banks. Loans had to be repaid and foreign bankers expected British governments to take measures to restrict demand from the British people, measures which brought hostility at home. Secondly, there was the problem of inflation, which affected not Britain alone, but most of the world. In addition to the rise in world commodity prices, domestic conditions in Britain added to the inflationary spiral. All the political parties subscribed to a policy set out in *Full Employment in a Free Society*, a report issued by the Beveridge Committee in

[1] See p. 299

1944. But full employment led to a strengthening of the bargaining power of those who were organised in strong unions, so that demands for higher wages had to be met. This meant higher prices and consequently more demands for pay rises. Governments were unable to do more than to check the inflationary spiral temporarily. Thirdly, there was a need to improve efficiency and productivity in order to increase the national wealth, at a time when the British people expected more of everything year by year. The more the British people consumed of the goods they made, the less there was for export; the less they saved, the less there was for capital investment.

The existence of these problems meant that governments had to play a greater part in the control of the economy. As the state now spent a greater proportion of the national product, governments could have some influence. Whereas in 1938 government spending accounted for 19%, in 1951 it had risen to 34.9%; between 1952 and 1962 it was 40 to 45%. The 'planned economy' had become a necessity, but it had to be put into practice by persuasion, by co-existing with private enterprise and with the free bargaining traditions of the trades unions. Governments were forced to go from one temporary expedient to another, and none was able to find a permanent solution.

THE YEARS OF AUSTERITY, 1945-51

A general election, the first for ten years, held in July 1945 resulted in a sweeping Labour victory. The Labour party, under Clement R. Attlee, remained in power until 1951, though from February 1950, as a consequence of another general election, its overall majority was only ten. The Labour government was faced with many immediate problems. The transition from war to peace had to be carried out smoothly and quickly; industry had to be re-equipped; the social reforms and the nationalisation programme promised in the election manifesto had to be implemented. But above all, the balance of payments problem, and especially an acute dollar shortage caused by the purchase of supplies from the U.S.A. during the 'cash and carry' period up to March 1941, had to be dealt with. The easing of some of these problems could be achieved only by worsening others. The Labour government's policy was not surprisingly lacking in consistency. Though it achieved much in the establishment of the welfare state, it failed to stabilise the economy. It might be said that the problems were so great that they defied a quick solution.

Dollar Loan, 1945

The dollar shortage was accentuated by the abrupt termination of lend-lease with the ending of the war. Britain was now faced with the immediate problem of paying for her imports by exporting. This task was rendered difficult by the need for time to convert industrial production to peace-time needs, which required considerable capital investment and, in particular, dollar aid. The government had no alternative but to ask the Americans for a loan in order to buy time. At the end of 1945 the famous economist, John Maynard Keynes, was sent to the U.S.A. to negotiate a dollar loan. The Americans were at first hesitant, as there were countries other than Britain needing help; but Keynes put the case for Britain with clarity and force. It is to the credit of the U.S.A. that, despite some misgivings on the part of some members of Congress, a loan agreement was reached. Britain received 3,750 million dollars from the U.S.A., and a further 1,125 million dollars from Canada, at the very low interest rate of 2 per cent. Britain was to start repaying the loan in 1951 by annual instalments for fifty years. Also, the U.S.A. insisted, as a condition of the loan, that Britain should honour the Bretton Woods Agreement by July 1947.[1] This meant that Britain had to play her part in I.M.F., and make her currency convertible two years earlier than had been agreed. The government was criticised for accepting this agreement, but they had little option. Beggars cannot be choosers. They had bought time, but due to circumstances beyond their control, not as much time as was required. A rise in raw material prices led to the exhaustion of the loan more rapidly than was expected.

Government Controls

In order to ensure that exports grew, the government had to curb domestic demand by the continuance of controls. As most goods had been rationed during the war, or had been unobtainable, the British

[1] See p. 301

people were in need of many of the things which we would regard as essentials. Also, many people had saved money during the war. Economists call this situation 'suppressed inflation'. The government had, therefore, to decide how much of the national product could be spent on housing, furniture, food, etc. and to keep down demand by controls. Food rationing was continued; in 1946, owing to a world shortage of food, the weekly allocations of bacon and eggs were even reduced. In the same year bread, which had been plentiful during the war, was rationed. Bread Units entitled all adults to the equivalent of two large loaves per week, and children under six to one large loaf. Critics were quick to point out that the Labour government had achieved something which Hitler's U-boats had failed to do.

"Now don't forget—anyone hanging around with a wistful · look in their eye—let 'em have it—bing, bang!"

Bread-rationing, avoided during the 1939–45 war, came into force in 1946.

The Winter Crisis, 1946–47

Industrial production was disrupted by bad weather in the winter of 1946–47, when a fuel crisis led to the loss of £200 million in exports. In the middle of December 1946 the bitter cold set in; five weeks later heavy snow fell over all the country—even in the Scilly Isles. Snowdrifts paralysed road and rail transport, disrupting industry. Coal supplies were already low when the blizzard struck. As coal deliveries became more difficult, with roads impassable and colliers sheltering in port from the gales, several power stations had to close. This meant more than hardship to people in home and factory. The lack of power caused some factories to close; by the end of the first week in February 1947 there were over two million men unemployed. In order to save power, greyhound racing and television were suspended, and people were forbidden to use electric fires in their homes during the daytime. The frosts continued throughout February, and after a slight thaw in early March, more snow came. Then, the thaw coincided with high winds and torrential rain, which flooded 600,000 acres of arable land, and ruined potatoes and wheat. This extreme weather was followed by an unusually hot and dry summer, which brought a water shortage. This was the year the American loan ended, when Britain was supposed to stand on her own feet.

Cripps and Devaluation

In 1947, owing to a boom in the U.S.A. which led to a reduction in American imports from Britain, Britain's foreign exchange situation grew steadily worse. In October 1947, Sir Stafford Cripps replaced Hugh Dalton as Chancellor of the Exchequer, and he began a policy which has been called 'austerity'. Britons were to be self-denying in order to help the balance of payments crisis. The situation was eased by the generosity of the United States. In April 1948, under the Marshall Plan, dollar aid was given to Britain together with fifteen other European countries, until 1952. But in 1949 Britain was faced with another financial crisis. Sir Stafford Cripps took many steps to save foreign currency, including the limitation of foreign exchange for inessential purposes, such as holidays abroad. Cripps then took the desperate course of devaluation, so that the pound sterling was valued at 2·80 dollars instead of 4·03. This devaluation, by making British goods cheaper abroad, temporarily helped the export drive. But the wisdom of devaluation was questionable, as the gains were short-lived. As raw materials and other imports became correspondingly dearer, in the long run Britain was no better placed.

Although the 'dollar shortage' and the balance of payments problem continued throughout the 1950's, the problems were not as acute as in the immediate post-war years, as British industry had recovered partially. Also, the price of raw materials fell, giving Britain more favourable terms of trade. During the 1950's it was possible to assuage the needs of the home market. The rationing of food came to an end by slow degrees. In 1948 bread, potatoes and jam were derationed. The rationing of clothes and shoes was ended in 1949; soap and milk in 1950; sugar and tea in 1952, and meat, bacon, fats, butter and eggs in 1954. Petrol rationing ended in 1950. Goods became plentiful, so that it appeared that Britain was prospering.

The Labour government which went out of office in 1951 was followed by thirteen years of Conservative rule. Whilst there was a difference in the policies of the two parties on public platforms—the Labour party advocated social justice and equality through state control, and the Conservative party urged an expanding economy through more freedom for private enterprise—in practice there was little fundamental difference between the practice of the two parties whilst in power. Both parties could be criticised for not taking action early enough, and for failing to initiate comprehensive long-term economic planning. This failure was due in part to political circumstances. As governments are in office only with the support of the electorate, they cannot flout public opinion. The British electorate was still distrustful of too much governmental interference in the economy.

Recurrent Inflation

From 1951 to 1956 the balance of payments situation was reasonably satisfactory, and the volume of exports was rising. But the country appeared to be caught in a spiral of inflation; rising prices, followed by wage increases, which caused a further rise in prices. The Bank Rate, which in practice controlled the interest rate, was raised from 2 per cent to 2·5 per cent in 1952, the first time that a British government had used this device to influence the economy. This move was in accordance with the theories of J. M. Keynes.[1] The intention was

[1] See pp. 304–5

to curb domestic demand for goods, as firms or private individuals borrowing money had to pay a higher interest rate.

In 1957, when Harold Macmillan succeeded Sir Anthony Eden as Prime Minister, Britain's economic situation appeared to be good. The balance of payments position was strong, and the country appeared to have solved its economic problems except for rising prices. Full employment had been achieved, the standard of life of the majority of the people was rising. The term 'The Affluent Society', coined by an American about his country, was apparently appropriate to England. Macmillan himself later used the phrase 'You have never had it so good'. But inflation was a serious problem. Expansion of the economy was taking place, but prices were rising more rapidly than was production. In September 1957 the Chancellor of the Exchequer, Peter Thorneycroft, raised the Bank Rate from 5 per cent to 7 per cent and advocated a reduction in governmental expenditure. His views were not accepted by the majority of the cabinet, and Thorneycroft resigned early in 1958. His successor, Heathcote Amory, lowered the Bank Rate, and followed an expansionist policy. The balance of payments position weakened in 1958, and was adverse in 1959. The government in that year applied what was known as a 'credit squeeze', i.e. restrictions on facilities for borrowing money. In 1961 the new Chancellor of the Exchequer, Selwyn Lloyd, was forced to take stronger measures. The Bank Rate was raised from 4 per cent to 7 per cent, customs duties and purchase taxes were increased; and government expenditure was cut. In addition, Selwyn Lloyd announced a 'pay pause', or an appeal to workers not to ask for wage increases. Critics of the government complained of a 'stop-go' policy, for so it appeared to be. The controllers of the economy appeared to be applying alternately brake and accelerator. But the government had made some positive achievements; it had avoided the devaluation of the pound at a time when speculators were converting their holdings of sterling into dollars; and it had given the nationalised industries a salutary warning that they should try to pay their way.

Devaluation, 1967

During 1963 and 1964 Britain's trading figures worsened. Harold Wilson became Prime Minister in 1964, and announced that priority would be given to solving the problem. The Bank Rate was raised, indirect taxation increased, restrictions were placed on the exchange of sterling for foreign currency, and government aid was given to exporters. A loan was obtained from I.M.F., and E.F.T.A. agreements for the reduction of duties were postponed. Cynics said that the Conservative policy of 'stop-go' had been replaced by one of 'stop-stop'. But even these stringent measures were not enough. After a slow improvement in 1965–6, despite a long seamen's strike, the trade gap widened in 1967. The closure of the Suez Canal, a long dock strike, foot-and-mouth in the midlands, restrictions on trade with South Africa and Rhodesia were contributory factors but not causes. The British people were living beyond their means. Following a 'run' on sterling in November 1967 the pound sterling was devalued by 14·3 per cent.

Prices and Incomes

The Labour government of 1964, like its predecessors, tried to tackle the vexed problem of wage demands. The Conservatives had, in 1963, set up a National Incomes Committee, hoping to link rising wages with rising productivity, and thus braking inflation. This failed, in the main because of the hostility of the trade unions, who argued that, since no attempt was made to control prices, it was an unjust approach to the problem. The Labour government tried to get the goodwill of both sides of industry by promising to consider both wages and prices, and formed, early in 1965, the National Board for Prices and Incomes. The Board had few teeth, and the voluntary approach proved ineffective. In July 1966, after a general election in which the Labour government was returned with a large majority, a compulsory 'freeze' of wages and prices was applied for a period of six months. At the end of that period trade unions and management agreed to try to make industry more efficient, to increase productivity, and to minimise the rise in wages and prices. The N.B.P.I. was empowered to act as an arbiter, and any rise in prices or incomes was to receive its approval. But by 1968 the effects of devaluation added to pressure from management and men for increases, and though the government tried desperately to contain the situation, the 'voluntary' policy was, by 1970, largely a dead letter.

The Conservatives were in power from 1970 to February 1974, and they tried a two-pronged attack on the problem. First, every encouragement was given to industry to expand, in the hope that increased activity could effect the maintenance of full employment and a greater gross national product. Secondly, by curbing the trade unions through the Industrial Relations Act and the application of of a compulsory prices and incomes policy, they hoped to keep wage demands within reasonable limits. But inflation became more rampant, and the situation was made worse by both external and internal problems. Abroad, world prices for raw materials rose rapidly, especially oil, when in late 1973 the oil producing countries formed a cartel and made dramatic increases. At home, a policy of non-co-operation with the government by some of the larger unions led to tension which was brought to a head in December 1973 with a strike of the coalminers. By the beginning of January 1974 the whole of industry was on a three-day working week, whilst shops, offices, and schools had to make do with severe reductions in power supplies. The government called a general election in February 1974, in the midst of industrial strife, and Harold Wilson became Prime Minister once more, at the head of a Labour govern-ment. The miners were immediately given all they had demanded, the three-day week ended, and the possibility of the compulsory control of wages appeared to be at an end. Critics of Heath's Con-servative government were quick to assert that their troubles had been partly of their own making. The government had applied legal sanctions to wage demands without sufficient popular support; they had increased the amount of money in circulation in order to help expansion, thus adding to inflation; the Bank Rate was raised in 1973 to 13%, partly as a consequence of a world-wide rise in interest rates, and this hit all debtors, including house mortgages; house prices had doubled in five years; not enough was done to curb prices. Defenders of the government blamed world prices and the sudden shock of the oil price rises. Whatever the rights and wrongs, by the end of 1974 the balance of payments had got almost out of hand, with each months' adverse figures forcing the government to borrow from abroad. The country appeared to be mortgaging its future.

The Common Market

Although it was clear that Britain had to 'export or die', the question of to whom she should sell was not so clear. The patterns of trade were changing, with the loosening of the ties with the Commonwealth. In 1957 six western European countries formed the European Economic Community (E.E.C. or 'Common Market').[1] At that time, Britain's trade with the sterling area was greater than that with the Common Market countries, although the latter was 17% of the total trade and was rising each year. Britain countered the Common Market by playing a leading role in the formation of the European Free Trade Association (E.F.T.A.)[2] in 1959 with six other European countries. But by then, some were convinced that Britain would have to join the Common Market eventually. There was a deep division of opinion on the question among both politicians and economists. The existence of the Common Market made it more difficult for British manufacturers to compete with those six countries; 'entry into Europe' would open up wider markets to Britain. On the other hand, entry would weaken further the ties with the Commonwealth, harm the valuable trade with the Scandinavian countries, lead to a rise in food prices, and, it was suggested, damage Britain's agriculture. It was a question of swings and roundabouts. As early as 1961 the Conservative government, with Edward Heath as negotiator, applied for membership to the Common Market, but this was rejected largely because of the opposition of France. In 1967 the Labour government made a further application, but once again France vetoed it, despite the unanimous wish of her five partners that Britain should become a member. When Heath became Prime Minister in 1970 he was determined that Britain should join the Common Market. By then the patterns of trade were clearer. In 1972 43% of Britain's exports were being sold in Western Europe, of which 23% went to the Common Market, whilst 24% of the sales were with the sterling area. The Conservative government began a protracted series of meetings, and Britain finally entered the Common Market on 1 January 1973. The Labour party, though divided, complained that the terms of entry were too severe, and when the Labour government came into power in 1974

[1] See p. 302   [2] See pp. 301–2

it decided to negotiate a revision of the terms and then to hold a referendum to allow all the people to vote on continued membership or withdrawal. The referendum, held in June 1975, resulted in a convincing vote in favour of membership of the E.E.C.

Military Contraction

Faced with this recurring problem of the balance of payments Britain was forced, after 1945, to take stock of her military expenditure overseas. From 1945 to 1947 she tried to maintain her pre-war rôle. British troops were kept in Europe, the Middle East, India and the Far East. In addition, she gave economic aid to Greece, Turkey, and parts of Africa. By 1947 it was evident that she could no longer afford to maintain these world-wide commitments. After 1947, the U.S.A. increasingly took over Britain's former spheres of influence, whilst Britain relied for her security upon international military organisations such as N.A.T.O. Britain gave up her bases in Egypt, and curtailed her forces 'east of Suez'. At the same time, many parts of the Commonweath became independent. India, Pakistan, and Ceylon did so in 1947, and by 1966 all former British territory in Africa except for Rhodesia and Swaziland had become independent. But because of the complex nature of modern weapons, military expenditure remained high. In 1974 defence accounted for 17% of the government's outlay, and late in that year proposals for further reactions were put forward, involving withdrawal from some bases and commitments overseas, notably in Singapore and the Mediterranean.

CHAPTER 24

Industry after 1945

'The Decisive Jump'

'During the Second World War, and not before, Great Britain took the decisive jump industrially from the nineteenth into the twentieth century. Before the war Great Britain was trying to revive the old staples. After it, she relied on new developing industries' (A. J. P. Taylor). The record of British industry after 1945 was impressive; there was another 'Industrial Revolution', as spectacular as that which occurred in the early nineteenth century. After 1945 the gross national product rose more rapidly than the number of people at work, i.e. there was greater productivity per head. But as productivity in other industrial countries was also rising, Britain's share in world production fell.

This industrial growth, engendered by the needs of the war, was fostered by the application of science and technology to industry. After the war, the 'boffin', as the back-room scientist was called during the war, became accepted as an essential part of industry. Large firms established their own industrial research departments, whilst the government carried out much useful work. The Department of Scientific and Industrial Research (DSIR) founded in 1916, extended its activities. The Agricultural Research Council, established in 1922, carried out work in all matters concerning food production. Government ministries developed research programmes which were of use to industry. The National Research Development Corporation, founded in 1949, assisted private inventors to develop their ideas. University science and engineering departments worked closely with industry, and new universities and colleges of technology were developed in order to train personnel.

After 1945 the old staple industries, such as cotton textiles and coal-mining declined. Expansion took place in chemicals, electrical engineering, iron and steel, machine tools, oil refining, and the production of motor-cars. These changes in production caused uneven demands for skilled labour. In general, it was short in the south and east, and in the new industries. It was essential for people to be prepared to move from one part of the country to another, and in some cases to change the nature of their occupation. Those who remained in their old craft needed to learn new techniques. For example, shipbuilding changed largely from riveting to welding, and the building industry from brick-laying to prefabrication.

NATIONALISATION

The public ownership of industry and services had long been one of the aims of the Labour party. During the war, the National government had in effect controlled the greater part of industry. When the Labour party assumed office in 1945 it began the gradual nationalisation of some sectors of the economy. This policy was the logical outcome of previous trends. There were some who feared that the Labour government intended to create a wholly 'socialist' state, but the effect of the many measures passed was to place about 20 per cent of the country's economic activity under the state, leaving the rest under private enterprise.

The nationalisation carried out in 1946 caused little controversy. First, the Bank of England was nationalised. As the Bank had always worked in co-operation with the government, this measure had only minimal effects. Under the Act, the Treasury was empowered to give instructions to the Bank of England, so that the Bank could be used to control the economy. For example, the Treasury could lay down the Bank Rate. The Civil Aviation Act of 1946 established two more government airlines, British European Airways, and British South American Airways; the latter was merged with British Overseas Airways Corporation in 1949. (B.O.A.C. was formed in 1939.)

The Coal Industry Nationalisation Act was also passed in 1946. The coal industry had been in the doldrums during the inter-war years, and its nationalisation had been considered then. The 1946 Act set up a National Coal Board, under the Ministry of Fuel and Power. This was a case of a 'sick' industry being given national assistance. There was a need for more mechanisation, but as many British coalmines had only narrow coal-seams, large capital outlay was needed for small rewards. The coal-owners were given compensation, and the N.C.B. began its existence with a large initial debt. Productivity rose, but very slowly, whilst the price of coal rose rapidly immediately after nationalisation.

The electricity and gas industries were nationalised by Acts passed in 1947 and 1948. The generation and supply of electricity was put in the control of the British Electricity Authority, whilst distribution remained with area boards. After 1947 a considerable number of new electricity generating stations were built, but it was not until the 1960's that demands at peak periods could be met. The gas industry was organised under twelve almost autonomous area boards. Both the electricity and gas industries were responsible to the Minister of Fuel and Power; the Minister controlled prices. One effect of the nationalisation of power was to ensure a greater uniformity of price. Before, both gas and electricity were considerably more expensive in rural areas than in the towns.

In 1947 the Transport Act created the British Transport Commission, which was to be responsible for rail, road, and canal traffic. The railways had been virtually under governmental control during the war, and, like the coal industry, had suffered hard times before the war. The four companies, Great Western, Southern, London Midland and Scottish, and London and North Eastern, became four regions of 'British Railways'. After nationalisation they found it impossible to make a profit. Long-distance road haulage services, except for furniture removals, were also nationalised, and operated by 'British Road Services'. As the railways already owned the two largest concerns, Pickfords and Carter Patersons, this measure caused little controversy.

The government's proposal to nationalise the steel industry did, however, provoke opposition. The steel industry was an expanding one, which did not need aid. The Iron and Steel Act was passed by the House of Commons in 1949. The House of Lords insisted on certain amendments, including a delay in the Act's enforcement until 1951, after a general election. The election took place in 1950, when the Labour party retained power with a bare majority. The Steel

Act came into force in 1951, the same year that the Labour Party went out of office.

The Nationalised Industries after 1951

During the Conservative ministries of 1951–64 little was done to change the balance between the nationalised industries and the private sector. Iron and steel were denationalised in 1953, but the return of the various firms to private ownership was gradual and incomplete. By 1955 50 per cent of the productive capacity was in private hands, and by 1957 86 per cent. The firm of Richard Thomas and Baldwins, which produced 9 per cent of the national iron and steel output, was still unsold in 1964, when the Conservatives went out of office. The Transport Act of 1953 made no radical alteration to the nationalised transport organisations. Canals and railways continued under public ownership, but private firms were allowed to operate in road transport. The Conservative party tried to make the nationalised industries pay their way, but in this they were only partially successful. Under the 'Beeching Plan' of 1961 many branch lines, small stations, and uneconomic railway services were closed. In 1966 the state and local government together employed three million people, and were responsible for 50 per cent of the building work done in Britain. In general the nationalised industries and services were accepted as a permanent feature of the economy.

Power

The major change in the sources of power was the decline of steam, and the expansion of electricity, oil, and atomic power. Some electrical power stations were still dependent on coal to create steam to drive the dynamos; some used oil. Due to the need to save dollars, Britain imported crude oil from the Middle East rather than refined spirit from the U.S.A. This led to a growth in oil refining. The small A.G.W.I. refinery at Fawley, near Southampton, developed into a large concern owned by Standard Oil (Esso). Other large refineries were built at Stanlow in Cheshire, Shellhaven, Partington, Grangemouth, Wilton, Billingham, Canvey Island, and Milford Haven. The use of oil as a source of energy grew so rapidly that by 1973 it comprised 46% of the total consumption. Thus Britain was hard

Nuclear power stations for generating electricity.

hit when the oil producing countries made substantial increases in the price of oil at the end of 1973. Whilst some of the electricity power stations could run on coal (which then supplied 38% of the total energy consumption), most of industry could not. Fortunately, large deposits of oil had by then been discovered under the North Sea and off other regions of the British Isles, so that by 1980 Britain should be an oil exporter. Natural gas, also abundant under the North Sea, was exploited throughout the 1960's, and by 1973 this source provided 12% of the total power supplies.

Another possibility was the use of nuclear power, and soon after the war the government began to develop this source. The first nuclear power station was built at Calder Hall, Cumberland. The others which followed can be seen on the map above. There were, however, technical problems, such as the disposal of dangerous waste material, and nuclear power stations were expensive to build and to maintain. Nuclear power remained an ancillary power source, making up only 3% of the total in 1973.

Coalmining

Before the war, miners were unemployed because of the decline in

58 The Esso refinery at Fawley, the largest in Britain, stands on a 1000 acre site on the
Southampton water, and produces 12 million tons of petroleum products annually. (p. 273)

59 The Steel Company of Wales plant at Port Talbot. (p. 276)

60 *An atomic power station under construction in Anglesey.* (p. 274)

61 *An atomic power station, Hinkley Point, Somerset. Why are both stations near the sea?*

the use of coal. When the war ended, there was a different situation. Production was insufficient to supply the demands for British coal for domestic and industrial use, and for export. Coal had to be rationed; for example, families in the south of England were allowed 34 cwt. per annum. This was a meagre allowance at that time, as few homes had central heating or other heating appliances. The open fire was still the usual means of house-warming. The National Coal Board, formed in 1946, faced the problem of raising productivity in an industry which needed rejuvenating. More mechanisation was needed, but this was not always suitable in all British coal-fields, where the seams were narrow. The labour force was ageing, and, in an era of full employment, it was difficult to recruit enough younger men. The bad winter of 1946–47 led to an acute shortage of coal. Britain was forced to import from the U.S.A. on average 23 million tons of coal a year from 1947 to 1956. Taking coals to Newcastle had become a reality. In 1950 the N.C.B. began a forward-looking programme. Uneconomic pits were closed, and new techniques were introduced. The plan envisaged that within ten years the annual output would rise to 240 million tons. But productivity did not reach expectations. In 1955 the plan was revised, and the aim was lowered to 230 million tons. The problem of the coal shortage was solved by the industry's customers. Industry and domestic consumers changed to oil or gas or electricity. Railways increased the number of diesel-electric engines. In 1958, although the coal industry had not yet achieved its target, there was a surplus. Former customers abroad, bereft of regular supplies of British coal for twenty years, had long since found other suppliers, or had turned to alternative sources, so that the problem could not be solved by exports. In 1959 the N.C.B. reduced the output to 216 million tons, but there was still a coal surplus. More mines were closed, the five-day week was introduced, recruitment was curtailed, and the output target was set at 200 million tons a year. This policy, which seemed right at the time, rebounded more than a decade later. During the 1960's the demand for power increased, and the electricity power stations, despite an increasing use of oil, also used more coal, so that by 1973 they took 76 million tons a year, compared with 52 million tons in 1960. Although the use of sophisticated equipment led to an increase in the output per man, the dangerous and unpleasant job of the coalminer did not appeal to a new generation, which could earn a better living in other occupations. In December 1973, at a time when oil supplies were being threatened by the producing countries, the miners began a strike which lasted until February 1974. The matter was not settled until a general election was held, which resulted in the fall of Heath's Conservative government, and the formation of a minority Labour government under Wilson. The new government ended the strike by meeting the demands of the miners for a rise in pay and improvements in conditions, but the coal industry remained troubled throughout 1974. The problem was one of a declining industry, but one which was essential at least until the 1980's, and probably beyond. The country still needed about 130 million tons of coal a year, a small amount compared with the hey-day of 1913, but it had to be won with a disgruntled labour force.

Textiles

The cotton industry thrived from 1945 to 1952, due to shortages caused by the war. After 1952, British cotton textiles faced intense competition from manufacturers in the Far East. But more serious competitors were the manufacturers of man-made fibres. The sharp decline in cotton manufacture was slowed but not stopped by government aid towards new machinery. In 1962 the cotton labour force had dropped to 150,000, and 40 per cent of British cloth production was in man-made fibres. Cotton was losing its dominant position.

Rayon accounted for 84·4 per cent of the output of British man-made fibres in 1960. Courtaulds and British Celanese were the most important British firms engaged in the manufacture of rayon. Nylon, made principally from benzene (a by-product of coal or oil), was first invented by the American firm of Du Pont. In Britain, the firms of I.C.I. and Courtaulds together formed British Nylon Spinners in 1940, in order to produce parachutes and tow-ropes. After the war, British Nylon Spinners built a large factory at Pontypool, Monmouthshire. Another important synthetic fibre is terylene, which was invented by two British chemists, Whinfield and Dixon, in 1941, in the laboratories of the Calico Printing Association. The war delayed the development of this new material, but production began in 1955, when I.C.I. opened a new factory at Wilton, near Middlesbrough. Terylene is made principally from ethylene (a petroleum product); it has the advantage of being warmer to the touch than nylon. A third group of synthetic fibres, polyacrylic, such as 'Orlon', 'Acrilan', 'Winyon', and 'Dynel', were developed in Britain from 1957 by Courtaulds and by Chemstrand of Belfast. In 1963 I.C.I. and British Petroleum formed a new company, Border Chemicals, and opened a new polyacrylic plant at Grangemouth.

Man-made fibres are used for a variety of things. Viscose rayon, (made from wood pulp and sulphuric acid), together with nylon, is used in the making of rubber tyres. Acetate rayon, produced mainly from cotton linters and acetic acid, is widely used in the manufacture of shirts, underwear, dress materials, and electrical insulation. Nylon is used by clothes manufacturers and by industry. Their development changed the nature of the textile industry. In the days of wool and cotton, the producers of the raw materials and the manufacturers were separate concerns. In the case of man-made fibres, raw materials and the manufactured article are produced by the same organisation. The development of man-made fibres benefited the British economy. In order to produce £300 worth of cotton or woollen goods, Britain had to import about £100 worth of raw material. With man-made fibres, £100 worth of imported raw materials produced £1,000 worth of exports.

Plastics

Plastics are synthetic materials which can be moulded into a given shape. In 1960 Britain was the third largest producer of plastics, which were used for a variety of purposes, but mainly as substitutes for heavier and less durable natural materials. Perspex was particularly useful as a substitute for glass in aircraft. Bakelite was used for car fittings where formerly wood was used. The whole range of plastic materials became so varied that they were used for radio and television sets, floor tilings, electrical fittings, and even as paint. As the plastics industry used by-products of coal and petroleum, many of the plants were situated near the mining areas or near the refineries.

Iron and steel works and coal fields in the 1960's.

Metals

The production of iron and steel grew steadily after 1945. Pig iron production grew from 7 million tons in 1945 to 15 million in 1964, and steel from 12 million to 25 million tons in the same period.[1] The development of the industry was especially marked in Corby, Northamptonshire, at Scunthorpe, Lincolnshire, and at Margam in South Wales. The industry was run by the Iron and Steel Board, which fixed prices, controlled production, and directed research. Iron and steel were nationalised in 1951, denationalised in 1953, and then nationalised once more in 1967. Despite this, Britain remained the fifth largest steel producer in the world, with an annual output of about 26 million tons.

Aluminium became the second largest metal industry in Britain. It grew after 1945 partly because of the high cost of tin and paper. Aluminium was cheap, light yet strong, resistant to rust, and a good conductor of heat and electricity, and was used in the electrical, motor car and building industries.

The Motor Industry

The motor industry developed very slowly in the immediate post-war years. It was hindered by petrol rationing, a hire-purchase tax, which kept home demand to a minimum, and the motor taxation system. Tax was assessed on horse-power, thus discouraging manufacturers from making large cars for which there was a ready export market. The annual production of private cars and commercial vehicles grew only from 365,000 in 1946 to 499,000 in 1948. In 1948 the motor tax was changed to a flat-rate, regardless of horse-power, which led to increased exports to the U.S.A. and to Europe. In 1950 the production of vehicles of all types had grown to 784,000, and in 1964 2·3 million were made. Impressive though this development was, it was in some ways disappointing. In the 1950's, Britain lost ground to foreign competitors, due in the main to the production of too many models, a neglect of servicing facilities and spare parts abroad, and a lack of consideration for the differing road conditions in other countries. Greater standardisation was brought about through amalgamation. In 1952 Austin and Morris Motors com-

---

[1] In 1973, steel output was 26 million tons.

bined to form the British Motor Corporation. Later the Jaguar Company amalgamated with Daimlers, whilst Standard, Triumph and Leyland formed another large combine, which eventually joined with B.M.C. to form the British Leyland Motor Corporation. These firms, like the American-owned Fords and Vauxhalls, increased mass-production, which enabled them to make sound cars at reasonable cost for home and export demand. Armstrong-Siddeley, one of the expensive quality cars, stopped production in 1960, but the rich man could still buy a Rolls-Royce, or a Jaguar. Designers revolutionsed the appearance of British cars in the 1950's, and black ceased to be the commonest cellulose colour. The problems of space for parking led to the development by B.M.C. of a small car, with low fuel consumption, a small turning circle, and a front-wheel drive engine. This car, the Mini-Minor, set a trend followed by other manufacturers. Many families bought two cars, a large one for family pleasure, and a 'Mini' for travel in towns.

The midlands, especially near the Birmingham, Coventry, and Oxford areas, remained the centre of the motor industry, together with Luton (Vauxhall Motors), and Dagenham, Essex (Ford).

The industry employed over 500,000 workers in 1973, and produced 1,700,000 cars and 400,000 commercial vehicles. As over 600,000 cars were for the export market, it had become very important to the economy.

Electronics

This industry, much stimulated by the war, made spectacular advances after 1945. It was especially beneficial to the economy as it required skilled labour and management rather than raw materials. The industry made radio, television, and recording machines; highly sophisticated navigational instruments, such as radar, for ships and aircraft, and computers for industry. The labour force, over 120,000 in 1951, had doubled itself by 1961. Its development was hampered, not by the lack of demand or materials, but by an insufficient number of people trained in special technical skills.

The main trends in British industrial production were the development of automation, and computerisation. Automation, a natural development of mechanisation, in which 'machines control machines', meant that new skills were required of the labour force.

The computer, which performed work previously done by clerks or calculators, was more widely used for a variety of tasks, from selecting winners of prizes of Premium Bonds to producing pay-slips. More advanced machines were used to help directors to arrive at decisions on policy. In short, whilst the machines of old replaced physical labour, the computer helped people to 'think'.

Agriculture

After the 1914–18 war, in which the British farmer had played a vital part in feeding the population, British agriculture declined. After 1945, British farming was given state help and encouragement to prevent it from withering. This difference in policy was due in part to the balance of payments problem after 1945. Britain had to pro-duce as much food as possible in order to save imports. The Agricul-ture Act of 1947 set up a system whereby the Minister of Agriculture, in consultation with the farmers, was empowered to guarantee prices annually, each February. Subsidies were given to encourage particular commodities, and marketing schemes were improved. The farmer was able to plan production, knowing that he could sell his produce at a guaranteed price. At the same time, farmers had to be efficient. County Agricultural Executive Committees, com-prising practising farmers, were set up in order to ensure that all farmers used their land efficiently. In order to encourage tenant farmers to 'improve' their land, tenure was guaranteed to those who proved efficient.

Although wages and conditions of work of those who were engaged in agriculture improved, they remained among the poorer sections of the community. However, in a country which became increasingly urban, the 'way of life' acted as a compensatory factor, whilst easier communications no longer meant that the countryman was isolated. Large capital investment, the increase in the size of farms, and mechanical aids led to increased productivity with a considerably smaller labour force. In 1945 Britain produced 3·34 million tons of corn from 19·2 million acres of arable land. In 1963 7·19 million tons were produced from 18·2 million acres. Meat production was doubled in the same period, whilst milk production was increased by over 50%. This greater efficiency meant that, despite the steady growth of population, more of the nation's food supplies were produced at home. In 1973 80% of meat supplies, 64% of the cereals consumed, and 40% of the sugar needed, were produced by Britain's farmers. Despite this apparent strength, entry into the Common Market led to some heartburning, because it was feared that the importing of European agricultural products would lead to a decline in Britain's own farming.

CHAPTER 25

Working and Living Conditions after 1945

The Welfare State

Plans to make Britain a better country to live in when peace should come were made by the National government during the war. It was almost as if statesmen, conscious of the failure of Lloyd George's promise made during the previous world war of 'a land fit for heroes', were determined that this time social reforms would be carried out. The National government prepared the ground. Before the war ended they had passed the Town and Country Planning Act, 1944; the Butler Education Act, 1944; the Location of Industry Act, 1945; and issued the Beveridge Report of 1942 as a white paper in 1944. The Labour government put the measures into operation after 1945.

The general aim was to ensure that all citizens who were willing to make some contribution to the country would be guaranteed the necessities of life. All who sought work ought to be able to obtain work. 'Full employment' became a principle which was adopted by all political parties after 1945. Those who were in need of help were to get aid from the state. The money for this welfare was to come from all citizens who were in employment. The Beveridge Report stated graphically that there were five giants to attack—Want, Disease, Ignorance, Squalor, and Idleness. These enemies were fought with vigour. The ten years after the war saw a social revolution, in which many of the evils of the previous generation disappeared.

The Beveridge Report, named after the chairman of the Committee, Sir William (later Lord) Beveridge, proposed a plan to

abolish Want 'by ensuring that every citizen willing to serve according to his powers has at all times an income sufficient to meet his
responsibilities'. The Report stated that poverty was due to two
main causes, (a) large families, and (b) an interruption in earning
power.

In 1945 a system of family allowances was begun. Five shillings a
week was paid to parents for each child other than the first. If there
were three children, then the allowance was 10s. a week. The
money was payable to the mother (as a safeguard against unscrupulous husbands) through the post office. In the same year, free
milk (one-third of a pint daily) was given to all children at school.

'Social Security from the Cradle to the Grave'

In 1946 the National Insurance Act and the National Health Service
Act were passed. They came into operation in 1948, and Aneurin
Bevan (1897–1960), Minister of Health, had much to do with
their final form. These measures were described by the press as
'social security from the cradle to the grave'. This social security was
to be administered by the Ministry of Health; everyone, regardless of
income, had to belong; all workers were to pay the same contributions, and to receive the same benefits. The Insurance Act ensured
that those who were unemployed or were sick received enough to
provide the bare essentials. Old Age Pensions, renamed Retirement
Pensions, were to be paid by the state to men at the age of 65, and
single women aged 60, if they gave up work. Other benefits were
widows' pensions, maternity allowances, and a small death gratuity
to help towards funeral expenses. By the National Health Service
Act, all medical services were provided free of charge. These included
treatment by general practitioners and by specialists, hospital treatment, drugs and medicines, dental and optical services. This Act did
much to remove hardship caused by ill-health. Before the 1939–45
war only people with an income of less than £260 p.a. were *allowed*
to contribute to a health insurance scheme to provide for free medical
attention (this maximum was raised to £420 in 1940). These par-
ticipants were known colloquially as being 'on the panel'. When
the wage-earner was taken ill, and he was not 'on the panel', his
family was likely to suffer hardship. At a time when his earning
power was interrupted, the sick man had to worry about how to pay

the doctor's bill or the hospital fee. In matters other than life or death, many people had tried to overcome physical ailments as cheaply as possible. Many of the poor bought ill-adjusted spectacles in chain-stores, or false teeth which fitted badly.

These measures were modified after 1948, but were not changed radically. When they first came into operation, there was such a hidden demand for medical treatment of all kinds that the service nearly broke down. A generation which had been denied proper medical care through lack of money decided to have its money's worth. The National Health scheme had other growing pains. Hospitals, taken over by the state and organised by regional boards, were inadequate for the demands. Doctors' surgeries were crowded. But gradually improvements were made. Although complaints were made about hypochondriacs and malingerers, the next generation, accustomed to nothing but a free medical service, learned to use it with discretion. The service was, after all, free only indirectly. The money was provided from three sources: central and local government, the employer, and the employee. In 1963 cash payments under all social security schemes accounted for 6·8 per cent of the gross national product, lower than in most other western European countries. In 1950 the Labour government imposed a charge for some items of medical care. Patients had to pay half the cost of dentures and spectacles, and a token sum for medicines. This measure caused a split in the Cabinet, and led to the resignation of Aneurin Bevan and Harold Wilson. In 1965, when Wilson was Prime Minister, the charge for medicine was abolished, only to be reintroduced after 1970 with a change of government.

The development of a National Health Service helped to take some of the terror out of illness. It meant that financial worries were not an accompaniment of sickness; all could be treated by the best doctors, and with the latest scientific methods. However, the National Health Service found it difficult to keep pace with the growing needs of the population. The money needed for new and bigger hospitals was hard to find, and the universities failed to provide enough doctors. The pay of nurses did not keep pace with that of other employment, so that the number of girls entering that profession was insufficient. But those problems were shared with other 'service' professions.

The Problem of the Old

Unfortunately, there was one group of people who were not shel-tered by these schemes. Those who had already retired in 1948, together with those who retired within three years of that date, were not eligible for state pensions. To cover them, a National Assistance Act was passed in 1948. Those in real need were to apply for help. In practice this did not work well, as many people were unwilling to apply, since they felt there was a stigma attached to receiving na-tional assistance. In 1965 there were still half a million old people who were not in receipt of state retirement pensions, living on their capital or on national assistance. Those who did receive pensions were hard pressed. As prices rose, the retirement pensions, though raised, proved inadequate. The winter of 1962–63 high-lighted the problem: many old people died because of a lack of food and inade-quate heating. As there were then over 6 million old age pensioners, over a million of whom relied solely on their state pensions, a sizeable proportion of the population still lived in comparative poverty in a so-called 'affluent society'. During the late 1960's and 1970's im-provements were made in the rate of pensions, and more of the recently retired by then had additional pensions from their place of employment. However, the number of those aged over 65 continued to rise, so that by 1973 there were 7·6 million in that age group, or 14% of the total population. This was due to the longer expectation of life, which then was 69 for men and 74 for women. Something was done by some local government authorities to provide small labour-saving flats for the elderly and widowed. A variety or clubs and societies were formed exclusively for the elderly. But the prob-lem of loneliness, in an order of society in which the younger generation were unable or unwilling to look after their parents, could not be solved.

Education

The Butler Education Act, passed in 1944, was put into effect after the war. Free secondary education was made available to all. Local authorities were left free to develop secondary schools as they wished. Most kept the 'grammar' schools, and pupils were selected for these by means of various ability tests. Some built large 'com-prehensive' schools, to which all pupils of eleven proceeded, regardless of ability. In 1954 there were 13 comprehensive schools in England, and in 1963 175. In 1965 the Labour government instructed local education authorities to move gradually towards a comprehensive system of secondary education.

This directive, '10/65', caused some controversy as it meant the ending of the selective grammar schools, which some argued had been the poor child's ladder to success. Others condemned selection as divisive in a society which needed to become united. From 1965 most local authorities gradually formulated plans for the reorganisation of secondary education, and by 1973 approximately half the school population were being educated in comprehensive schools. As always, the money needed to do the job properly was not forthcoming, so that many children were still using old and inadequate buildings. The school leaving age had been raised to 16 by the 1944 Education Act, but due to the shortage of teachers and buildings this could not be put into effect immediately. The step from 14 to 15 was taken in 1947, and the leaving age was raised to 16 in 1970. By that time a considerable proportion of schoolchildren were already remaining at school beyond the age of 15 voluntarily. The 1960's saw a rapid increase in the number staying at school until the age of 18 or beyond in order to take 'Advanced' level subjects, and to seek university places.

The number of university places was increased, partly by expanding existing univiersities, and partly by the establishment of new ones. In 1938 there were 49,000 university students; in 1963 there were 126,000, and in 1973 244,000. So that no one should be prevented from going to a university through lack of money, grants to students, scaled according to parental income, were given to all who obtained places. In addition to universities, a number of polytechnics were founded, and Colleges of Technology and technical colleges were expanded. All these measures were aimed at producing the enlightened and skilled population necessary to an industrial nation.

Housing Shortage

The housing problem was acute in 1945. Many cities had suffered extensive damage from aerial bombardment; over 200,000 houses had been destroyed, and over four million damaged. The building of houses had virtually ceased during the war, so that in 1945 the country needed another 1·25 million homes. But the building industry could not concentrate entirely on the building of private dwellings. Damage had been done also to factories, schools, and other public buildings. In addition, there was a shortage of building materials, especially wood, which could not be overcome by large-scale importation because of the balance of payments problem. Also, the labour force in the building industry had to be increased. In the first year after the war 55,000 permanent dwellings were built; in 1947 140,000; in the years 1948–50 200,000 were built each year. In addition, between 1946 and 1948 148,000 temporary pre-fabricated houses were erected. These 'pre-fabs', designed to last ten years, were single-storey buildings grouped usually in an open plan. In 1954 300,000 houses were built, in 1956 284,000, and in 1966 396,000.

The housing problem was intensified by an increase in the number of households. Earlier marriage led to a greater number of families, each wanting a home of their own. The household comprising different generations went out of fashion. This meant more homes per head of population, and a demand for smaller houses. This change, together with a steady increase in the total population, meant that the housing shortage was not completely solved. In 1939 there were about 10 million occupied private houses; by 1951 there were 13·3 million houses. But by 1951 there were 14·5 million families. During the 1950's and 60's many large old houses were demolished, and replaced by blocks of flats; other large houses were divided into several residences. The small house became the normal dwelling place. Because of the housing shortage, rents would have risen sharply if uncontrolled, so the Labour government of 1945–50 placed a restriction on the rent of unfurnished accommodation, but furnished houses were not included. An intensive new house building programme in the 1960's did something to ease the situation.

The rise in living standards and continuing inflation together produced an unwelcome backlash in increased housing prices. More people became owner-occupiers, buying through mortgages, as the value of the house offset the interest payable. Between 1970 and 1973 the price of land soared, partly through speculation by large organisations, and partly because of scarcity, so that the price of new houses doubled in three years. As the building societies had to lend more money per house purchase, they had difficulty in raising enough for the demand, even though the interest rates were raised dramatically. This sudden increase once more made it difficult for the young married couples to 'own' their own house. However, during 1973, the housing market became steadier, whilst continued inflation made the price of new houses seem not so high. The new houses were labour-saving, light, and cheerful, but lacked the space and graciousness of those built before the war. As land was expensive, gardens became smaller, so that children had to rely more and more on public open spaces in which to play. Privacy was at a premium, as housing became denser. By 1973 four out of every five people lived in towns.

Industrial and Urban Planning

Measures were taken to try to prevent unplanned growth in towns and in industry. The Distribution of Industry Act, 1945, empowered the Board of Trade and the Treasury to acquire land, to give loans, and to make grants to firms willing to build new factories in certain parts of the country. These special areas, the north-east (Durham and Northumberland), west Cumberland, South Wales and Scotland, were known as 'development areas'. These were the regions where unemployment had been so rife during the inter-war years, and where there was room for expansion. But despite this and other measures, new industries continued to develop in the already crowded south-east of England.

The problem of the ever-growing towns was also considered. Two reports, those of Scott and Uthwatt, had considered the future, and their advice was embodied in the first Town and Country Planning Act of 1944. This Act gave local government greater powers to acquire land for slum clearance. The second Act, passed in 1947, controlled the use of all land. Local Planning Authorities had powers to decide which land should be used for private houses, which for industrial undertakings, and which for agriculture. Further, they had to approve the plans of any building. The aim was to ensure the most economic use of all land, to prevent the further sprawl of towns, and to preserve some open spaces. Green belts were placed round many towns, so that one town should not merge with its neighbour. This scheme, however, meant that new housing

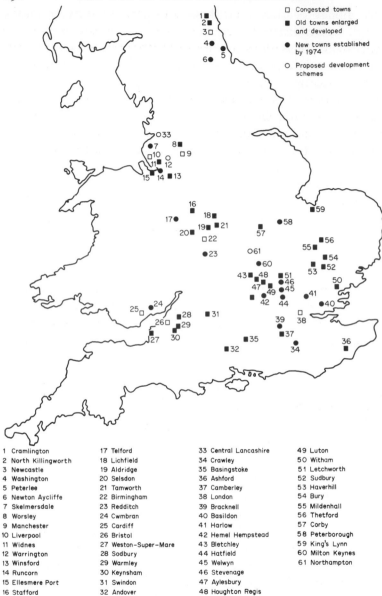

Key:
- □ Congested towns
- ■ Old towns enlarged and developed
- ● New towns established by 1974
- O Proposed development schemes

1 Cramlington	17 Telford	33 Central Lancashire	49 Luton
2 North Killingworth	18 Lichfield	34 Crawley	50 Witham
3 Newcastle	19 Aldridge	35 Basingstoke	51 Letchworth
4 Washington	20 Selsdon	36 Ashford	52 Sudbury
5 Peterlee	21 Tamworth	37 Camberley	53 Haverhill
6 Newton Aycliffe	22 Birmingham	38 London	54 Bury
7 Skelmersdale	23 Redditch	39 Bracknell	55 Mildenhall
8 Worsley	24 Cwmbran	40 Basildon	56 Thetford
9 Manchester	25 Cardiff	41 Harlow	57 Corby
10 Liverpool	26 Bristol	42 Hemel Hempstead	58 Peterborough
11 Widnes	27 Weston-Super-Mare	43 Houghton Regis	59 King's Lynn
12 Warrington	28 Sodbury	44 Hatfield	60 Milton Keynes
13 Winsford	29 Warmley	45 Welwyn	61 Northampton
14 Runcorn	30 Keynsham	46 Stevenage	
15 Ellesmere Port	31 Swindon	47 Aylesbury	
16 Stafford	32 Andover	48 Houghton Regis	

New towns and the expansion of small towns were planned under the New Towns Act (1946) and the Town Development Act (1952), in order to ease the problems of London and other overcrowded areas. Other developments were suggested in the Buchanan Report (1965).

estates had to be built further and further from the centres of the towns. This caused people to travel longer distances from home to work—contemporary jargon described them as 'commuters'. The new housing estates tended to become dormitories, dead places during working-hours.

The growth of London created many problems. By 1939 Middlesex, and parts of Essex, Surrey and Kent were already part of the greater London area. Other counties, and especially Sussex, Hertfordshire and Buckinghamshire were in danger of becoming predominantly 'London commuter country'. In order to relieve London and its immediate environs eight new towns were created, or existing towns much enlarged, at Crawley, Bracknell, Basildon, Harlow, Hatfield, Hemel Hempstead, Welwyn Garden City, and Stevenage, These plans proved insufficient, so that Basingstoke was enlarged in order to help the overspill of London. The influence of London was being felt as far as Dorset and Norfolk. Government encouragement to industry to leave the south-east had no great effect. The other great centres of urban population also felt the need for relief, and measures were taken to create overspill towns for Birmingham, Liverpool, Manchester, and Newcastle.

Work, Wages and the Trade Unions

When the war ended in 1945, 4·5 million men serving in the forces had to be demobilised. Plans for resettlement and demobilisation were carefully made during the war. The Reinstatement in Civil Employment Act stated that employers had to reinstate those service-men who were in their employ before mobilisation. Also, the employer had to offer the ex-serviceman a post which it would be reasonable to assume that he would have attained if he had not been called up. For example, a police constable might be reinstated as a sergeant. Where possible, servicemen were given courses of educational and vocational training before they returned to civilian life. Demobilisation was carried out by stages. Those who were urgently needed in civilian life were released first under 'Class B'; then the remainder on the principle of 'first in, first out' under 'Class A'. As servicemen released under Class A were given eight weeks' pay and gratuities, their passage into civilian life was more smooth than that of the previous generation of temporary soldiers. This transition, together with the transfer of 3·25 million workers from the war industries, was almost complete by the end of 1946.

After 1945, partly due to the economic policy of full employment, and to the expansion of industry, there was a shortage of labour. Despite this strong bargaining position, between 1945 and 1950 wages rose more slowly than prices. But from 1950 to 1964 wages rose more rapidly than prices. Government departments tried to educate the working population in the simple economic proposition that wages must be tied to productivity. Between 1953 and 1963 wages rose on average 6 per cent a year; productivity rose only by 2½ per cent a year. The average wage for men, £6. 18s. in 1948, and £10. 4s. in 1954, had risen to £21 a week in 1967, and to £44 in 1973. 'Average wage' can be misleading; in fact, the wages of the semi-skilled and the young rose more rapidly than did those of the skilled older worker, i.e. there was a levelling out of incomes. This was due to deliberate governmental policy, which demanded a fairer society; to full employment which caused labour shortages, specially in the south and the Midlands; and to the bargaining strength of some of the larger trade unions.

The position of the trade unions was strengthened by full employment, as the age-old employers' counter-weapon of dismissal was no longer possible. Moreover, more of the working population were members of unions. In 1945 trade union membership was 7·8 million; this had risen to 9·9 millions in 1963, and to 11·2 millions in 1972. As eleven unions had over 60% of the total as their members, these large unions, and especially those whose members performed vital services, were able to wield power. Despite this, Britain's record during the 1960's for strikes was better than that of most non-communist countries. However, various attempts were made to improve industrial relations, to reform the trade unions, and to curb the free-bargaining jungle law of pay negotiations. The Donovan Report of 1968 suggested the establishment of a Commission for Industrial Relations, but this did not prove successful. In 1969 the Labour Party's ideas, contained in a pamplet *In Place of Strife*, received a cool reception from the rank and file and had to be abandoned. When the Conservatives were returned to office in 1970, they passed an *Industrial Relations Act* which was greeted with overt hostility from a few of the larger unions, especially the A.E.U., whose secretary was Hugh Scanlon. This Act indirectly led the Conservatives to a collision course with the miners' union in 1973, and the prolonged miners' strike at the end of that year. When the Industrial Relations Act was repealed in 1974 by the new Labour Government, its demise was mourned by few. It was apparent that Britain was not yet ready for legal curbs on the unions.

The legal position of the unions was affected by two important events. In 1946 the Trade Disputes Act of 1927 was repealed. In 1963, in the case of *Rookes v Barnard*, it was ruled that strikers were liable to prosecution for acts of intimidation against fellow workers unwilling to strike. In 1965 the *Rookes v Barnard* judgment was reversed by a new Trade Disputes Act.

As a result of all the trade union legislation during the past hundred years, trade unions were left in a unique position: they were immune from civil damages; sympathetic strikes were legal; peaceful picketing was permissible; contracts between Employers' Associations and the unions were not legally enforceable. Only by the implementation of a special Emergency Powers Act could governments intervene in order to maintain essential services. This immense power led to a great need for responsible action, which was more forthcoming from the leaders of the unions than from the shop stewards. Much had changed since the days of the Tolpuddle Martyrs.

Changes in Work and Leisure Habits

The average weekly working hours of factory workers were 54 in 1910; in 1963, 44.[1] The greatest reduction in hours came about after 1950, through more and more workers obtaining the five-day working week. Saturday morning work became less common. In the building industry, however, Saturday morning work remained the rule. Large stores which remained open in Saturdays adopted the practice of closing on Mondays. Also, hours became more standardised. This led to an increase in the number of people travelling to and from work during the 'rush hour'.

The reduction of working hours, together with the increase in the number of married women at work, and a rise in real incomes,

[1] In 1973, though the average official working week was 40 hours, overtime made the actual average 46.7.

caused changes in everyday life. The use of pre-packed food, which could be cooked quickly, became common. Husbands performed domestic duties, and helped with the shopping. More children stayed to dinner at school. Attendances at cinemas declined as families, out all day, preferred to stay at home and enjoy television. Attendances at football and cricket matches did not grow with the population. But the new opportunities for active pastimes, such as yachting, rock-climbing and golf, led to a greater variety in the use of leisure hours. An increase in the numbers owning their homes led to more 'do-it-yourself' jobs about the house; car cleaning and polishing became almost a ritual in suburban streets. Bingo, a revival of the game known in the Services as 'Housy-Housy', became popular with the masses during the 1960's. But Britain was not altogether a materialist society. With the general introduction of 'holidays with pay', more families took an annual holiday abroad, to Europe and beyond. A better educated population led to an increasing interest in good music and good books. The younger generation, with money to spend, found a new culture of their own with the introduction of 'pop' music and art.

The years after 1945 saw the widening of the opportunities for leading a full life for the great majority of the British people, regardless of their age. The Giants mentioned in the Beveridge Report were in retreat. For most life was more than the mere getting of a bare subsistence.

SEQUENCES

Poor Law and Social Security

1601	Elizabethan Poor Law.
1782	Gilbert's Act.
1795	Speenhamland System.
1834	Poor Law Amendment Act.
1905–9	Royal Commission on Poor Law and Unemployment.
1908	Old Age Pensions Act.
1911	National Insurance Act.
1942	Beveridge Report published.
1945	Family Allowances Act.
1946	National Insurance Act.
	National Health Service Act.
1948	National Assistance Act.
1959	Graduated Pensions.
1966	National Insurance Act—earnings-related benefits scheme.

Commercial Policy

1703	Methuen Treaty with Portugal.
1721–23	Walpole simplified tariffs; introduced excise system.
1776	Adam Smith's Wealth of Nations.
1784–89	Pitt the Younger simplified tariffs.
1823–27	Huskisson's reduction of duties.
1838	Formation of Anti-Corn Law League.
1842–45	Peel's 'free-trade' budgets.
1846	Repeal of Corn Laws.
1849	Repeal of Navigation Acts.
1853/1860	Gladstone's budgets: Britain a free-trade country.
1906	Joseph Chamberlain fought the election on a 'tariff-reform' platform.
1932	Import Duties Act (end of free trade).
1959	Britain joined E.F.T.A.
1967	E.F.T.A. became a free-trade area.
1973	Britain joined E.E.C.

The Industrial Revolution

Year	Cotton	Iron	Steam	Transport	Agriculture
1701					Tull's seed drill
1709		Coke for furnaces (Coalbrookdale)			
1711			Newcomen's atmospheric engine		
1733	Kay's Flying Shuttle (weaving)				Tull's *Horse-Hoeing Husbandry* Norfolk Rotation (Townshend)
1742		Crucible steel (Huntsman)			
1761				Bridgewater Canal	
1764	Hargreaves' Spinning Jenny				
1766		Reverberatory furnace (Cranage Brothers)			
1769	Arkwright's Water Frame (spinning)		Watt's steam engine		
1777				Grand Trunk Canal	
1779	Crompton's Mule				Coke and Bakewell
1784	(spinning)	Puddling process (Cort)			
1785	Cartwright's power loom (steam)				
1793	Whitney's cotton gin				Board of Agriculture established (Young)
1802			*Charlotte Dundas*	Roads and bridges (Telford, McAdam)	

GLOSSARY

Balance of payments: a statement of accounts showing all financial transactions between citizens of the U.K. and the rest of the world. Exports and imports comprise the greater part of these dealings, but the 'balance of payments' is wider than the 'balance of trade'.

If a country receives more than is paid out, there is a 'favourable' balance of payments; if less, then there is an 'adverse' balance of payments.

Balance of trade: one component of the 'balance of payments': the difference between a country's exports (visible and invisible) and its imports. If more is imported than exported, there is an adverse balance.

Bank Rate: the rate of interest charged by the Bank of England to the discount houses if they should wish to borrow. This in turn affects the interest rate charged by other banks, building societies, hire-purchase firms, etc. The Bank Rate is announced every Thursday morning. Between 1932 and 1951 the Bank Rate was kept low (at 2 per cent). This is called 'a cheap money policy'. Since 1951 the Bank Rate has been used to influence the economy.

Banking School: those who, in the period before the 1844 Bank Charter Act and after, believed that the number of Bank of England notes to be issued should not be tied solely to the amount of gold held. Thomas Tooke was a prominent member of this group. They were opposed by the 'Currency School'.

Corn: in Britain this is a generic term for various kinds of grain or cereal. In the U.S.A. corn means one particular crop, maize or 'indian corn'.

Enclosures: entailed (1) the putting of a hedge of fence round hitherto open fields *or* (2) the consolidation of each owner's land in compact holdings *or* (3) the enclosing of common or waste-land.

In the eighteenth century, most enclosures were for arable farming to be carried out more efficiently.

Exports—invisible: receipts from services, such as carrying goods in ships, insurance, banking. If people from other countries holiday in Britain, their expenditure becomes 'invisible exports'. If an Englishman goes abroad, he is 'importing'.

Exports—visible: receipts from sales of goods from Britain to other countries.

Farming—arable: the growing of crops, producing food directly from the soil.

Farming—pastoral: the production of food by using the land as animal pasture.

Gross National Product: the total value of the goods and services produced by a country (usually in one year).

Manchester School: a group of men, or 'school of thought', who advocated free trade and *laissez-faire*; active in mid-nineteenth century, e.g. Anti-Corn Law League.

Piece-rates: payment of a specific sum for a specific task; used in industry to increase productivity. The danger of this system is the possible decline in quality.

Real wages: income related to prices. The bare statement of wages without knowing 'what money will buy' is of little value. If prices have doubled in 10 years, and wages have also doubled, then real wages are the same.

Tariffs: duties imposed on imports; customs duties. Excise duties are taxes on home-produced goods for sale inside the country, e.g. wines and spirits.

Taxes—direct: are taxes levied directly on the tax-payer, e.g. income-tax.

Taxes—indirect: are taxes levied on a commodity, and included in its price to the purchaser, e.g. taxes on cigarettes and tobacco.

INTERNATIONAL ECONOMIC AGREEMENTS SINCE 1945

Bretton Woods
A conference in New Hampshire, U.S.A., attended by 44 nations in 1944. They agreed to establish the International Monetary Fund (I.M.F.) and the International Bank for Reconstruction and Development. The former was intended to stabilise foreign exchange and the latter to provide money for under-developed countries.

Organisation for European Economic Co-Operation (O.E.E.C.)
Established in 1948 to help non-Communist countries which had suffered in the war to co-operate in order to restore their economies. The U.S.A. loaned money to members under 'Marshall Aid'. O.E.E.C. was superseded by O.E.C.D.

Organisation for Economic Co-Operation and Development (O.E.C.D.)
Set up in 1961, with headquarters in Paris, by eighteen European countries together with the U.S.A. and Canada. The aim was to achieve economic growth, full employment, and a rising standard of living in member countries, and to assist non-member countries to develop their economies.

European Free Trade Association (E.F.T.A.)
Established in July 1959, and came into force by the Treaty of Stockholm in 1960. Members were Austria, Denmark, Norway, Portugal, Sweden, Switzerland, and the United Kingdom, with a total population of 90 million or about half that of the U.S.A. or of the E.E.C. countries. They agreed to reduce by stages import duties and other barriers to industrial trade between member states, and intended to arrive at free trade by 1970. However, all went so well that it was agreed that final reductions should take effect on 31 December 1966. E.F.T.A. had its offices in Geneva. It was called 'the Outer Seven'. It was established after the European Economic Community ('the

Common Market'), established by the Treaty of Rome, 1957, which came into force in 1958.

European Economic Community (E.E.C. or 'The Common Market') Britain was *not* a founder-member of E.E.C., which was part of a general movement towards the unity of Europe resulting from the war. There were some who advocated that western Europe should become a political unit, a 'united states of Europe'; others advocated economic unity, whilst preserving present political boundaries. E.E.C. was established in 1957 under the Treaty of Rome, which came into force in 1958. The members were Belgium, France, West Germany, Italy, the Netherlands, and Luxemburg, with a total population of 170 millions in 1959. Its headquarters was in Brussels. These six countries had already formed the European Coal and Steel Community in 1950, and under the Treaty of Rome set up the European Atomic Energy Community (Euratom). Britain was invited to join but refused. Then in 1961, Britain negotiated to enter, but agreement was not reached and her application was refused in 1963, and again in 1967, owing to French opposition. Further negotiations, begun in 1970, resulted in Britain's entry on 1 January 1973, together with Denmark and the Irish Republic. E.E.C. aimed to abolish all duties between member countries, and to allow free movement of capital and labour.

APPENDIX IV

FIVE ECONOMISTS AND PHILOSOPHERS WHO HAVE INFLUENCED POLICY AND THOUGHT

Adam SMITH (1723–90)

He was a student at Glasgow and Oxford Universities, and later returned to Glasgow as lecturer and professor. His most important book was *An Inquiry into the Nature and Causes of the Wealth of Nations* (1776). Whilst other economists argued that a country's wealth was its land, or its balance of trade, Smith said that wealth was labour, and that labour was more productive if specialised. He attacked excessive regulation of economic affairs by central and local government, and advocated freedom for individuals to pursue their own economic interests. This would lead to greater productivity. The *Wealth of Nations* influenced Pitt the Younger and others who reduced tariff barriers. The book helped to cause the collapse of what Smith called 'The Mercantile System', i.e. government restrictions, and led the way to *laissez-faire*.

Thomas Robert MALTHUS (1766–1834)

He was educated at Cambridge, was ordained priest, and after some years as a country clergyman spent several years in Europe. From 1806 until his death he was a professor at Haileybury College. His most famous work was *Essay on the Principle of Population as it affects the Future Improvement of Society.* He argued that whilst the means of subsistence (i.e. food supplies) increased by an arithmetic progression (i.e. 1, 2, 3, 4, 5 ...), the population was growing in geometric progression (i.e. 1, 2, 4, 8, 16 ...). Therefore, unless checked, the population would outstrip food supplies. Nature checked the population by means of war, disease, or famine. Man should not allow wages to rise above bare subsistence level, or Nature could not hold the rise in population in check. He forecast that over-population would become a great problem in industrial countries. His gloomy forebodings proved wrong, because he could not foresee the changes in transport, agriculture, and technology which made it possible to feed a growing population. It is still possible that the world will become over-populated, and many people today are prophesying disaster. The more optimistic suggest that new methods and sources of food supply will be found. Malthus had a profound effect on his age and contemporaries, e.g. the Poor Law Commission of 1834.

Jeremy BENTHAM (1748–1832)

He was educated at Westminster School and Oxford. He carried Adam Smith's ideas of a free economy further. He argued that man was governed by two masters—pain and pleasure; that where the individual could pursue his own self-interest, he would achieve more than under strict controls. Economic progress was greater in a free society, so the government should interfere as little as possible. The government should follow *laissez-faire* (leave alone) principles wherever possible, and should aim at 'the greatest happiness of the greatest number'. 'Every person is in the main the best judge of his own happiness.' As Bentham applied the principle of 'What is its use' to any suggested measure he and his followers are sometimes called 'Utilitarians'. Bentham's ideas were developed by James Mill (1773–1836), and John Stuart Mill (1806–73). The Utilitarians influenced reformers such as Chadwick.

William Henry BEVERIDGE (1879–1963)

W.H. Beveridge was knighted in 1919, and raised to the peerage in 1942. He had a varied career, including periods of public service and as Director of the London School of Economics and Master of an Oxford college. His writings had a great influence on governmental policy in his life-time, especially on problems of unemployment and social security. He had much to do with the creation of the 'Welfare State'. At the beginning of the century he advocated labour exchanges and the reform of the Poor Law. In 1941 he was appointed Chairman of the Committee set up to enquire into existing social insurance schemes. Its Report, issued in 1942, is often called the 'Beveridge Report'.

John Maynard KEYNES (1833–1946)

J.M. Keynes was an economist whose writings helped to end *laissez-faire*. He was educated at Eton and Cambridge. After a short period in the Civil Service, he became a Fellow of King's College, Cambridge, in 1908, and four years later became the editor of the *Economic Journal*. During the 1914–18 War he worked in the Treasury. He attended the peace conferences in Paris, but resigned in 1919 as he disagreed with the policy of reparations. He stated his views in *The Economic Consequences of the Peace* (1919). The depression of 1929–33 caused him to reconsider traditional economic theories, and in 1936 he published the then revolutionary *General Theory of Employment, Interest, and Money*. Earlier he had written *A Treatise on Money* (1930). Keynes argued that unemployment and depressions would not cure themselves, and advocated governmental action. The government needed to act according to the state of the economy. Credit and facilities ought to be controlled; interest rates should be kept low in times of unemployment and depression, and high in times of overemployment and inflation. In order to stop unemployment the government needed to 'prime the pump' by financing 'public works'. Unemployment could also be alleviated by making the distribution of income more equal; this would increase the demand for consumer goods. Put simply, if there is one very rich man, and four men who can only just survive, only one motor-car will be sold. If the government taxes the very rich man, and gives to the poor men, then five motor-cars will be sold.

Keynes' views were accepted in Britain only after the beginning of the 1939–45 War. His ideas had a great influence on the plans made for social security and full employment. Post-war governments have applied his theories in their use of the Bank Rate, taxation, and public expenditure.

In 1939 Keynes rejoined the Treasury, and he was raised to the peerage in 1942. In 1944 he attended the Bretton Woods conference, and in 1945 negotiated the U.S.A. loan to Britain.

APPENDIX V

STATISTICAL TABLES

A. *Transport from 1935*
(all figures in millions)

| Year | Road vehicle licences | | Railways: passenger miles |
	Commercial	Private	
1935	0·4	1·5	19,000
1938	0·5	1·9	20,000
1945	0·48	1·5	35,000
1946	0·47	1·8	29,200
1947	0·68	1·9	23,000
1950	0·92	2·3	20,200
1953	1·0	2·8	20,600
1956	1·2	3·9	21,100
1959	1·3	5·0	22,300
1963	1·5	7·5	19,600
1973	2·7	13·4	15,200

B. *Population and Unemployment*
(all figures in millions)

Year	Total population of United Kingdom	Unemployed
1900	41·1	0·4
1904	42·6	1·1
1906	43·3	0·7
1908	44·1	1·5
1911	45·2	0·6
....		
1921	44·0	2·5
1922	44·3	1·6
1926	45·2	1·5
1929	45·7	1·2
1931	46·0	2·7
1932	46·3	2·8
1933	46·5	2·5
1935	46·9	2·0
1939	47·8	1·5
1948	49·6	0·3
1958	51·7	0·5
1961	52·8	0·3
1963	53·7	0·5
1967	55·0	0·4
1973	55·9	0·5

Note: figures above the dotted line include southern
Ireland (now the Republic of Ireland) which was then
part of the United Kingdom.

C. *Trade Unions and Strikes*
(all figures in millions)

Year	Total trade-union membership	No. of women included in previous column	Total working days lost through stoppages
1900	2·0	0·1	30·0
1912	3·4	—	40·8
1913	4·1	0·4	9·8
1920	8·3	1·3	26·5
1921	6·6	—	85·8
1926	5·2	—	162·2
1932	4·4	0·7	6·4
1945	7·8	1·6	2·8
1962	9·8	2·0	5·7
1972	11·2	2·8	—

Index

Aaron Manby, 120
Abingdon, 111
Acts of Parliament:

agriculture
enclosures, 16–17; (1831) modification of
Game Laws, 95; (1836) Tithe Commutation, 95; (1868) abolition of Gang System,
96; (1875) Agricultural Holdings, 101;
(1896) Land Rerating, 101; (1907) Smallholdings, 101; (1947) Guaranteed Prices,
283–4.

banks
(1708), 209; (1816), 211; (1826), 211; (1844)
Bank Charter, 212; (1946) Nationalisation,
273

education
(1870) Forster, 205; (1880) Mundella, 205;
(1889) Technical Instruction, 156; (1902)
Balfour, 205–6; (1918) Fisher, 226; (1944)
Butler, 288–9.

factories and mines
(1802), 161; (1833), 162; (1842) Collieries,
163; (1844), 162; (1847), 163; (1850), 163;
(1864–74), 163; (1864) Climbing Boys,
163; (1901) Factories and Workshops, 164;
(1909) Trade Boards, 166; (1930) Coal
Mines, 238, 276–7

friendly societies
(1793), 200; (1855), 178

housing and planning
(1919) Town Planning, 227; (1923)
Chamberlain, 228; (1924) Wheatley, 228;
(1944) Town and Country Planning, 291–3

location of industry
(1945) 285, 291

nationalisation
(1946) Bank of England, 273; (1947)
electricity, 274; (1948) gas, 274; (1947)
transport, 274; (1949) iron and steel, 274;
(1953) iron and steel, 275; (1953) transport,
275

poor law
(1601) Elizabeth I, 185; (1662–97) Settlement, 186; (1722) Workhouse, 186; (1782)

Gilbert, 186; (1834) Amendment, 188;
(1948) National Assistance, 288

public health
(1848), 193–4; (1850) Metropolitan Burials, 196; (1875) Disraeli, 196

railways
(1844), 108; (1846), 109; (1854), 109;
(1921), 244; (1947), 274–5

reform of Parliament
(1867), 177; (1884), 181; (1918), 226

repressive
(1709) Unlawful Oaths, 171; (1819) 'Gag',
169

roads
(1835) Highways, 114; (1865) Locomotives, 114; (1924) London Traffic, 247;
(1930) Road Traffic, 245

social security
(1908) Old Age Pensions, 191; (1911)
National Insurance, 191; (1946) National
Insurance, 286; (1946) National Health, 286

trade and tariffs
(1651) Navigation, 75, 134, repealed, 135;
(1701–21) prohibition of Indian calicoes,
39; (1751) duty on spirits, 7; (1815) Corn
Law, 131, repealed, 133; (1823) Reciprocity of Duties, 131; (1931) Abnormal Importation, 230

trade unions
(1799–1800) Combination, 57, 168; (1867)
Master and Servant, 177; (1871) Gladstone,
178; (1871) Criminal Law Amendment,
178; (1875) Disraeli, 178; (1875) Employers' and Workmen's, 178; (1906) Trade
Disputes, 182; (1913) Trade Union, 182;
(1927) Trade Disputes, 238; (1965) 269,
Industrial Relations, 294

wages
(1906) Trade Boards, 166

war
(1914) Defence of the Realm, 220; (1937)
Air Raid Precautions, 253